*The languages of criticism
and the structure of poetry*

R. S. CRANE

The languages of criticism and the structure of poetry

THE UNIVERSITY OF CHICAGO PRESS • Chicago & London

The University of Chicago Press, Chicago 60637
The University of Chicago Press, Ltd., London

Copyright, Canada, 1953, by University of Toronto Press
All rights reserved. Published 1953
Midway Reprint edition 1986
Printed in the United States of America
95 94 93 92 91 90 89 88 87 86   5 4 3 2 1

Library of Congress Cataloging-in-Publication Data

Crane, Ronald Salmon, 1886–
   The languages of criticism and the structure of
poetry.

   (Midway reprints)
   Reprint. Originally published: Toronto : University
of Toronto Press, c1953.
   Includes index.
   1. Criticism.   2. Poetics.   I. Title.   II. Series.
PN81.C83   1986   801'.951   86-11387
ISBN 0-226-11797-9 (pbk.)

TO MY COLLEAGUES

in the University of Toronto, Easter Term, 1952

PREFACE

THIS BOOK IS a considerably revised version of the Alexander Lectures for 1951–52 which I gave at the University of Toronto in March of this year. I have kept the original lecture form and much of the original text but have restored several passages I was compelled to omit in delivery and added a good many others especially in the first and last parts.

It is always presumptuous in this psychoanalytical age to aspire to know more about one's own secret thoughts than others can easily infer from one's printed words. I cannot feel sure, therefore, that I am aware of all the prejudices that lurk beneath what I have been trying to say in these lectures. It may well be that in taking the position with respect to critical principles which I call pluralistic, I will be thought by some readers to be far gone, in spite of myself, in scepticism and by other readers to be merely concealing thus a deep desire for authority and metaphysical certitude. It may well be, too, that in attempting to discriminate different kinds of problems and methods in criticism, I will seem to have fallen into the error of those "rationalists" who assume that the concrete multifariousness of life or literature can be enclosed neatly and finally in ordered schemes of ideas. I can only say that if I understand what is meant by these various attitudes, they are all attitudes which, in my conscious moments, I deeply abhor, whether they show themselves in criticism or in philosophy, politics, or morals; and I should be unhappy if anything I have said in this book should be supposed to lend encouragement to any of them. At the same time I do not wish to avoid responsibility for the several long-standing prejudices of a somewhat different sort which I do clearly recognize are present in what I have written.

The first is a prejudice which I doubtless owe to the fact that I have been educated as a scholar and have spent most of my life in university teaching. It is natural for me to think of criticism in the context not of literary journalism or of general cultural discussion but of humanistic learning—as a form of inquiry to be cultivated in the same questioning spirit, for the sake of a disinterested understanding and appreciation of its objects in their own natures, as is proper to the study of history, language, and ideas, and with an approach to the same rigour of analysis and statement. I should want to distinguish, with Northrop Frye in his essay on "The Function of Criticism at the Present Time," between the criticism which thus aspires to be "a learning" and two other kinds: the criticism that takes the form of cultivated *causerie*, after the manner of Hazlitt, Sainte-Beuve, Matthew Arnold, and their many descendants; and the criticism that results from the interested application to literature of general systems of religious, philosophic, or political ideas, after the manner of the later Eliot, the Marxists, Liberals, Humanists, Kirkegaardians, and Existentialists; though I should not insist on calling the "learned" criticism, as Professor Frye does, "genuine criticism" or "criticism proper." The prerequisites, techniques, and ends of the three kinds are not the same, and their utilities for readers of literary works are of very different orders; all are good things when responsibly done—that is, with a serious concern for principles and facts; and I can find no defensible grounds on which any one of them can be given precedence in intrinsic value over the others, since any such ranking presupposes—what can never be the case—that the question of what criticism in general is or should be has been authoritatively settled. My attachment to the first kind is thus a prejudice, but not, I believe, an invidious one; I have written with this kind chiefly in view because it is the kind in whose prosperity I have the most immediate interest; but I do not oppose it, in any polemic way, to the others or indeed to any manner of dealing with literature whatever that goes

viii

beyond mere dogmatic assertion or the reduction of criticism to a journalistic play with current commonplaces and sectarian slogans.

A second prejudice that I am clearly aware of is reflected in what will surely seem to many the undue importance which these lectures assign to questions of critical method and theory. I call this a prejudice because the final defence I should have to make of it would be simply, I suppose, that such questions happen to be greatly to my taste, or at any rate that they have always forced themselves upon me whenever I have tried to estimate the meaning and validity of what either I or someone else has written about any subject. I call it a prejudice, also, because I recognize that there is a kind of criticism—sometimes, as in Matthew Arnold, of great excellence and power—which is able to do its work with a minimum of theoretical inquiry into the nature of its objects, its controlling principles being identical, so to speak, with the moral insight and literary tact of the critic himself. This, however, is the criticism of genius, and what holds true of it does not necessarily hold true, to the same extent at least, of the criticism which most of us attempt to practise, in which considerations of the objective subject-matter of the critic's discourse are of central concern; and with respect to criticism of this more common sort—the criticism with which I mainly deal in the following pages—I do not believe that I need to fall back upon my ultimate defence. Let me try to say, then, what I think can be said for a preoccupation with theory and method in criticism in opposition to the counter-prejudice that manifests itself either in a thorough-going impatience with anything that is not "concrete" in literary discussion or in the assertion that criticism is not nearly so dependent on theory as the devotees of general principles appear to think. In the context of these lectures, the question is really a double one, as it relates, on the one hand, to theorizing about literature or poetry and, on the other hand, to theorizing about criticism itself.

It can be said, first of all, that, whether we like it or not, theory of some sort is an unavoidable necessity whenever we proceed to set down, even in the most particularized practical criticism, statements about literary works. For in the making of any such statements, and still more of a connected series of them, we inevitably bring into play three variable factors: our perceptions of the concrete text before us as an object of common sense understanding or historical learning; our assumptions as to the kind of thing, critically speaking, it is—that it is a poem, for example, or a lyric poem, or a drama; and the power we have—our sensibility and taste—to join the other two together in an intelligible and appropriate way. The second of these factors is the peculiar object of theory; and how essential this factor is can be seen if we consider what a great difference it would make, for everything we might write about a given poem, whether we assumed its nature to be that (say) of a statement communicating something to us, or of an art work to be responded to emotionally for its own sake as its construction dictates, or of a composite of memorable passages, or of something that makes us feel the presence behind it of a distinctive mind or culture. It is clear, on this view of the matter, that there can be no good practical criticism in which all three factors—particular knowledge, conceptual definition and analysis, and sensitive response—are not present and operative, each in its best possible state; and it is therefore a false analysis that isolates any one or two of them as all-important or sets up an antithesis between the "concrete" elements of knowledge and sensibility and the "abstract" element of theoretical commitment. This much is true: that without sensibility and taste, no criticism can be good at all, however learned the critic or deeply versed in theory; it is also true that we praise certain critics, and rightly, for the excellence of their particular perceptions whose stated theories of poetry seem to us narrow or confused. These are wholly just discriminations; but they do not warrant any general inference that concern with theory is either negligible or, still less, a hindrance to the operations of the other two causes. Dryden is a much better critic than Thomas Rymer, for all the latter's reputed skill in theory, but there is no implication in this of the relative unimportance in criticism of general principles; for it is surely the case that Rymer's theory is as bad as the taste with which he applies it, and that Dryden, along with his superior sensitivity, is also by far the better theorist of the two, and might have been an even better practical critic than he is had his theory been of a more sharply discriminating kind. All such disjunctions, I am bound to say, seem to me to distort the facts, and to have, besides, an abstract and academic character such as can lead only to vain disputes without showing critics how to be better than they are. This is not to say, though, that we cannot properly take one or more of our three factors as constants in any particular discussion—as I have taken taste and sensibility as a constant in these lectures—and centre our attention on the variability of the others while in no way implying that what is left out is less important for the practising critic than what is included.

Theory, then, is inescapable, but it may of course be present in any critical writing, not as explicit and argued assertion, but merely as a complex of unstated assumptions and habits of procedure. There have been great critics of both kinds: there is Johnson, for instance, whose critical system must be inferred in large part from the remarkably systematic operations of his mind on particular literary questions; and there is, at the other extreme, Coleridge, for whom the long philosophical preliminaries of the *Biographia Literaria* were an indispensable means to saying cogently what he wanted to say about poetic diction and the poetry of Wordsworth. Tastes will differ, but I cannot think of any objective criterion that will justify us in saying that the practical criticism of either one of these two very different writers is intrinsically better than that of the other. Whether we take time out to talk in general terms about the nature of our literary objects or merely assume this and go on with the business of making particular judgments, is clearly, therefore, only a question of which of the two courses we think more useful for our purposes at a given time. If I have taken the first course, it is mainly, as I have tried to explain in the opening lecture, because I think that we are now faced with a situation in criticism in which a little more explicit inquiry into principles might well lead to better or at least more varied critical practice.

I am encouraged in this view by what has happened in other fields. I cannot but think that the cult of the "concrete" in contemporary criticism—when the "concrete" is opposed to a concern with theoretical analysis—is a counterpart of the state of affairs in medicine when the so-called "empirics" ruled; and we all know that the period of greatest progress in detailed observation and understanding in the medical arts began only after their reign was ended. It has been so, too, with the notable advances of the present century in physics, genetics, psychology, economics, political science, and linguistics: they have all been preceded and accompanied by theoretical revivals; and in any university the subjects which are now most alive are those in which there is the least indifference to general ideas and the least inclination to find an incompatibility between a concern for them and the pursuit of particular facts.

To say this is not to aspire in any way to assimilate criticism, in its concepts or methods or the character of its results, to any of these other subjects. The point is not that we should try to be like the sciences in any of their distinctive aspects but merely that we can perhaps come to have the same kind of history they have had by going about our tasks in similar though not identical ways. In spite of everything, we cannot avoid commitments to theory; we may keep them hidden from ourselves, with no great risk, possibly, so long as our general concepts are adequate to all the particular things we want to do, but with considerable risk, if this is not the case, of writing confusedly or of shutting ourselves off from observations we might otherwise make or of lapsing into stagnation and routine. Good as our criticism may be now, it is surely not good enough; and it would therefore seem the better course to try to emulate the most active minds in these other fields and to bring our commitments out into the open, without fear that our sensibility will be impaired thereby or our capacity for dealing with particulars interfered with. We might then find that we had missed many significant discriminations in our most studied authors merely by not having had the terms in our possession by which they could be made; and we might discover also what I should like to call the duplicity of the "concrete"—the striking fact, which much contemporary criticism illustrates, that any attempt, in the name of concreteness, to get along with only a few concepts and distinctions in practical criticism inevitably results in making our statements about particular works excessively general and abstract.

The great danger in all this is, of course, that in becoming more overtly theoretical we may become more closely wedded than we otherwise might be to the particular version of our subject-matter which, for one reason or another, we have made our own. There is likely to be a certain dogmatic ring in any appeal, in practical criticism, to general principles, and often enough the dogmatism is more than a fashion of statement. Nothing would be gained, naturally, if the revival of critical theory I am urging resulted merely in a further multiplication of doctrinaire critics. But the safeguard against this is not, I think, to remain innocent of theory but to see to it that our theorizing is done in a spirit of philosophic comparison between the principles we ourselves prefer and the principles which other critics, past and present, have used, for the sake of discovering as precisely as we can the sources of the differences among them and the extent to which these differences can be resolved. Such a comparative examination of critical concepts and methods would not lead immediately to more or better practical criticism, but it would have, I think, a number of indirect benefits that could be as important in the long run. It would serve as a discouragement to vain sectarian disputes between critics of different schools and between critics and scholars, as a way to a more sympathetic understanding of what other critics are doing and hence to a fuller use of their findings, as a stimulus to self-criticism and to reconsideration of our cherished but perhaps only half-true positions, and, generally, as a powerful challenge to us to rise, at least occasionally, above our own limited intellectual habits.

These, it is true, we can never transcend completely, and it is probably better that we cannot, since how, otherwise, could we ever get anything done? We must all remain prejudiced by temperament or training with respect to what we want to do in criticism and, therefore, also, with respect to the kind of critical theory and method we prefer to use; and the best we can do is to try not to exalt our prejudices in these matters into religious dogmas or to expect them to be shared by more than a reasonable number of our contemporaries. The character of my own bias has been fairly clear to me for many years. It amounts, negatively speaking, to a fascinated distrust for that variety of theorizing about the concrete phenomena of human affairs, whether in criticism, politics, morals, or history, which I have called in these lectures, after David Hume, "abstract." It was the first kind of critical and historical theorizing to which I was introduced, in a Hegelian form, as a student, and I have never ceased to feel the charm of its schematic symmetry and neatness. I had hardly learned to practise it in an elementary way, however, before I began to have sceptical doubts; it was not at any rate, I soon saw, the kind of method that would give me answers of the sorts I wanted to the sorts of questions I felt more and more impelled to ask about historical events and literary works; and so, while the fascination has persisted, the distrust has progressively grown. I am persuaded philosophically that my distrust is one which no one else is obliged to share, at least in relation to the method itself as distinct from inappropriate applications of it; it is an indispensable method for getting at one aspect of the truth about things if that is the aspect one wants to get at; my difficulty has been all along that I have wanted to know something quite different. For what has chiefly interested me in a positive way, in all the fields in which I have tried to study, has not been the patterns of ideas which particular things reflect but the immediate causes, in the literal sense of that word, which have made the things what they are and rendered them capable of affecting our minds as they do, and more especially those causes which involve the efforts of human beings, whether politicians, scientists, philosophers, or artists, to solve successfully the particular problems inherent in their situations and tasks. I have therefore sought for principles and methods of inquiry that might give me, as fully as possible, knowledge of this kind and provide a basis, at the same time, for judgments of value appropriate to the various sorts of ends which such a consideration would reveal. I have discovered these in no one source, ancient or modern; and if in these lectures I emphasize what I have found useful in Aristotle rather than in (say) Longinus or Johnson or the masters of historical criticism or philosophic analysis, that is because my subject here is the structure of poetry rather than any of the many other aspects of the literary arts that lend themselves to exploration in broadly similar causal terms. I have thought it

xiv

only fair to call this taste for the literal and causal in criticism a prejudice, since I know of no way in which it can be defended, on ultimate philosophic grounds, against other different critical tastes. It can be discussed, therefore, only as one valid approach among others, and be recommended for what it can accomplish only to those who, like myself, want to accomplish this kind of thing.

After what I have just said, I cannot avoid mentioning gratefully the name of the scholar, though he would probably have hesitated to approve many of the things I say in this book, who first set me on the way of thinking which it reflects—my teacher in medieval history at the University of Michigan, the late Earle Wilbur Dow. My most immediate and particular debts, however, are to the friends and colleagues at the University of Chicago with whom I collaborated last year in a volume called *Critics and Criticism: Ancient and Modern*; the many references to their work in my notes sum up only in the meagerest way what I owe to them, and particularly to Richard McKeon and Elder Olson, for guidance and correction during many years; these friends will not, I hope, hold themselves responsible for my errors and confusions. I have learned a great deal also from my students both at the University of Chicago and at the University of Toronto, and some of them will doubtless recognize themselves in a number of my points and illustrations. And finally, among those at the University of Toronto to whom I have ventured to dedicate these lectures, I must give special thanks, for much benevolent encouragement, to A. S. P. Woodhouse and Gordon Roper.

R. S. C.

Ephraim, Wisconsin
August, 1952

ACKNOWLEDGMENTS

THIS BOOK owes much in detail to the suggestions and criticisms of my friends Professors M. H. Abrams and W. R. Keast, of Cornell University, and John Lucas, of Carleton College, who have been so kind as to read it in manuscript or proof. I wish to express my gratitude also to the following for their generous permission to quote from copyrighted materials:

The Bollingen Foundation, Inc., New York, for permission to quote from *Contributions to Analytical Psychology*, by C. G. Jung.

Mr. Robert Graves, for permission to quote two stanzas of his poem "To Juan at the Winter Solstice" (*Poems 1938–1945*).

Harcourt, Brace and Company, New York, for permission to quote from *The Well Wrought Urn*, by Cleanth Brooks (copyright 1947).

New Directions, Norfolk, Connecticut, for permission to quote from *The Anatomy of Nonsense*, by Yvor Winters (copyright 1943 by New Directions).

Longmans, Green and Company, New York, for permission to quote from *Character and Motive in Shakespeare*, by J. I. M. Stewart (copyright 1949).

CONTENTS

*The languages of criticism
and the structure of poetry*

The multiplicity of critical languages

I HAVE THOUGHT that I could best show my sense of the great
honour which the invitation to give these lectures has brought to
me by selecting a subject as close as possible to those central and
permanent issues of literary study from which Professor Alexander,
as I have often been told, never allowed himself to stray very
far. The problem of the structure of poetry, it has seemed to me,
is such a subject, especially when the word "poetry" is used, as I
shall use it throughout what I have to say, to stand for the whole
range of artistic creation in words. The structure of poetry, in
this large sense of the term, was the dominating interest of
Aristotle in the beginnings of systematic criticism; and there have
been few critics in any subsequent period, however great their
concern with other questions, who have not found it necessary
to deal, if only subordinately, with the obvious fact that poems
are ordered compositions exhibiting characteristics which require
to be discussed under such heads as "form," "synthesis," "unity,"
"disposition," "arrangement," "construction," or "design." And it
is a further sign of the perennial importance of the question that
it has again become, for many of the most influential critics of
our day, the focal problem of their "new" poetics, the preoccupation which appears to them to distinguish their inquiries into
poetry most sharply from those of critics in the past. Whereas
earlier critics, we are often told, had erroneously assumed that
the values of poems could be identified with the qualities of their
parts and had concentrated their observations, accordingly, on

3

the "local" beauties of language and sentiment or, as in the older criticism of Shakespeare, on the merely human attributes of characters considered apart from the plays in which they appear, the best critics of the twentieth century have reversed this view. They have discovered that poems, or at least good poems, are patterned wholes, the parts of which necessarily have "an organic relation to each other," so that poems are adequately described only "in terms of structure," and the proper critical question about any element in a poem is "not whether it is in itself pleasing, or agreeable, or valuable, or 'poetical,' but whether it works with the other elements to create the effect intended by the poet."[1] It is not strange, therefore, that the first task of critical theory has been taken by many of these critics to be the definition of the nature of the "structure" by which poetry is differentiated from other uses of language, or that they have found in the term "structural analysis" the most appropriate description of their dealings with individual poems, novels, and plays, or that the pages of their books and essays have been liberally sprinkled with words like "organic unity," "pattern," "rhythm," "movement," "thematic development," "recurrent imagery," and "total meaning."

My subject is thus both ancient and up-to-date; but that very fact, while guaranteeing its significance for literary and humanistic studies, might well suggest that nothing particularly new or useful can be said about it. After so many centuries of discussion, what can now be added? Little enough, I should agree, if what is to be attempted is a direct answer, in didactic terms, to the question of what poetic structure in general, or in any of the several branches of poetry, really is. For that is the form which the problem has taken in the writings of all the critics who have considered it from the Greeks to our time. And the result has been, and is still today, a chaos of solutions of the most varied and apparently contradictory kinds, in the face of which it must surely seem futile or presumptuous to look for still another.

It is hard, indeed, to think of any aspect of the question about which critics have not radically disagreed. We read Aristotle and Mr. Cleanth Brooks and note that matters of structure, for them, are all-important, each of the other terms and distinctions they

4

find it necessary to use being subsumed in one way or another under this, so that their whole discussion is directed, though in quite divergent fashions, to problems of how poems are put to‐ gether. And then we read on and discover that for many more critics, both ancient and modern, the idea of structure, in the sense of the artistic organization of materials, either has a rela‐ tively minor significance in their theories of poetry (as in Samuel Johnson, for instance) or else plays the role of a secondary term in a pair of concepts of which the primary concept—to mention only a few examples—is sometimes "substance" (as in A. C. Bradley), sometimes "function" (as in Kenneth Burke), some‐ times "texture" (as in John Crowe Ransom), sometimes even "life" (as in the celebrated debate of H. G. Wells with Henry James). The differences are equally striking, also, between those critics, such as Aristotle, for whom poetry exhibits a multiplicity of structures not capable of reduction to any single type and those critics, like Cleanth Brooks again, who insist that the essential structure of poetry is one, and devote their efforts to defining the common pattern which organizes works as dissimilar in other respects as *The Odyssey* and *The Waste Land*, "Tears, Idle Tears," and *The Rape of the Lock*.[2] Nor do these last two groups form homogeneous schools. For critics of the first group the structural principles of tragedy, for example, are necessarily dis‐ tinct from those of comedy or lyric, but it has seldom happened, in this tradition of criticism, that the distinctive structure of tragedy has been given exactly the same statement in the many formulations of it attempted since the *Poetics*; and the diversity has been no less great among the critics of the second group, in their search for the universal principle of structure which dis‐ tinguishes poetry as a unitary whole from other things. Whether the essential structure of poetry is taken to be many or one, what it is thought to be in any particular instance obviously depends on the character of the terms in which it is defined; and these have been chosen sometimes on the assumption that poetic struc‐ ture is *sui generis* and hence must be analysed by means of terms —such as Aristotle's plot, character, thought, peripety, recogni‐ tion, and the like—that have technical meanings restricted to poetics alone; and sometimes on the assumption that its nature is

5

such that an adequate description of it is possible only through analogies borrowed from other arts or fields of knowledge. The great majority of critics have held the second view; and inasmuch as the possibilities of finding illuminating analogies for anything are unlimited, structures of the most varied kinds have been attributed to poetry in general or to its particular species, depending on whether the terms used in constituting them have been drawn (say) from grammar, or from logic, or from painting, or from music, or from analytical psychology, or (as very frequently in our day) from the anthropological study of ritual, folktale, or myth.

Such divergences in theory are bound to be reflected in the judgments of critics on individual works; and there can be few of us who, after examining what different critics have to say about the structure of any poem, are not often tempted to exclaim that surely these commentators could not all have been reading the same text! As compared with *Hamlet*, for instance, Shakespeare's *Macbeth* would not seem to be a particularly difficult work. Yet it would take more words than I can spare to do even partial justice to the rich variety of answers that have been given, in the criticism merely of the past twenty years, to the question of what precisely is its unifying form. According to one school of interpreters, the principle of its construction is the concrete human action which it represents—an action to which we are intended to respond emotionally as we would respond to a similar action in life by virtue of the illusion the drama creates that the hero and most of the other *dramatis personae* are in all essential respects men and women like ourselves. It is, on this view of its structure, a literal tragic imitation, to the discussion of which the distinctions provided by Aristotle in the *Poetics* are accordingly relevant. But then when we ask what exactly the imitated action is and in what sense it is tragic, we find that it has been possible for different critics of this school to conceive of the plot of *Macbeth* in two radically opposed ways: on the one hand, as a modified tragedy of the Aristotelian type, in which the spectacle of a potentially good man's suffering and moral ruin under the stress of great temptation excites in us at least qualified pity and fear;[3] and, on the other hand, as a tragedy of retribution, some-

6

what similar to *Richard III*, only more profound, in which a sequence of criminal acts leads the hero to deserved misfortune, and the climactic emotion is not pity but punitive satisfaction.[4]

By many other critics during these years, however, the assumption on which both of these contrasting views are founded has been called sharply in question. It is an error, we are assured, that does little credit either to Shakespeare's genius or to our understanding of his age or of poetry to think of *Macbeth*—or for that matter of any of the major tragedies—as primarily a drama at all, at least in the sense ordinarily given to the word "drama" from Aristotle to Bradley and William Archer. But if not a drama, or at any rate not a "realistic" drama, what is it, we ask? And here again we are offered various answers, which have in common only the presupposition that if *Macbeth* is as great a work as we have always thought, its controlling structure must be one not of literal actions, as in the criticism of the other school, but of meanings. The pattern, says one critic, is twofold—a moral or religious allegory of "the onslaught of evil upon the human personality and the murder of the soul" and a political allegory in which the forces of natural-supernatural evil, using the Macbeths as both agents and victims, succeed in killing the divine-king and triumphing in the state, until the time is once more set free by the victorious instruments of God and of the pious Scotland of St. Columba.[5] For another critic, the play is not so much an allegory in the strict sense as a poetic shadowing-forth of two universal myths: in one of its aspects it is Shakespeare's Descent into Hell, his *Inferno*, in its other aspect his spring-myth, the tyranny of Macbeth between the two beneficent reigns of Duncan and Malcolm being but "winter come back after the promise of spring only to be overcome in turn by spring itself."[6] For a third critic, the play is best described as a "poem" in dramatic form of the order of *The Waste Land*; in reading it, he tells us, we ought to concern ourselves not with the human qualities of its actions and characters but with the fashion in which Shakespeare's peculiar use of language gives unity and emotional force to its themes of good and evil, order and disorder, reality and appearance, certainty and doubt.[7] And lastly, for still another critic, the true form of *Macbeth* is the metaphysical vision of death and

7

life forces which is conveyed to our imagination more completely through its static pattern of images than through its narrative plot; we come to realize, when we submit our minds to these, that the whole play "is a wrestling of destruction with creation: with sickening shock the phantasmagoria of death and evil are violently loosed on earth, and for a while the agony endures, destructive; there is a wrenching of new birth, itself disorderly and unnatural in this disordered world, and then creation's more firm-set sequent concord replaces chaos. The baby-peace is crowned."[8]

And so I might go on indefinitely. But the moral for our inquiry is perhaps clear. It is simply that before we can embark, with any assurance, upon a fresh approach to the subject of these lectures, we must first attempt to account in some fashion for the extraordinary confusion of opposing doctrines and interpretations in which the problem of poetic structure, as it presents itself to us in this late age of criticism, appears to be involved.

II

There would seem on first thought to be only three ways of doing this. The easiest way would be to draw the same negative conclusion from our list of disputes that sceptical writers like Montaigne or Bernard Mandeville drew from their similar lists of the controversies and contradictions of philosophers—namely, that no solution to the problem can be hoped for inasmuch as criticism, like philosophy, is only a matter of opinion. Or, secondly, following the example of many natural scientists, of a majority of the most advanced modern students of language, and of those contemporary philosophers who think it a waste of time to read any of their predecessors before Bertrand Russell and G. E. Moore, we might distinguish between two historical phases of our subject—a past, or pre-scientific, phase, in which confusion and error were inevitable since the right method of inquiry had not yet been found, and a present or future phase in which, thanks to the discovery of the correct procedure and to the emergence of the necessary auxiliary disciplines, such as psychology, modern linguistics, or anthropology, criticism is at last on the point of

8

attaining real solutions to this as well as its other problems. We should then be able to dismiss what earlier critics have said about poetic structure as a mere collection of errors or fragmentary truths founded on assumptions such as can hardly survive the age of Freud and Jung and Bloomfield and Frazer; and we could then subscribe, with an easy conscience, to the eloquent declaration of modern independence in the first chapter of I. A. Richards' *Principles of Literary Criticism*: "A few conjectures," he tells us, "a supply of admonitions, many acute isolated observations, some brilliant guesses, much oratory and applied poetry, inexhaustible confusion, a sufficiency of dogma, no small stock of prejudices, whimsies and crotchets, a profusion of mysticism, a little genuine speculation, sundry stray inspirations, pregnant hints and random *aperçus*: of such as these, it may be said without exaggeration, is extant critical theory composed."[9] Or, thirdly, should this seem a bit extreme, we might attempt to do for the conflicting theories of critics respecting the structure of poetry what Cicero, for example, undertook to do for the not less conflicting theories of earlier and contemporary philosophers respecting morals: seek out, that is, such partial insights into the truth about the subject as they may appear to afford and find a means of reconciling these with one another within the confines of a new and more comprehensive critical scheme.[10]

Let us consider, however, whether these three ways of interpreting and dealing with oppositions in critical doctrine and judgment are indeed the only available alternatives. And we may observe, to begin with, that, distinct as they seem to be, they yet all rest upon a common assumption. What they presuppose, in effect, is that the question at issue, in the various conflicting statements of critics about the structure of poetry or of individual poems, is a single question, to which, accordingly, unless it be a question that can't be answered objectively at all, we have a right to expect, in the long run at least, as knowledge accumulates and techniques improve, a single correct answer. When it is asked, for instance, what kind of structure poetry or tragedy has, or what is the unifying structure of *Macbeth*, or what functions are served in that play by the repeated imagery of badly fitting clothes or by the long scene between Malcolm and Mac-

9

duff at the end of Act IV, it is taken for granted that these are all problems of the same univocal sort, though requiring different means for their solution, as is, let us say, the problem at the present time of the structure of the atom or of the human eye or the problem of how the first quarto of *Hamlet* was put together. The striking thing, however, about these latter problems is the very considerable body of conclusions upon which scientists and bibliographers have been able to agree; and it is therefore only natural to infer from the absence of such agreement among the critics who have written about tragedy or *Macbeth* or the structure of poetry in general either that criticism itself is a vain pursuit or that critics have not yet learned, or are only just beginning to learn, what is their proper job.

The inference is indeed a natural one—provided we grant the assumption. But it is precisely this I would question, at any rate in the naïve form in which it has usually been entertained, on the ground that it leaves out of account one of the three independently variable factors which determine the character of any critical writing that goes beyond mere appreciation or the expression of emotional responses to literary works. Of these factors, one is the critic himself, as a man endowed with a certain set of interests, a certain intellectual capacity, a certain range of reading and information, a certain kind or degree of taste and sensibility; and a second factor is the subject upon which he is engaged, in the ordinary sense of the objectively existing text or body of texts to which he refers us when he speaks, for example, of *Macbeth* or Shakespeare or tragedy. These are obvious determinants of what any critic may elect to say; but it is an inadequate view of criticism—and one bound to lead to misinterpretation and injustice—that is satisfied to dwell on the interaction, in any critical writing, of these two factors only, without recognizing that the "facts" or "objects" the critic is talking about are what they are in his statements of them as a consequence not merely of their "real" or objective nature modified more or less radically by the critic's human equation but, at the same time and independently, of the internal necessities and possibilities of the discourse which he is constructing about them. Any critical book or essay that makes coherent sense is a body of propositions the meaning and validity of any one of which cannot be properly judged until we have uncovered the precise question in the critic's mind to which the proposition is intended to be an answer. This again is obvious; but what is commonly forgotten is that no question or problem, in turn, has any absolute status or isolable meaning, but is always relative, as to both its content and the conditions of its answer, to the total context of the discourse in which it occurs—a context that exists independently both of "things" and of the critic himself once he has chosen or constructed it, as a particular and finite structure of terms in which the referent of any term is conditioned by the logical relation in which it stands to all the other terms, or conceptual elements, employed in the discussion, and ultimately to the special set of basic assumptions concerning subject-matter and method upon which the discourse rests.

It can be said for this view of criticism that it receives strong encouragement from one of the major intellectual developments of our time, although I should not wish to ground the case for it on that fact alone. The primary emphasis in philosophy, as we all know, has tended to shift in the twentieth century from a preoccupation with the nature of objective things or with the powers and forms of the mind to a predominant concern with the character, organization, and uses of symbols. The immediate results of this revolution have undoubtedly included a considerable narrowing of philosophic curiosity and a setting up of dogmas quite as rigid in their way as any dogmas of the past; but among its more fruitful consequences we must certainly number the fresh appreciation it has brought of the fundamentally important role played by language no less in the determination than in the expression of our knowledge. We have come to see more clearly perhaps than before that language is not only a means of communication and artistic creation but also, as Edward Sapir remarked, an instrument of discovery and understanding, and this not merely in the simple sense suggested by the fact that we can move by the aid of common or collective nouns from thought of individuals to thought of classes and groups, but likewise "in the much more far reaching sense that its forms predetermine for us certain modes of observation and interpretation."[11] And from

11

this starting-point we have been led to conceive of any science or discipline as first of all a highly specialized linguistic construction—a coherent "framework" (to use the current slang) of selected terms and distinctions and of rules for operating with them, into which we must translate all our observations of particular objects if we are to succeed in making verifiable sense out of their characteristics and relations. We are thus, in all our inquiries into things, the more or less willing and productive prisoners of the special system of "language" (in this derived sense) we have chosen to employ; it is only in relation to this system that we can assert anything as a meaningful "fact" or give determinate significance to any question we ask; and our problems and solutions will differ widely, even when the ostensible subjects remain the same, according to the peculiar conceptual and logical constitution of the "framework" we happen to be using. They will be of one kind, for example, if its elements are names for everyday objects like tables and chairs, of another kind if its controlling terms are restricted to the immediate data of the senses, and of another kind still if its distinctive vocabulary, as in mathematical physics, is confined to space-time-event relations of a wholly abstract sort.[12]

Now among the various frameworks or systematic languages within which our reasoned knowledge of the world is contained and by which it has been shaped, some may happen at a given time to exhibit a more stable character than others. There is a large measure of stability—to recur to my former examples—in present-day nuclear physics, in modern ophthalmology, and in the bibliographical investigation of printed texts; with the result that questions like those of the structure of the atom or the human eye or of the origins of the first quarto of *Hamlet* can be said to have in a real sense the same definition for all qualified students of these subjects. On the whole, however, throughout intellectual history, situations of this kind have tended to be the exception rather than the rule. The unity of science, except in the most general and useless statements of its method, is still a remote and probably unrealizable ideal; and in the many disciplines having to do not with external nature but with man's behaviour and productions, the characteristic spectacle has always been one of instability and the rivalry of competing frameworks. That is one reason why, for instance, the debate on foreign policy which has gone on continuously in the United States since the First World War has been so difficult to resolve. For although the participants have seldom realized the fact, there has been implied in that debate from the beginning, over and above the many perplexing circumstantial issues, a basic question of the kind of language in which such matters ought to be discussed—whether this should be a language composed primarily of moral terms, so that the politics of nations are turned into something like the plot of a melodrama, or a language modelled on that of domestic penal law, so that the central problem of policy becomes the prevention or punishment of international crimes, or a "realistic" language (as the phrase is) in which thinking is typically directed to questions of national interest and the balance of power.

III

What I would propose, then, as a major premise of these lectures, is that literary criticism is not, and never has been, a single discipline, to which successive writers have made partial and never wholly satisfactory contributions, but rather a collection of distinct and more or less incommensurable "frameworks" or "languages," within any one of which a question like that of poetic structure necessarily takes on a different meaning and receives a different kind of answer from the meaning it has and the kind of answer it is properly given in any of the rival critical languages in which it is discussed.[13] It is not a sufficient objection to this view of criticism that it has rarely been entertained even by the most self-conscious of critics. For the diversities of language we are here concerned with are matters of assumed principle, definition, and method, such as are not likely to show themselves, save indirectly, on the surface of a critic's discourse, and hence not likely, even in controversy, to force themselves on his attention. They pertain rather to what he thinks *with* than to what he thinks *about*—to the implicit structure and rationale of his argument as a whole than to the explicit doctrines he is attempting to state. And both the reality and the importance

13

of the diversities have been further disguised, in the criticism of our European tradition, by the persistence of a large body of terms and commonplaces—like the word "structure" itself or "poetry" or "tragedy" or "plot"—the verbal identity of which in different critics tends effectually to conceal the often sharp oppositions of principle and method that separate their discussions from one another. It takes some effort after all to realize that a writer may not be talking about the same things I am, or reasoning about them in the same way, merely because he happens to use the same customary formulae in the statement of his points! The true state of affairs, however, often reveals itself whenever, on being confronted with an extreme clash of doctrines between two obviously serious and intelligent critics employing the same vocabulary, we undertake to pry into the hidden structures of definitions and assumptions which their respective arguments presuppose.

An illuminating case is the attempt of Mr. L. C. Knights, in his well-known essay on "How Many Children Had Lady Macbeth?", to correct what he regards as the errors imposed on readers of Shakespeare by A. C. Bradley's classic lectures on *Shakespearean Tragedy*.[14] The most damaging of these, he tells us, is the dogma that Shakespeare was "pre-eminently a great 'creator of characters' " and that the main task, consequently, of students of the plays consists in laying bare the marvellous insights into human nature in crisis which the tragedies, in particular, embody. Eminent critic as Bradley was—so the argument runs—he did a grave disservice to Shakespeare when he devoted so many of his pages to detailed psychological and moral analyses of the characters of the plays, to the exclusion of any serious concern with their language and verse, and especially when he continued the bad tradition of writing about Shakespeare's *dramatis personae* as if they were real persons whose lives could be properly thought of as extending beyond the plays in which they are involved. To write thus, according to Mr. Knights, is to disregard the essential fact, which has been revealed to us by C. H. Rickword, that the "characters" of a drama or novel, as well as its "plot," have no existence except as "precipitates" from the reader's memory of the successive words he has read and that, as

14

such, they are mere critical "abstractions" to which we can attend only at the cost of impoverishing our "total response" to the work. And it is also to forget that a play of Shakespeare is not a drama simply but a "dramatic poem," the end of which is "to communicate a rich and controlled experience by means of words"; and accordingly that the only profitable approach to it must be by way of "an exact and sensitive study of the quality of the verse, of the rhythm and imagery, of the controlled associations of the words and their emotional and intellectual force, in short by an exact and sensitive study of Shakespeare's handling of language."

I have selected this controversy because it seems to me a comparatively easy one to resolve in the terms of my hypothesis. Let us suppose that we are critics for whom the primary object of concern is something we call "poetry" and let us further suppose that we have defined "poetry" in such a way as to make it distinct from "drama" in the sense in which an ordinary prose play depicting "real" characters in action is drama, and that we have, moreover, conceived of a poem, of whatever sort, as essentially a certain definitive arrangement of words, or rather as the sum total of emotional and intellectual responses—corresponding to the experience the poet wished to communicate—which this arrangement of words is calculated to evoke in the mind of a properly trained reader. It would then follow, naturally enough, that in writing of one of Shakespeare's plays, we would direct attention, as Mr. Knights does, mainly to its key words and metaphors and the pattern of associated and contrasted meanings these suggest, and would be no less convinced than he is that "to stress in the conventional way character or plot or any of the other abstractions that can be made, is to impoverish the total response to the poetry." It would be unthinkable, indeed, for us to take any other line. But now let us suppose that we have started with concepts and terms of quite a different sort. We have taken as the genus of our subject-matter not "poetry" or "poetic drama" but "Shakespearean tragedy" (in which "poetry" in Mr. Knights's sense is one of the technical means) and have identified this, not with a specific art form or with a particular kind of effect to be produced in audiences, but with a certain imaginative conception in the mind of the poet—the conception of "the tragic

15

aspect of life" which Shakespeare sought to embody dramatically in different ways, but always in terms of actions issuing from and expressing moral character, in *Hamlet, Othello, King Lear,* and *Macbeth.* Wouldn't it follow from this that our central problem in discussing the plays would now be, as it was for Bradley, the recovery for each of them of what was in Shakespeare's mind when he wrote it, so that, as Bradley said, the action and the personages engaged in it "may assume in our imaginations a shape a little less unlike the shape they wore in the imagination of their creator"?[15] And wouldn't it also follow that in effecting such a recovery, we would be justified in concentrating on the characters as the main source of "the tragic fact" and in considering them not as "abstractions" from the words of the plays as finally written but as the concrete semblances of real men and women, each with a being more or less independent of the particular actions he performs in the completed drama, which they undoubtedly were for the imagination of the poet who conceived them? It would be unthinkable, once more, given the scheme of terms we have chosen to use in discussing the tragedies, that we should take any other line.

What I have been saying, in short, is that the opposition between Bradley and Mr. Knights on the issue of the nature and importance of character in drama is not at all an opposition of the kind which requires us to assume that if one of the two propositions is true, the other must be false. It would be such an opposition only if the two propositions were answers to the same question about the same object; and we have seen that this is not the case, inasmuch as Bradley is talking about the plays as reflections of their author's imaginative view of what is tragic in life, whereas Mr. Knights is talking about them as effects in the right reader of certain determinate arrangements of words on the printed page. It is therefore possible to affirm without contradiction both that the characters of Shakespeare are individual men and women possessed of a reality analogous to that of living people and that they are merely (in Rickword's phrase) "precipitates from the memory" that have "emotive valency" only "in solution."[16] The opposition, in other words—though this is largely concealed by the similarities in vocabulary—is not one of

16

conflicting interpretations of the same facts, to be settled by an appeal to a common body of evidence, but of two distinct worlds of discourse, in which the "facts" cited by each critic in support of his position have been determined differently for the two of them by their prior decisions to constitute the subject-matter of Shakespearean criticism in essentially different terms.

IV

It should be clear from this example that the real subject-matter of any critic can never be accurately defined by noting merely that he is talking about such things as dramatic poetry or tragedy or Shakespearean tragedy or *Macbeth*. His real subject-matter is not any of these things in itself (whatever that may mean), nor is it necessarily any of these things as conceived by us or by any of the other critics whose errors are being exposed. Rather it is simply that aspect, or those aspects, of his indicated subject upon which our attention is focused by the semantic and logical constitution of his discourse; it is what, in short, he has thus *taken* his subject to be. And the range of possible critical subject-matters, in this sense, that may lie hidden under the various familiar names for literary entities is extraordinarily great. This is only to be expected, perhaps, when we consider that the typical subjects of criticism are such as lend themselves peculiarly to diverse and shifting modes of consideration. Although they have a basis in human nature, they are not invariant natural phenomena but contingent human constructions, so that their "true" character is always relative, as that of the objects of physical science is not, to what men have designed or thought them to be; and that character, besides, has often been affected, in the course of history, by the very attempts of theorizing critics to say what it is. They differ, moreover, from such artificial products as dwelling houses, automobiles, and atomic bombs in having a far wider variety of significant uses and hence in permitting a much greater diversity of interpretations and of criteria for judging their success or failure. It is little wonder, therefore, that critics in all periods—writing under the influence of varying practical aims or philosophic preoccupations—should have felt

17

free to constitute literature or poetry or any of their individual monuments as widely discrepant kinds of things, the differing natures of which are bound to be reflected, in many subtle but decisive ways, in the differing structures of terms they employ in making statements about them.

I know of no historian or theorist of criticism who has succeeded in exhibiting the full range of such differences, but it is clearly much greater than our usual classifications of critical approaches—for example, as historical, biographical, psychological, aesthetic, moral, sociological, and the like—would suggest. It is common, thus, to say that both Longinus and Coleridge are psychological critics; but the subject-matter of Longinus, in the sense of that which gives determinate reference and intelligibility to his propositions and arguments, is a certain general quality of writing, amenable to art, the character of which is best described in terms of its effect on readers, whereas the subject-matter of Coleridge (when he talks about "poetry") is primarily the manifestation in poems of a natural power inherent in poets and best described in terms of the mental faculty in which it resides—"that synthetic and magical power," as he calls it, "to which we have exclusively appropriated the name of imagination."[17] And so also with many of the general words which critics themselves have used to designate the subjects or characteristics of subjects they are engaged in discussing—it can never be safely assumed in advance that their common use by two different critics is a sign that these critics have constituted the effective subject-matters of their discussions in the same way, so that it is possible to make direct comparisons between their conclusions and to say that one is more nearly adequate to the real state of affairs than the other. The term "imitation" is of crucial importance, as we all know, for the discussion of poetry in both Plato and Aristotle; but whereas for Plato it is a universal and unifying term applicable not only to art but to human actions and knowledge and to the natural world itself and hence a term that brings the objects of criticism into organic relationship, in the dialogues, with all other objects, its function for Aristotle, on the contrary, is that of a differentiating term by which poetry, or rather a certain class of poems, is distinguished from nature, action, and knowledge, and

18

constituted, for the purposes of the *Poetics*, as a body of concrete objects presupposing peculiar principles of construction and subject to evaluation in ways not relevant to either actions or propositions.[18] This is a radical difference in subject-matter between the two philosophers, in the light of which it is surely not fair to Plato to say that Aristotle "refuted" his condemnation of poetry in *The Republic* or fair to Aristotle to say that Plato took a sounder view than he did of the relation between poetry and morals. Or consider, again, the discussions of "metaphysical poetry" in Dr. Johnson and Mr. Ransom. In spite of the fact that Mr. Ransom writes in full awareness of Johnson's use of the term and that both critics refer to some of the same seventeenth-century poets, the real object of discussion in the two is only nominally identical, the object envisaged by Johnson being a historically determinate "race" of poets in the generation before Dryden, to whom he attributes certain excesses and defects in the light of his general criteria for poetry of any kind, whereas the object of concern for Mr. Ransom, as constituted in the terms of his essay, is strictly not a particular school of poets at all but a universal kind of poetry, the nature of which is determined, in his definition, by the opposition he establishes between it and the two contrasting extremes of "physical poetry" on the one hand and "Platonic poetry" on the other.[19] One term, again, but two subject-matters that overlap at no essential point; and though we may prefer, with Mr. Ransom, to use the name "metaphysical poetry" in a more honorific sense than it has in Johnson, we must not allow ourselves to suppose that we are honouring the same thing.

This will suffice as an indication of one basis of divergence among critical languages, of which we shall see a good many other examples as we proceed in these lectures. A critical language, however, is more than a finite set of basic and often implicit definitions which, as a conceptual scheme of a determinate sort, constitutes its literary objects as the particular subject-matter that is being talked about. It is also a special set of assumptions as to how the principles and distinctions needed in the discussion are to be derived and as to how they may be used to give valid and relevant knowledge concerning whatever

19

the subject-matter is taken to be. There can be no critical writing that makes coherent sense which does not rest upon such a double commitment; but the two aspects are so related that what literature or poetry or any poem is for a given critic may be conditioned quite as much by his preference among possible ways of investigating or arguing about subjects of this sort as his selection of a method of inquiry or demonstration is conditioned by what he assumes literature or poetry to be.

Of the various differences of basic method discernible in the history of criticism, I can deal here, illustratively, with only one. It is a difference that emerges clearly enough when we contrast the procedure of a critic like Mr. Ransom in his essays on poetry with the procedure of Longinus in his attempt to construct an art of the "sublime." Such an art is possible, Longinus argues, because the "sublime" exists as a concrete effect or quality actually achieved and hence achievable in language—an effect, quite distinct from that of rhetorical persuasion, which we all experience whenever, in reading works of poetry, philosophy, oratory, or history, we come upon a passage that transports us out of ourselves and makes us, in a sense, one with the writer or speaker. For the art which Longinus envisages, this empirically verifiable effect, the nature of which can be defined in general terms by distinguishing it from its various possible opposites (turgidity, frigidity, and *parenthyrson*), becomes the end to be sought and hence the starting-point or first principle of his inquiry. That inquiry, since its object is a practical one, must follow an *a posteriori* course from the nature of the effect to be achieved to its necessary causes or conditions in what a writer must do if he wishes to attain "sublimity" of utterance; and the problem is solved when Longinus has discriminated the five essential sources of "sublime" effects in literature (noble conception, strong emotion, and a proper employment of figures, diction, and rhythmic and harmonic composition), has demonstrated that these exhaust the possible causes, and has shown for each that it is a means conducive to the end desired.[20]

Strikingly different from this is Mr. Ransom's procedure in the argument that serves to support his well-known contention that any good poem is a composite of a "logical structure" and an

20

"irrelevant local texture," the first being a prerequisite of the second though only very loosely determinative of it. If we ask why we must accept this as a description of what the objects of poetic criticism are, one answer that might be given is that it works in practice. We have only to read Marvell's "To His Coy Mistress," for example, to see that behind the poem is "an easy argument to the effect that a lover, after pointing out the swift passage of time, reasons with his mistress that they had better love at once," but that the poem itself gives us "a good deal more than we had hoped for"—that the detail of its various parts has assumed "a good deal more of independent character than could possibly have been predicted" from a consideration of the "logical argument" alone.[21] This, however, is not altogether satisfactory; for it is clear that much of what, in Mr. Ransom's analysis of Marvell's poem, is "irrelevant texture" (in other words, "poetry" as distinguished from "prose") would at once become part of the "logical structure" had he only made his paraphrase of the "argument" a bit more precise—for example, by qualifying the lover as "impatient" and "witty" and the mistress as "coy"; and it is equally clear that the poem could be satisfactorily analysed, as it has been, in terms of many other pairs of contrary terms than the one he has seen fit to employ. The important question, therefore, is why we must accept this particular opposition of "logical structure" and "irrelevant texture" as a necessary formulation of the nature of this and all other poems.

The necessity is plainly not of the same order as that which leads from Longinus' isolation and definition of the "sublime" as an effect possible in language to his distinction of noble conception and strong emotion as the two "natural" conditions of its existence in any piece of writing. It is not, that is to say, the hypothetical necessity that joins, in practical experience and the arts, something taken as an end with the means requisite for its achievement, but rather, we may suspect, the kind of necessity that compels us, once we have granted the premises of a given argument, to assent to whatever conclusions are drawn from them. And our suspicion that the necessity behind Mr. Ransom's analysis of poetry is of this dialectical sort is confirmed when we examine the foundations of his poetic theory as set forth especially in the essays collected in *The World's Body*.[22] For here we discover, at the basis of all his reasoning about particular literary questions (for example, in the discussion of "metaphysical poetry" already referred to), a general hypothesis or supposition concerning man and his possible relations to the world of concrete things, according to which the fundamental opposition in human life is between the impulse to use, take, and "devour" things in the interest of conceptual knowledge and practical or "economic" action and the impulse to contemplate and love things in all their "wild" particularity for their own sake. This is the starting-point of all his speculations; and from the structure of primary terms and relations thus fixed upon he proceeds to generate, by strictly logical disjunction and equation, a whole series of more particular oppositions—between "idea" and "image" ("An idea is derivative and tamed. The image is in the natural or wild state, and it has to be discovered there, not put there, obeying its own law and none of ours"); between science, as one extreme, and religion, manners, and art, as the other; between poetry "of the feelings" (in which "the subject does not really propose to lose himself in the object") and "metaphysical poetry" (which, starting with feelings, tends to "objectify these imaginatively into external actions"); and so on. The two original impulses, and all their derivatives, remain in dialectical opposition throughout, but in such a manner that the two must be present somehow, and in some ratio of one to the other, in any human act or production. Science and art are thus necessarily contraries but not wholly exclusive of one another: "Science gratifies a rational or practical impulse and exhibits the minimum of perception. Art gratifies a perceptual impulse and exhibits the minimum of reason." And so with poetry. "The poetic impulse is not free"—there must be some element of "science" in it if only in its metre—"yet it holds out stubbornly against science for the enjoyment of its images." A poem must be therefore, by necessary inference from the preceding argument if from nothing else, a composite of "logical structure" (since we must have some concepts if we are to grasp anything) and of "irrelevant texture" (since the differentia of poetry is that it gives us, in opposition to science, the "world's body" rather than merely ideas about it).

22

Here then are two sharply contrasting methods of deriving critical principles and solving critical problems; and it is easy to see that much will depend upon which of them a critic chooses. The one is a "matter of fact" method (as Hume would say) that seeks to render an account of empirically distinguishable literary phenomena in terms of their essential and distinctive causes of production. Its starting-point is always some literary form or actuality that has been and hence can be achieved by art (whatever other prerequisites may be involved), and its procedure consists in reasoning back from this to the necessary and sufficient conditions of its existence or of its existence in the best possible state. The distinctions it looks for and employs are distinctions of "nature" rather than of "reason" inasmuch as their relevance is determined not by the exigencies of the critic's hypothesis but by some kind of inductive consideration of the particular phenomena he is studying: for example, of the various kinds of wholes that poets may construct (as in Aristotle's differentiations of tragedy, comedy, and epic), or of the different elements necessary to the production of an effect or of a work of a certain kind (as in Longinus' analysis of the sources of the "sublime" or Aristotle's discrimination of plot, character, thought, diction, melody, and spectacle as the constitutive parts of tragedies), or of the alternative devices or procedures available to poets with a view to certain ends (as in the modern distinction between symbolic and literal modes of representation in the novel), or of distinguishable factors in the responses of audiences (as in Johnson's resolution of the general conditions of literary pleasure into "truth" and "variety"). And it is characteristic of the method that it prefers multiple and overlapping classifications of literary things to classification on the basis of a single principle of division to which all of the particular distinctions developed in the critic's discourse may be referred.

The second method is in most respects the contrary of this. It is that "other scientific method"—to quote Hume again—"where a general abstract principle is first established, and is afterwards branched out into a variety of inferences and conclusions" which are then made to apply to the immediate subject in hand.[23] Its starting-point is always something laid down as a basic truth

23

from which, if it is granted, consequences can be inferred by logical equation and opposition that are assumed to be appropriate in some way to literature or poetry through one or another or some combination of its causes in the minds or creative processes of writers, in the language they use, in the things or actions they represent, or in the effects their works are capable of having on readers. The essential first step is therefore to fix upon some kind of general structure discernible in things or actions or mental faculties or symbolic expressions (for example, the creative powers of God, the universal relations of man and nature, the character of discourse or of science, the nature of metaphor or synecdoche, the operations of the libido, the manifestations of primitive myth and ritual) which can be taken as a model or analogue in the discussion and which, being simpler or better known than poetry, can be used to supply the critic with principles and distinctions wherewith to mark off poetry from other things or to assimilate it to them and ultimately to make statements about the structures and values of individual poems. In the procedure thus determined, once the "general abstract principle" is established or the model chosen, the basic oppositions it makes possible necessarily persist, in however qualified or disguised forms, throughout the critic's discourse, with the result that his account of poetry, no matter how sharply he may wish to set it apart, is always framed in patterns of terms that can be applied with more or less equal relevance to other things (as we have seen in Mr. Ransom). This cannot be avoided, but at the same time it is possible for a critic who uses this method to employ it in two different ways: either reductively, by arguing that the literary object he is concerned with is "nothing but" the more simple or general model to which it is referred (as in much contemporary psychoanalytic and "archetypal" criticism), or constructively, by retaining the basic oppositions afforded by the model but showing that they are inevitably particularized and qualified as they manifest themselves in more differentiated forms (as, for the most part, in Mr. Ransom). In both of its two modes, finally, it is a method that can be described, in contrast with the other method, either as hypothetical, in the sense that its starting-point is a general supposition chosen more or less arbitrarily for its assumed explana-

24

tory powers; or as dialectical, in the sense both that the relevance of its initial premises is something to be granted rather than established inductively by inspection of concrete literary phenomena and that it proceeds typically by dialectical devices of division and composition; or as "abstract," in the sense that its essential distinctions (like the Marxist conception of the "inner contradictions" in capitalism) are "relations of ideas" or distinctions of "reason" rather than of "nature."

Any critic who wants to make coherent sense about literary questions must evidently choose between these two methods of procedure, even if he remains unconscious that he is making the choice; and as he chooses the one or the other, so will what he is talking about, under the name of "tragedy" or what not, be one kind of thing or another, and few of the statements he may make about it will have the same meaning or possess equal validity in the two cases. For clearly what may be true of tragedy, or of any tragedy, when "tragedy" is taken, in the first method of consideration, as a name for a particular species of concrete artistic productions that are distinguished, among other things, by having such-and-such a plot-form as a necessary condition of producing such-and-such an effect, will not be true, or true in the same sense, when "tragedy" is taken, in the second method of consideration, as the name of a universal attitude or "vision" of life the distinctive nature of which is defined in dialectical opposition to another similarly universal attitude or "vision" of life for which the word "comedy" is thought to be the appropriate symbol.[24] And so with any other literary thing that is susceptible of formulation in either "matter of fact" or "abstract" terms; it must inevitably suffer a change of nature in passing from the one language to the other—so inescapable, in criticism, is the mutual interdependence of the subject-matter the critic actually talks about and the method of inquiry and argument by which it is constituted for him in his discussion.

V

From this view of the nature of critical discourse we may derive certain consequences of major importance for our problem in these lectures as well as, I think, for the practice of criticism in general. The essence of the view—to adapt what has been said of science and philosophy as a whole—is that the same critical "sentence" about no matter what subject "may be demonstrably true or demonstrably false, empirically confirmable or not, significant or nonsensical"—and, we may add, relevant or irrelevant, of central or only marginal importance—"depending upon the framework to which we appeal."[25] There is, in other words, a strict relativity, in criticism, of statements to questions and questions to "frameworks"; and as for the status of variant comparable "frameworks" with respect to one another, it is clear that we must take the position recently urged upon his fellow logicians by Professor Carnap.[26] Concerning the substance of any crucial statement in a science, he says, we can ask questions of two different kinds. The first kind consists of questions "internal" to the framework before us: for example, the question of how the structure of poetry differs from that of science in a framework which assumes that poetry is essentially a kind of discourse and which disposes, accordingly, only of terms that signify such a subject-matter; these are questions of fact or theory to which true or false answers can be given within the conceptual and logical bounds of the framework. The questions of the second kind are "external" in the sense that they are really questions not about propositions within a framework but about the justification of the framework itself: for example, is it true that poetry is essentially a kind of discourse? And these, says Professor Carnap, are not theoretical but practical questions, which are stated correctly only when they are put in the form, Shall I use this or some other alternative framework, applicable to the same sphere of objects but constituting them as different kinds of things, for the inquiries I wish to pursue? Shall I, in criticism, for instance, employ a language which will necessarily lead me to dwell on characteristics that relate poetry to other things or a language which will necessarily cause me to emphasize characteristics peculiar to poetry or to one or another of its kinds? The issue, plainly, cannot be decided by a direct appeal to facts, for it is equally true that poetry is organically connected with everything else in life and that it is something with a distinctive reality of its own. I cannot, however, use the same conceptual language to exhibit both the organic interconnections and the specific differences; hence I must choose; but I can justify my choice only by arguing, and possibly persuading others to agree with me, that by means of the particular framework I have selected certain important questions about poetry (in the common sense reference of the term) can be answered which I could not even raise, much less answer intelligibly, in a framework of the other sort. There is thus a strict relativity, in criticism, not only of questions and statements to frameworks but of frameworks to ends, that is, to the different kinds of knowledge about poetry we may happen, at one time or another or for one or another reason, to want. And who is there with authority sufficient to entitle him to inform critics what these must be?

It is hardly necessary, perhaps, to point out the difference between this pluralistic view of critical languages and the various other views, including those mentioned earlier in this lecture, which attempt to account for the many divergences and apparent contradictions in doctrine or interpretation so familiar to us in the history of criticism. To insist that the truth about literature or poetry is not and cannot be enclosed within any particular scheme of terms and principles of method is by no means, in the first place, to give oneself up to scepticism about criticism itself or the capacity of any mode of critical approach to yield observations or general propositions the truth of which we can verify for ourselves once we have noted accurately what it is that the statements are intended to refer to. The plain fact is that, despite all the conflicts of doctrine and critical philosophy from the Greeks to ourselves, real knowledge of literature has been advanced, though never in a straight line.

Again, although I have used the word "relativity" in describing the status of critical questions and answers, the relativity inherent in the view of criticism I am proposing is a very different thing from what those critics have in mind who describe themselves as historical or sociological "relativists."[27] I shall not dwell on the fact that relativism in this sense, at least in its more consistent statements, is a self-refuting doctrine when applied to philosophic positions, inasmuch as the determination of all ideas

27

by circumstances which it asserts must necessarily hold true of this assertion itself. But the matter is much simpler than that, for if there were indeed any fixed causal relation between the languages which critics have used and the social and cultural conditions of their times, the very diversity of critical languages which confronts us in every period or civilization in which criticism has flourished would have been impossible, and the co-existence in classical Greece of Plato and Aristotle would be a miraculous event. A critical language is indeed something developed in historical time, but once it has been invented and made to yield useful and verifiable results within its sphere, it remains thereafter, despite changing conditions, as one of the permanent resources of critics for solving the particular kinds of problems it is fitted to solve should these again seem important.

There have been, I suspect, few real sceptics or historical relativists in criticism as compared with the many critics who have dealt with the problem of diversity in critical positions in one or another of two other ways, both of them clearly incompatible with the view I am suggesting. The first are those who yearn for a more comprehensive "synthesis" or "integration" in criticism than yet exists, and propose to achieve this by a more or less eclectic putting together of various distinct systems or approaches or at least of what appear to be their sounder parts. No one, perhaps, has committed himself more ardently to this natural aspiration than Mr. Stanley Edgar Hyman, in his portrait of the "ideal critic" who would combine in his work the best insights and techniques of Edmund Wilson, Yvor Winters, T. S. Eliot, V. F. Parrington, Van Wyck Brooks, Maud Bodkin, Christopher Caudwell, John L. Lowes, G. Wilson Knight, R. P. Blackmur, I. A. Richards, William Empson, Kenneth Burke, Jane Harrison, John Crowe Ransom, Cleanth Brooks, etc., while discarding what is "irrelevant, worthless, or private to them"; the "actual critic," he confesses, would be satisfied to aim at a more modest kind of integration.[28] A less ambitious critic of this school is Mr. R. P. Blackmur, who has recently proposed, as one remedy for the narrowness of contemporary criticism, an "alliance" or "marriage" between Aristotle and Coleridge: from the one he would take "the notions that still live in the following set of six terms,"

28

namely, *praxis, mimesis, mythos, ethos, pathos, katharsis,* together with such "formal terms about the plot" as *desis, crisis,* and *lysis*; from the other, "the notions in the set of three words—not any one or any two but the set of all three words"—namely, *esemplastic, coadunative,* and *synergical.*[29] The result, he implies, would be something better than either of the two critics taken separately, since, whereas the terms of Aristotle apply "to the behaviour of the things indicated by the words" of poetry, the terms of Coleridge, which "apply to the behaviour of words and are the attributes of imagination in words," would give us, as a supplement to Aristotle's account of the subject-matter of poetry, "a free heuristic psychology of poetry, a rich partial means for finding out what is in the words of poetry, and an equally rich partial means of putting the maximum meaning into the words we use ourselves." And this sort of synthesis would be in harmony, he says, with "the rhetorical tradition of the European mind which reached its true heights of articulate imaginative richness in St. Augustine and Dante: to whom all the modes of the mind were equally parts and instruments of aesthetic experience, and each with a warrant to correct, modify, complete, and incarnate each of the other modes." I am quite unable to imagine what the "integrated" criticism proposed by Mr. Hyman would be like; but it is surely evident that the offspring of Mr. Blackmur's suggested alliance would have only the most remote resemblance to either of its parents: it might or might not have important virtues of its own as a newly invented language, but these would be no adequate substitute for the separate and distinctive virtues of either Coleridge or Aristotle, and we should end, were his suggestion to lead to the rise of a new critical orthodoxy, in being worse off in analytical resources than we were before, just as criticism in the Neoclassical period was rather impoverished than enriched, on the whole, by the similar effort of the Renaissance to "marry" Aristotle and Horace.

What, however, is most of all incompatible with the pluralistic account of criticism I have been developing in this lecture is the common assumption that underlies all the verbal wars between critics in different traditions and inspires the frequent assertions that this, whatever it may be, is the "proper" or "only profitable" way of studying poetry or reading Shakespeare. There is of course an important sense in which all of us, if we are to accomplish anything in criticism or any other science, must be dogmatists. We must, that is, attach ourselves to some particular set of first principles in which we have faith, at least for the task in hand, and proceed to use these in the solution of such problems as they allow us to deal with; and we cannot be required to demonstrate the "truth" of the principles we adopt any more than the physicist is required to prove that matter or atoms exist; it is enough if we are able, by working with them, to achieve positive and verifiable results of the kind we want. This is dogmatism, but of an indispensable and salutary sort, without which no progress could ever take place in any of the sciences or arts; and it ought not to be confused with the negative and preclusive type of dogmatism that shows itself so often nowadays in the mutual recriminations of aesthetic critics and historical scholars, in the many attempts to legislate against critical "heresies" and "fallacies" (the "intentional fallacy," the "affective fallacy," the "didactic fallacy," and so on), in the numerous debates as to what poetry "really" is or as to whether there is one "myth" or many. Much sincere fervour and eloquence, and often much bitterness over the refusal of other critics to agree, have gone into the assertion of these exclusionist positions, and much valuable paper has been consumed; and all to no purpose except the stultifying one of making communication among critics of different schools unnecessarily hard and depriving them of both inclination and ability to learn from one another. For what lurks in all these and similar quarrels among critics is a confusion of the second with the first of Professor Carnap's two types of questions; they are actually controversies not about problems and statements but about frameworks; and they would be impossible except for a tacit identification of the "real" or metaphysical nature of the objects the critic is talking about with the particular terms in which he has chosen to discuss them—of poetry, for example, with what he can get out of a scheme of concepts in which poetry is equated uniquely (say) with the poetic process, or with the poet's imaginative vision, or with the expression of a certain type of knowledge, or with language of a certain kind; whence it naturally follows that the critic who thinks in this way is not content to assert propositions more or less warranted by his chosen scheme but must insist on denying, at least by implication, the truth or relevance of any propositions not so derived.

The pluralistic critic, on the other hand, would take the view that the basic principles and methods of any distinguishable mode of criticism are tools of inquiry and interpretation rather than formulations of the "real" nature of things and that the choice of any special "language," among the many possible for the study of poetry, is a practical decision to be justified solely in terms of the kind of knowledge the critic wants to attain. He would be no less zealous than the dogmatic critic in going about such positive tasks in criticism as he might wish to pursue; he would merely waste less time in controversies of the invidious kind I have spoken of. For he would understand that critical approaches of the most diverse sorts can coexist without implying either contradiction or inconsistency. He would know that if he found it essential or useful for his own purposes to conceive of poetry as communication or expression of meaning or as a form of cognition or as "symbolic action," this would in no sense invalidate the analytical devices or the conclusions of another critic who started from the hypothesis that poetry, or some poetry, is a mode of imitation; for he would see that completely different aspects or relationships of poetry are involved in the two cases and that there is no way of impugning the "truth" of either view except in terms of assumptions peculiar to the other. He would know, similarly, that in a critical discussion centring in the creative processes common to imaginative writers or in general qualities of language and thought (such as the "sublimity" of Longinus or the "maturity" of Mr. Leavis), distinctions of literary kinds might well be irrelevant, but that this would not entitle him to say that such distinctions are in themselves meaningless or without basis in reality, or that other critics, concerned with inquiries into the nature of poetic products, are in error when they assign to them major importance. In practical criticism, again, he would know that poetic works are bound to appear as different kinds of structures and to suggest quite different observations when they are placed in different analytical contexts, and he would be careful to ask what context has been chosen and for what reasons before dismissing a critic's observations on a given poem as false or beside the point. He would expect, for instance, that the structures discovered in Shakespeare's plays would not turn out to be the same in a critical context in which the plays are considered as dramatic works designed to please contemporary theatregoers, as in a context in which attention is focused on the analogies between them and their archetypes in ritual or myth; but he would see no reason for condemning the second type of study as such because it is not as useful as the first for the literary critic or historian or for condemning the first type because it is not as useful as the second for critics interested in analysing poetry, as Miss Bodkin does, for the sake of the insights it can give us into the "universal forces" operating in our natures. He would, in short, look upon critical principles, whether his own or others', not as sectarian dogmas to be defended on metaphysical grounds, but as instruments of research and appreciation, any set of which is necessarily limited in relation both to the aspects of poetry it brings into view and to the kinds of conclusions it permits the critic to reach. He would still be a dogmatist in the first of our two senses; but he would understand that the truth of any statements he may make is relative not only to the objective facts to which his principles are applied and in the light of which their relevance is guaranteed, but to the nature and scope of the principles themselves, and he would take care not to indulge in assertions as to what poetry or poetic structure "really" is or as to what is the "proper" way of approaching it that imply any supposition that what is "real" or "proper" in his scheme of principles is "real" or "proper" absolutely.

VI

All this does not mean, however, that there are no general standards for distinguishing the better from the worse in the performances of critics or for making comparative valuations among the different existing languages of criticism. In the first place, whatever the character of a critic's language, we have a right to hold him to the accepted canons of reasoning and

32

hypothesis-making, as well as of common sense, that apply in any branch of inquiry dealing with particular things. It may be highly useful, for certain purposes, to consider poetry as a special kind of language; but something is surely amiss when the differentia of poetic language the critic chooses concentrates attention on devices which are demonstrably not peculiar to the particular body of works he has agreed to call "poetry," or when the inherence in all poems or all good poems of the characteristic he has selected—whether it be "ambiguity," "paradox," "irony," or something else of the same sort—depends largely or solely upon his having applied to them a technique of reading determined by the very hypothesis he is attempting to establish.[30] Or, again, although we can have no quarrel with an approach to classical poetry or drama that seeks to trace the survivals in it of its origins in primitive myth and ritual, there can be no sound inference from the fact, or supposed fact, that myth and ritual are symbolic structures to the conclusion that Greek epic or tragedy is therefore likewise symbolic; for to argue in this way is to assume that the developed state of anything can be fully known from a consideration of its initial state; and this *is* a fallacy whether in criticism or in anything else.[31]

Of the requirements of proof in practical criticism and interpretation, little need be said. It is no doubt possible to justify the most extreme "liberty of interpreting" when criticism is frankly concerned with the practical uses to which poems may be put by readers irrespective of their authors' intentions in composing them; they can then be made to say or to mean whatever is most relevant to our interests or needs; and who can rightly object if this is what we want to do and is plainly advertised as such? But most modes of criticism, however different their languages, have assumed that their theories are applicable to poems in ways that require some sort of verification in terms of what was actually put into the poems by their poets; and when such is the case, there can clearly be no sufficient excuse for any "critical" interpretation of a poem that cannot be reconciled, except by special pleading, with the results of an independent and properly conducted grammatical and historical inquiry into the probable intentions of its writer and the meanings of his

33

words. Here criticism and philology can never be at odds, whatever the critic's principles, although it must be said that when the philological evidence conflicts with itself, the critic may have to decide in the light of the best hypothesis he can form concerning the artistic intent of the poem or passage. And any such hypothesis—again whatever the critic's principles—is subject to scrutiny according to the general rules for hypotheses which most scholars instinctively know but which many critics cheerfully disregard. There is the rule, for example, that any hypothesis must be verifiable by the reader in terms of evidence which he can examine for himself by means of his ordinary faculties supplemented by the relevant information; this is inconsistent with all those not infrequent arguments by critics (of which we shall see some examples in a later lecture) to the effect that the truth of their contentions should be evident to any one who has the requisite sensibility for reading poetry or who will think about the matter as long or as hard as the critic himself has done. Critical insights into poems are not worth having on these terms. And only less shocking, though even more often to be met with, are the arguments that require us, as a condition of receiving the new truth the critic has to offer, to disregard our natural emotional response to the poem when we read it naïvely without benefit of the critic's hypothesis. An instance of this that deserves to become classic is Mr. Wilson Knight's essay on *Hamlet*, in which we are told that, if only we will "refuse to be diverted from a clear vision by questions of praise and blame, responsibility and causality, and watch only the actions and reactions of the persons as they appear," and if only we will refuse, in reading the play, to "think in terms of logic," we shall then "observe a striking reversal of the usual commentary" on what is going on in Shakespeare's tragedy: we shall see, among other things, that Hamlet himself, throughout the action, is a figure of death and evil, an incarnation of "bitterness, cruelty, and inaction" which "spreads its effects outward among the other persons like a blighting disease," whereas Claudius, in spite of his original crime, is a person whose faults "are forced on him" and who is "distinguished by creative and wise action, a sense of purpose, benevolence, a faith in himself and those around him, by love

34

of his Queen. . . ."[32] But why, we are bound to ask, must we make these refusals? And there seems to be only one possible answer: because, without them, there could be no "striking reversal of the usual commentary." The whole procedure, in short, is one designed to save, not the phenomena, but the hypothesis about Shakespeare and dramatic poetry to which Mr. Wilson Knight has attached his faith.

But we can go farther than this and, still in an undogmatic and pluralistic spirit, raise questions concerning the comparative efficacy of critical "languages" themselves. And we can do this because, although all organized knowledge of literature is necessarily contained in particular and widely differing formulations of its nature and characteristics, we all of us possess, in addition, a more or less extensive subcritical or common sense acquaintance with literature or poetry in the light of which we may judge the relative adequacy and appropriateness of the various systems of terms that have been developed to explain it. We know that poetry, however we may define it, is an integral part of life, in complex relationship with other things, but that it is, at the same time, something which we prize for its own sake as distinct from nature, human action, religion, science, philosophy, history, or rhetoric, though all these may be involved in its genesis and content. We know, too, that what we call poetry is not all alike, even if collectively it appears to constitute one distinctive branch of human activity; we value different poems for the different peculiar pleasures they give us, and we are aware that these differences are determined, in no simple way, by interrelated differences in language, subject-matter, technique, and principles of construction. And we know that poetry, like everything else, has had a long history from its origins in human activities which we are accustomed to call by other names than poetry to its present highly diversified state as a kind of art.

Here then are the material objects of criticism; and they are of such a nature, and criticism itself, as we have seen, is of such a nature, that it is futile to look for any critical language which, in constructing, as it necessarily must, a particular set of terms capable of directing attention to a certain aspect of literary phenomena and in using this as the source of its data, will not at the same time exclude from consideration other aspects equally important. Such specialization is the price of knowledge in any field; wherefore criticism can be said to flourish in a given period in proportion as the languages available to critics tend to be collectively commensurate with the diversity of aspects which literature or poetry presents when looked at with the eyes of common sense. That is why the lust for orthodoxy or the "proper" approach in criticism is so pernicious a passion. But short of this collective adequacy of criticism to its objects—which we may hope for but never expect to see—we may recognize degrees of adequacy as between the particular critical languages with which different individual critics are content to work. The power of any critical method is a function at once of the analytical precision and the range of the compendent concepts it affords within the confines of its special view; and those are, generally speaking, inferior and relatively unfruitful methods which have terms for dealing with only one or a few of the many causes of poems, confining their effective distinctions, for example, only to the psychology of the poet or to poetic subject-matter or language;[33] or which are capable only of distinguishing poetry from other things but not of differentiating precisely the variety of poetic structures and effects;[34] or which permit the consideration only of the conventional and historical aspects of poetic works in abstraction from their artistic principles or, conversely, make difficult a consideration of poems in terms of circumstances and history; or which rest upon such a general or simple hypothesis that they invariably tend to reduce the particularities and developed structures of poetry to a common denominator of universal and hence aesthetically insignificant human traits. Of this last kind of inadequacy no one has spoken more sharply than C. G. Jung in his comment on the psychoanalytical reduction of poetic works to "the sphere of general human psychology, whence everything else besides art may proceed." "An explanation of a work of art obtained in this way is just as great a futility as the statement that 'every artist is a narcissist.' Every man who pursues his own line to the limit of his powers is a 'narcissist' . . . hence such a statement says nothing; it merely elicits surprise in the style of a *bon-mot*."[35] And what is true of the Freudian pro-

36

cedure is surely true, for the same reason, of such other reductions in criticism as those of poetry to myth or of all art to symbolic expression: they never allow us, in our discourse about poetry, to go beyond the simple and undifferentiated terms in which their premises are framed, so that we gain in universality at the cost of being unable to say anything to the point.

There are doubtless no absolutely inappropriate schemes of critical terms, since it is hard to think of any which have not permitted critics to make statements that can be seen to be relevant, in some sense and however remotely, to our experience of works of art. But I would raise the question, finally, whether what I have called the "matter of fact" criticisms (of which there have been a good many varieties) are not less likely, in general, to do violence to our common sense apprehension of literature or poetry than the "abstract" criticisms I have contrasted with them. The "abstract" method, as Hume said, apropos of its use in morals, "may be more perfect in itself, but suits less the imperfection of human nature, and is a common source of illusion and mistake in this as well as in other subjects."[36] It is a method, for one thing, that encourages the invention of occult qualities and the preoccupation with problems that arise from the relationship of these to one another in the critic's dialectic rather than from any empirically verifiable connections among things, with the result, very often, that theoretical debates are set going which admit of no possible resolution since they define no concrete facts to which we may appeal. This is the case, I think, with all the discussions in recent years, especially among Shakespeareans, about the general nature of "tragedy" and the implications of this nature (which is defined variously by different critics but always as a kind of Platonic essence) for such questions as whether or not "the tragic picture is incompatible with the Christian faith, or with any form of religious belief that assumes the existence of a personal and kindly God."[37] But both "tragedy" and "the Christian faith" are here abstractions, or constructs of the critic, having little to do with what individual poets were engaged upon when they composed serious plots of one or another kind and called some or all of them "tragedies" or with what individual men and women at different times have thought about God or about what they took tragedy to be; and the issue can never be settled because it is a pseudo-issue, one which is made to look like an issue of fact but which really has no identifiable reference outside the game of dialectical counters in which it has arisen. And other difficulties appear when schemes of literary values thus derived are used in the examination of particular works. For we then get typically judgments by reason rather than sentiment, in which the critic's predetermined scale of better and worse rather than the peculiar intent and form of the poem inevitably conditions what is said; as in Mr. Ransom's strictures on Shakespeare's seventy-third sonnet[38] or Mr. Leavis' objections to the metaphors in Shelley's "Ode to the West Wind."[39] From all which I conclude, not that the "abstract" method has no justifiable uses in criticism, but that there are many questions to which it ought not to be applied if we are interested in something more than the play of the critic's ideas and sensibility.

I have had to say these things about criticism in general in order to make clear the nature of the language—or rather, in the current slang I have been using, the "metalanguage"—in which I intend to deal in these lectures with the question of the structure of poetry. The consideration, for the reasons I have given, will necessarily be an indirect one, through the medium of the variant worlds of critical discourse, or some of them, which have determined what the problem has meant and how it has been solved. I shall attempt, in the next three lectures, to bring the radically different ideas about the structure of poetry to be found first in the *Poetics* of Aristotle and then in the dominant school of contemporary critics, into logical relation with the radically different types of language in which Aristotle and these moderns have approached not only this but all other critical questions; and I shall consider, in the final lecture, at least one of the ways in which the existing languages of practical criticism need, it seems to me, to be supplemented if we are to attain a more adequate understanding than we now have of the complex problem of poetic structure.

Poetic structure in the language of Aristotle

W E   C A N   S E E   H O W important the question of the structure of poetry was for Aristotle by considering the opening words of the *Poetics*. With respect to poetic itself and its various forms or species, he will inquire, he says, concerning what power (*dynamis*) each form has and how plots ought to be constructed if the poetry is to be good (*kalos*); concerning also the number and nature of the parts of which poems are composed; and similarly concerning other questions such as are proper to this line of inquiry (*methodos*). I shall come back to other parts of this statement later on, but for the moment I want to direct attention to its final clause: "and similarly concerning other questions such as are proper to this line of inquiry." We cannot well understand, I think, either what the structure of poetry is for Aristotle or why he makes the problem of structure so central in his poetic theory or why he treats it as he does, unless we keep in mind, to begin with, how the peculiar "line of inquiry" undertaken in the *Poetics* is related to the various other inquiries which make up his philosophic system.

The character of this relation can be exhibited most simply, perhaps, by contrasting Aristotle with nearly all the other philosophers of comparable scope who have included poetry or the fine arts among the subjects to which they have given serious attention. If we look into Plato, for instance, we find that, although poetry and music are treated rather differently in different contexts in the dialogues, the fundamental language of the dis-

39

cussion is always the same, and it is the same, also, as the language in which Plato discusses all other questions: no matter what the subject, the dialectic is invariably controlled by his central proportions of being and becoming, knowledge and opinion, and by the reference of everything ultimately to the One and the Good. There is a similar unity, also, in David Hume, although the underlying scheme of terms could not easily differ more widely: no matter what particular aspect of poetry or any other subject is being discussed, the premises of Hume's arguments are always derived, directly or indirectly, from his basic distinctions of impressions and ideas, the understanding and the passions, abstract relations and causes and effects. And so too with philosophers as diverse in other respects as Hobbes, Hegel, Croce, Dewey, and the contemporary theorists of symbolic structure: there is in all of them only one language for talking about poetry and the arts either in themselves or as they are related to other things. With Aristotle, on the contrary, almost the opposite is true. He is the great multilingual philosopher, who constructed his whole system on the assumption that, while everything in the world, including poetry, is inextricably connected with everything else, the essential condition of knowledge is a strict division of labour among the various sciences and arts and the constitution of any science or art as a distinct line of inquiry differing from other inquiries by having some specific and limited aspect of nature or human life as its special subject-matter and some specific and limited kind of knowledge as its end.[40] The system of terms used in any science or art, therefore, and the principles of reasoning it employs are necessarily relative to the particular aspect of things it deals with and to the particular kind of knowledge it pursues, and they will not be the same, except by analogy, in any other generically distinct art or science. This, however, is a division not of things but of sciences; and since any distinguishable existing thing, such as poetry, presents a multiplicity of aspects and relations, it can be taken as a possible subject of inquiry or source of data in many different sciences or arts, in each of which the character of the discussion will be determined by the distinctive aims and the distinctive basic truths, hypotheses, and methods of the art or science itself.

40

If we wish, consequently, to extract a general theory of poetry from Aristotle, we must proceed much as we would have to proceed if we wanted to find out what theory of poetry is taught in this University. We would not in that case confine our questions to the departments of literature but would consider also what is being said or implied about poetry, in their different languages, by the professors, let us say, of religion, ethics, logic, psychology, sociology, anthropology, linguistics, and cultural history; and what we would arrive at would obviously not be a single unified explanation, like that, for instance, of Croce, but a large number of insights into discrete but complementary aspects of poetry such as could hardly be afforded by any one treatment of the subject, however systematically comprehensive. The case of Aristotle, though in a much less extreme way, of course, is analogous to this. If we are interested in learning the truth, as he saw it, about poetry and the other related arts, we must read not only the *Poetics* but also the *Rhetoric,* the *Nicomachean Ethics,* the *Politics,* even the *Physics* and the *Metaphysics.* And it is characteristic of his philosophic method that the scattered propositions about poetry, music, or art in general which occur in these various treatises cannot be put together in any simple fashion to reconstruct for Aristotle an independent aesthetics or philosophy of art, such as many other philosophers have given us. The different inquiries do indeed converge, but they converge upon objects which, though empirically the same, are given by no means exactly the same conceptual status or definition in the varied "methods" which Aristotle brings to bear upon them. It would be a serious error, thus, to read the statements about the catharsis of pity and fear in the *Poetics* as logically continuous with the discussion of the cathartic power of poetry and music in Book viii of the *Politics,* inasmuch as in the *Politics* poems are being considered (in anticipation of Mr. F. R. Leavis) as instruments of education and hence as efficient causes in relation to the good of citizens, whereas their character in the *Poetics* is that of final or intrinsic goods in relation to the art of the poet as their efficient cause. There is no contradiction between the two accounts; but only confusion can result from assuming that the concept of catharsis must have the same meaning and implications in the one as in the other.

41

There are, then, in the philosophic system of Aristotle, a good many different languages for talking about poetry, among which the language of the *Poetics* is only one. It is so described, as we have seen, in the statement which opens the treatise. But when this has been said, it remains true that among the various ways in which poetry can be discussed by Aristotle—more ways, certainly, than he himself exemplified in his surviving works—the way determined for the *Poetics* has a special status, since it is only through the peculiar terms and the peculiar method of poetic science that it is possible to attain knowledge of those aspects of poetry which distinguish essentially what a poet does *as poet* from anything that he might do, in poetry, as psychological organism, moral being, philosopher, scientist, political propagandist, or member of society.

It is important to observe, therefore, how the terms which make up the special language of poetics in Aristotle have been chosen and put together. And we cannot but be impressed, in the first place, by the fact that a large number of them are terms drawn from one or another of the non-poetic sciences or arts. Some of them—like "whole," "part," "unity," "completeness," "magnitude," "beauty," and "imitation"—are general and analogical terms from metaphysics; others—such as "probability" and "necessity"—are terms borrowed from physics; others, again—such as "hamartia" and the various words used to define the actions and characters necessary to the tragic plot—are terms originally of ethics; still others—namely, "pity" and "fear" and the distinctions employed in discussing poetic "thought"—are terms whose primary definitions are in rhetoric; and a few others—notably, the expressions "soul" and "organic unity" as applied to plot in tragedy and epic—are clearly metaphors from biological psychology. There is nothing, of course, that need surprise us in this fact when we consider that poetry, however distinct it may be from other things, has its necessary basis and origin in human nature, derives its subjects from the ethically discriminable activities of men, and affects us, in large part, through our capacity for drawing inferences from words or actions and for reacting to these emotionally as we react to similar statements or situations in practical life. It is therefore connected through its causes with every aspect of our experience; and the special science which treats of it can be made truly comprehensive, accordingly, only if it is constructed as a composite science dependent upon many other sciences or arts for its subsidiary principles; as Aristotle explicitly recognizes, for instance, when he remarks that the subject of "thought" in tragedy falls under the arts of politics and rhetoric.[41]

The Aristotelian expert in poetics, in short, must know a good many different things besides poetry, but it is equally true that he becomes an expert in poetics by virtue precisely of his ability to subordinate the terms and premises he derives from metaphysics, physics, ethics, politics, rhetoric, psychology, and so on, to the peculiar principles of his own science. What these are, and why, we must now go on to consider.[42]

II

The primary aim of poetics, for Aristotle, is the discovery and statement of the principles which govern poets when they make good poems; these, it is assumed, will also be the principles by which the specifically *poetic* qualities of existing poems are to be judged.[43] Its end accordingly is not knowledge for its own sake but knowledge for the sake of a certain kind of human activity, the purpose or good of which determines the character of the data with which it is concerned and the method to be employed in dealing with them. Poetics is not, that is to say, a theoretical science like mathematics, physics, or psychology, but a practical science much more closely related to ethics, in which, as Aristotle remarks, we inquire not merely in order to know what virtue is but in order to become good men and be able to perform good actions.[44] It differs, nevertheless, from ethics in one essential respect, namely, that the good it aims at is not to be found in the activities to which it leads but rather in products that persist beyond the actions which produce them and have values in themselves which are independent of the character and motives of the agents who brought them into being, in the sense at least that knowledge merely of the agents and their actions will never enable us to judge adequately what they have done.[45] Nor, again, is poetics simply an instrumentalist art like logic, dialectic, or rhetoric, inasmuch as the constructions it envisages have their sufficient reason for existing in themselves; and by the same token it stands apart from the merely useful arts such as medicine or house-building. Its status, in short, is that of a productive science,[46] as Aristotle would call it, of which the end is the making of products that have beauty of some sort as their distinguishing characteristic, being things to which we attribute value for the intrinsic excellence of their making rather than for any further utility they may be made to serve.

But what does productive scientific knowledge of such things consist in, and how may it be obtained? They are, to begin with, like the objects of the biological sciences, things generated out of pre-existent materials by a certain process. Hence they exist and are fully knowable only as "concrete wholes"—as things, that is, of which we can give an adequate account only when we specify both the matter or elements of which they are composed and the form, or principle of structure, by reason of which this matter has the character of a definite existing thing, the two aspects of matter and form being inseparable in fact but separable analytically in our account;[47] and in all such things the form, or synthesizing principle, is most completely expressed, for any specific whole, by its peculiar *dynamis* or "power."[48] A good instance is the human eye, a complete understanding of which, as a distinctive kind of biological *synolon* (when it is viewed as the subject-matter of ophthalmology), depends on our taking account not only of its basic matter of bodily tissues and of the complex structure of organs that gives definite shape to these even in a corpse, but above all of the power of vision, which, in a living person with good eyesight, is the animating form or function of the whole material structure. Of such wholes, however, there are two major kinds—those which come to be by nature, that is, by a moving principle inherent in their matter (as acorns grow into trees), and those which come to be by art, that is, by a principle, outside the matter, in the mind of the human being who brings them about: "from art," says Aristotle, "proceed the things of which the form is in the soul of the artist."[49] These last are productions in the strict sense of "things made," and it is with wholes of this kind—and with knowledge relevant

44

to their making rather than (say) to their uses or history—that the productive sciences are concerned.

The knowledge they seek, moreover, at least as their ideal, is "scientific" knowledge; and that means for Aristotle knowledge of causes or necessary connections among the attributes of objects within any field of research.[50] There can be no science short of this; but necessity, as Aristotle frequently points out, is of several different sorts; and the kind of necessity which is possible in the productive sciences or arts is the same as that which is looked for in any of the sciences that deal with the generation of concrete wholes of whatever type. There is, he says, "absolute necessity, manifested in eternal phenomena; and there is hypothetical necessity, manifested in everything that is generated by nature as in everything that is produced by art, be it a house or what it may. For if a house or other such final object is to be realized, it is necessary that such and such material shall exist; and it is necessary that first this and then that shall be produced, and first this and then that set in motion, and so on in continuous succession, until the end and final result is reached, for the sake of which each prior thing is produced and exists. As with these productions of art, so also is it with the productions of nature. . . . The fittest mode, then, of treatment is to say, a man has such and such parts, because the conception of a man includes their presence, and because they are necessary conditions of his existence, or, if we cannot quite say this, which would be best of all, then the next thing to it, namely, that it is quite impossible for him to exist without them, or, at any rate, that it is better for him that they should be there; and their existence involves the existence of other antecedents."[51] Or, again, if a piece of wood is to be split with an axe, "the axe must of necessity be hard; and, if hard, must of necessity be made of bronze or iron."[52] This is the kind of necessity—dependent upon reasoning back from the nature of an achieved result to its necessary or desirable conditions—with which the natural scientist, according to Aristotle, must deal primarily if he is to go beyond the inadequate explanations of those earlier philosophers who attempted to generate the configurations of things in the universe out of the assumption of some underlying material principle, such as water, fire, or

45

earth, and of some moving principle, such as heat and cold or love and strife.[53] And the necessity appropriate to the productive sciences is no different: if we are to know what the parts, and their characteristics, of a house or a poem of necessity are, and how they must be arranged, our starting-point cannot be the materials of bricks or language we are using, it can only be a conception of the house to be erected or the poem to be composed as a completed whole of a certain kind, since it is only in the light of this, as a first principle, that we can attribute necessity to anything we may do or refrain from doing in writing the poem or building the house.

It follows from all this, in the first place, that the primary concern of poetics will not be with the actual process of poetic creation but rather with the poetic reasoning—from the character of the end to be achieved to the necessary or desirable means—that is reflected in this process when it terminates in an artistically successful product; for it is only of this rational element in art that we can have any scientific knowledge.[54] We can know, for example, as a matter of hypothetical necessity, that if a tragedy is to be composed that will exert its full characteristic power, it must have as its principal part a plot of a certain kind and quality and, subordinate to this, elements of appropriate character, thought, and diction; but it is obviously not necessary, in any sense of the word, that all good tragedies should come into being by a process of making that begins with the invention of a plot and then goes on to the invention of the characters and their thought and only as a final step discovers the words; it is often the case, indeed, that the last thing a poet actually comes to perceive in writing a successful poem is its distinctive form or power, although this is still, from the point of view of the reasoning upon which the completed poem rests, the first principle of his work. It follows also, in the second place, that the productive science of poetry (as of any other class of highly diversified productions) will deal with necessities of two kinds—those which can be identified as essential conditions or parts of all poems, once "poems" have been distinguished from other things, and those that are specific to different poetic forms; and that, moreover, since knowledge of the former is incomplete without knowledge of the latter, poetics will aim characteristically at a causal analysis of poetic species, or at least of those that differ most radically from the others in their peculiar structures and "powers." And it follows, lastly, that since poetics is a practical science, the end of its inquiries must be the discovery of what is the best possible state, consistent with their specific natures, to which different kinds of poems and their parts may be brought; and this means, as we shall see more fully later, that it must occupy itself not only with the necessities but also with the possibilities of the forms it treats in so far as these can be known at any given time.

These are, then, the major assumptions upon which the line of inquiry pursued by Aristotle in the *Poetics* appears to rest. We should expect him to begin accordingly, not with an "abstract" model or analogue from which the character of poetry in general might be deduced, but simply with the notation of a well-known fact—that there do exist certain differentiable concrete things which are commonly called "poetry"; and with respect to these, we should expect him to lay down, as the governing hypothesis of his inquiry, a proposition stating their collective nature such as will permit him to reason by hypothetical necessity to the conditions of their successful production. And this is what in fact he does in the second sentence of the treatise when he mentions epic poetry and tragedy, comedy, dithyrambic poetry, and most flute-playing and lyre-playing and says of them that they "happen all to be imitations" (the important word here is "happen"). The specific subject-matter of his inquiry is now determined: what he proposes to investigate are those existing varieties of "poetic" works—and those alone—of which the essential nature and productive causes can be most fully understood on the assumption that they are all, though in different ways, "imitations" of human actions.

The implications of this starting-point need to be carefully examined if we are to make sense of what follows; and the question evidently turns, in the first place, on the meaning of *mimesis* in Aristotle's usage. It is clearly a metaphysical term, in the sense that it can be predicated of a good many generically distinct things; but just as clearly it is not, as in Plato, a term of universal applicability capable of being used to discriminate

47

degrees of reality or value with respect to no matter what sub-jects.[55] There are no "imitations," for Aristotle, outside the sphere of human productions, and not all of these are imitations in the stricter sense in which the word is used in the *Poetics*. For generally, as he says in the *Physics*, "art partly completes what nature cannot bring to a finish, and partly imitates her";[56] and sometimes, as in medicine, the first function is more completely explanatory of what the artist does than the second. In the stricter sense an "imitation" is brought about whenever we succeed, by means of art, in producing an analogue of some natural process or form, endowed with similar powers to affect other things or us, in materials which are not naturally disposed to assume of them-selves any such process or form; any poem can thus be said to be an "imitation" when it is sufficiently intelligible, as a concrete whole, on the assumption that the poet, in making it, was intent on using certain possibilities of language in order to create in us, by certain devices of technique, the illusion of human beings more or less like ourselves doing or undergoing something, for the sake of the emotional effects naturally evoked by such characters, passions, or actions in real life when we view them as disinter-ested but sympathetic spectators. This, I take it, is what the term means, and all that it means, as Aristotle uses it in the *Poetics*. He is simply saying, in effect, that the various kinds of "poetic" works he intends to inquire into are wholes of the particular variety in which the patterns that organize the artistic matter of rhythm and speech, and thus account most completely for what the poet has to do *as poet* and for the distinctive "powers" of his creations, are patterns recognizably similar to one or another of the morally determinate patterns of human behaviour we are aware of in life. In saying this he is not committing himself or us to any particular doctrine concerning the bases of our knowledge of things (whether "epistemological realism" or anything else) or concerning the peculiar value of concrete things as opposed to abstractions, or to any dogma of art such as would lead us to prefer "idealized" to "realistic" representations or the reverse (for imitative poems are equally "imitations" whether they render things as they are, or as they are thought to be, or as they ought to be); nor is he basing poetics on a "theory of imitation" in any sense that would question the possibility of novelty in poetry or deny to the poet the honourable name of "creator." His proposition, in short, is merely a statement of the inductive hypothesis upon which he proposes to base his inquiry; and it is not intended—and this is most important to observe—as a hypothesis applicable to all the productions which men at the time were in the habit of calling "poems" but only to such kinds as "happen to be imitations" in the above sense of that term. The resulting science of poetry will therefore be far from all-inclusive, and there will remain for consideration in some other line of inquiry, more closely similar perhaps to that of the *Rhetoric*,[57] all those other species of "poetic" productions—no less admirable in their kinds—of which the organizing principle is not "imitation" but some variety of argument or persuasion.

It should be noted, finally, that no proof is offered in the *Poetics* that the kinds of poetry being considered are indeed "imitations." The hypothesis is simply laid down as a basic truth of the science to be constructed, for which there can, in fact, be no demonstration within the science itself any more than there can be a demonstration, in chemistry, of the "chemical" nature of the compounds it deals with. This does not mean, however, that the hypothesis is merely arbitrary or that a good defence cannot be made of it. That it is a fruitful hypothesis, the many distinctions it gives rise to in the *Poetics* which are obviously relevant to the productive problems of poets must leave little doubt; and its appropriateness to the facts it is being used to explain can easily be seen if we attempt to work with it ourselves as writers; for if we succeed in doing in any composition what the notion of *mimesis*, in Aristotle's sense, implies, the result will inevitably be a piece of writing, however mediocre, which has the same generic kind of structure and obeys the same necessities in its making as any of the poems treated as "imitations" in the *Poetics*.

His hypothesis laid down and the data of poetics thus determined, Aristotle is now in a position to embark upon the line of inquiry outlined in his opening sentence. His subject-matter is imitative poetry; but this presents itself, he recognizes, not as one homogeneous thing but as a number of more or less distinct

49

species of things, each of which constitutes an art by itself in the sense that skill in one of them does not necessarily imply skill in any of the others: there is thus an art of tragedy and a different art of epic, an art of comedy and an art of dithyramb, and so on. It is true that these different forms of imitative poetry have in common a good many problems and principles, but if we are to know how any of them is made when it is made well, we must have something more specific to reason from than the very general principle of imitation: we must also grasp the form of each in a definition of its peculiar nature as an artistic whole which will allow us to infer what its particular necessities and possibilities are. We can grasp in this way, it is evident, only the forms poets have already achieved, so that the basic definitions in poetics must be *ex post facto* and inductive; but we can know in advance what our definitions, in general, must consist in if they are to apply essentially and not merely accidentally to poems considered as products of art. They must, since poems are "concrete wholes," be definitions not simply of the form the poet aims at and not merely of the matter he uses but of the two as synthesized; and they must specify in appropriate terms what is distinctive of the species of poems being considered in both its matter and its form.

The first question, therefore, is what are the essential respects in which imitative poems may differ from one another in their material constitution? This is Aristotle's problem in the first three chapters of the *Poetics*, and the analysis he arrives at is of the greatest importance for the whole of the ensuing inquiry. The different groups of poems he has mentioned, he says, differ from each other in three ways: either in that they imitate in different matters or media or in that they imitate different objects or forms or in that they imitate differently and not in the same manner. The derivation of these three bases of differentiation among imitative poems—or these three generic or material "parts" of any such poem—from the nature of "imitations" in general is obvious once we consider that we cannot imitate without having a certain natural form in mind which we are attempting to embody in a medium of our own rather than of Nature's choosing, and that the result, further, will necessarily vary according to

50

the technique we use in effecting the actual fusion of the two. There must be, then, these three "parts" or structural elements in all imitative poems; and a little reflection will make clear that besides these, there can be no other material determinants of poetic structure of equal importance. In any individual poem, of course, the three elements can be separated only in an analytical sense; but that they represent distinct principles in imitative poetry is clear from the fact, to which Aristotle refers, that the same type of poetic medium may be used to imitate different kinds of objects (as when a combination of rhythm, melody, and verse is employed in both tragedy and comedy), that the same object may be brought before us in different manners (as when the action of a serious epic or part thereof is dramatized in a tragedy), and that the same manner is consistent with widely differing poetic means (as when a prose drama is rewritten in verse). They are, therefore, independent variables, all of which must be discernible in some determination in any poem, but no one of which, when determined in a particular way for a given poem, necessitates any particular determination of any of the others, although it is true that, with respect to the imitative arts in general, the selection of one kind of medium rather than another inevitably conditions the kind of objects that can be imitated in it—for example, in speech, primarily actions, passions, and the manifestations of character; in line and colour, primarily figures; and so on. As principles constitutive of the generic nature of imitative poems, moreover, they are all "poetic" or "aesthetic" principles in equal degree, since poetry, for Aristotle, is a character that inheres in the nature of poems as "concrete wholes" of a certain kind rather than peculiarly in any of their component elements. All of them, consequently, must be analysed with respect to their possibilities of independent variation if we are to be able to attain a properly specific knowledge of any given form of poetry; hence the resolution, in *Poetics* 1–3, of the poetic medium of rhythm, discourse, and harmony into the possibilities of using these means separately or in combination and, if in combination, simultaneously or in succession; of the objects of imitation into the possibilities of imitating the actions of men better than we are or worse than we are or like ourselves; and of

51

the manner of poetic imitation into the possibilities of representing the object dramatically throughout or narratively throughout or by some mixture of these two techniques. The discussion here is restricted to the basic possibilities only, as these follow from a consideration of the natures of the three elements supported by historical examples; and a more fully developed poetics would find room for many other subordinate and more refined possibilities of variation with respect to each.

Essential, however, as are all these three determinants of imitation to the conception or definition of any species of imitative poetry, they are not sufficient by themselves to give us the primary knowledge we need. Each of them, to be sure, implies a certain range of necessities and impossibilities, as well as of possibilities, for the poet. The art of dramatic imitation is not the same in what it demands or excludes as the art of imitation in any of the many kinds of narrative; the writing of a play in verse imposes very different requirements from the writing of a play in prose; the things that must be done or avoided in imitating a comic action are by no means identical with the things that the poet must do or refrain from doing if his subject is "serious"; and the necessities and possibilities of a lyric or a short story are of a widely different order from those of a full-length drama or a novel. That is why, for Aristotle, these distinctions define the spheres of different generic poetic arts. His primary interest, however, is in the making of individual works which are formally distinct in the more concrete sense of being unified composites of a particular kind of object, a particular kind of means, and a particular kind of manner; and in order to be able to reason adequately to the poetic of any of these, he clearly needs to discover, for any distinguishable species of them, what is its distinctive synthesizing principle. That principle is what he calls, in his first sentence, the peculiar *dynamis* or "power" of the form—that which animates its parts and makes of them one determinate whole, as the "soul" is the most formal principle, in this sense, of the living being, and hence the starting-point of any biological inquiry into its parts and their functions.[58] It is the same in any of the sciences or arts of production, as Aristotle's example of the axe will show. We may say that an axe, defined

52

in material terms, is a wedge-shaped piece of steel fastened to a wooden handle of an appropriate length and size; but this, though an adequate general account of the parts of an axe, would obviously be insufficient for any one, ignorant of axes, who proposed to make one, without the addition of the further specification that the piece of steel must be of such a character and the handle so designed and attached to it as to enable the user to cut wood: only with this last as a starting-point of his reasoning, would the axe-maker know precisely what and what not to do. And so, too, with the making and judgment of imitative works of literary art, even though these need have no uses beyond our contemplation of their beauty. We can thus define a certain kind of novel as an imitation of a serious action of some length involving people more or less like ourselves, in a moderately stylized prose, by means of a mixture of dramatic dialogue and narrative; and this, up to a point, would apply (say) to both *The Portrait of a Lady* and *The Master of Ballantrae*: it would distinguish them, for example, from novels like *Joseph Andrews* or short stories like "The Dead." It would not, however, enable us to account for the very different kinds of pleasure we derive from the two works or to state with any exactness the very different artistic problems faced by James and by Stevenson in composing them. Or consider, again, *Tartuffe* and *Tom Jones*— two works which are plainly comedies, though in different manners, inasmuch as they both imitate actions having the ridiculous, in Aristotle's sense of "a mistake or deformity not productive of pain or harm to others,"[59] as their basis: it is only when we distinguish the unmistakably different comic "powers" of the two works that we can perceive how distinct were the obligations as to incident, character, dénouement, and so on, which Molière had to observe from those which his commitment to a variant comic form imposed on Fielding.

And so it is that when Aristotle defines tragedy in Chapter 6 of the *Poetics* he gives us a formula which specifies not merely the three material components necessary to the existence of wholes of this kind but also the distinctive *dynamis* which is the actuality or form of their combination. A tragedy, he says, is a form of imitation of which the object is a serious action, complete as having magnitude; the means, language using all the resources of the poetic medium, each kind separately in the different parts of the play; the manner, dramatic rather than narrative representation; and the *dynamis*, "effecting through pity and fear the catharsis of such emotions." I shall say later what this last clause seems to me to mean; but its function in the definition is indubitably that of a first principle of poetic reasoning, derived inductively from certain of the individual things included in the science by its hypothesis, in the light of which Aristotle, or any poet, can make necessary inferences concerning the writing of tragedies as concrete imitative wholes.

The poetics of tragedy and its structure now follows, but it will be useful, before considering that, to look somewhat more closely at certain general features of the critical language in which its principles are stated.

III

We have seen that what Aristotle is aiming at is a productive science of poetry having as its primary subject-matter the various necessities involved in the making of poetic wholes of one or another specific kind; and we have seen that he finds a basis for the hypothetical necessity he needs by concentrating on the poetic product as distinguished from the process of its composition, by investigating the product in terms of the reasoning which constitutes peculiarly the art of its making,[60] and finally by restricting himself to those classes of "poems" which happen, when viewed in their concrete wholeness, to be imitations. The field of poetics is thus a severely restricted one. It excludes from consideration, for one thing, a good many types of productions which we are wont to call "poems" (its principles will not apply, for instance, to works like *The Divine Comedy*, *The Faerie Queene*, *The Dunciad*, or *The Prelude*), so that we need not look in Aristotle for any unitary theory of poetry such as most later critics have sought to erect. And poetics necessarily abstracts, for another thing, from the whole range of accidental or extrinsic causes of poetic production that inhere in the characters and intentions of poets, the state of poetic language, the prevailing

54

conceptions of poetic subjects, and the tastes and demands of audiences. Such causes are the special domain of the literary historian, and they are of interest to the poetic theorist, as Aristotle indicates in a number of places, as a means either of testing the conclusions of theory or of explaining why poets do not always do what their art requires. They can have, however, only a secondary place in poetics since they can obviously provide no grounds for necessary inferences as to what the poet ought to do or not to do if he is to realize such-and-such a form in his work.

The poetic theorist, nevertheless, can hardly shut his eyes to the fact that poems, being contingent human productions, are always the result, in reality, of a convergence of causes which in themselves have no necessary interconnections. Poets have intentions, but there is no inevitable correspondence between what a poem turns out to be and the original purpose that led to its writing; the language of poetry usually differs from the language of everyday life, but there are no properties of language that always go with poetry or with poetry of a given kind; there are a good many possible techniques of poetic representation, but any one of these can be used with almost any type of object or poetic means; and although some subjects have been characteristic of tragedy and others of comedy, the history of poetry makes clear that there are no subjects which are intrinsically either tragic or comic apart from what poets make of them in poems. The theorist of poetry, as Aristotle clearly saw, must take account of this contingency in the phenomena with which he deals. And that means, in the first place, that he must content himself with definitions of poetic species which specify separately all of the causes that must unite somehow if a distinctive poetic whole is to result: thus it is that in the definition of tragedy the first clause points to the poet's subject, the second to the kind of language he has chosen to use, the third to the technical process by which he has decided to put these together, and the fourth to his intention or end in writing; and we have seen how all these may vary independently of the others in different poems. But something more positive than this is also implied; for if we are to be able to reason scientifically from the definition, the various causes distinguished in it must be given an internal status comparable to that of the causes dealt with in any of the sciences of natural objects. And this Aristotle is able to do by virtue of his hypothesis of imitation. Poems are not natural things, but the varieties of poems he proposes to speak of do have a kind of nature, that of being imitative structures made out of the mimetic possibilities of language. Their matter, as completed wholes, is a determinate selection and arrangement of words, and all the other elements are in a fundamental way contained in this medium and have no *poetic* being apart from what it permits. The object imitated is internal and hence strictly "poetic" in the sense that it exists only as the intelligible and moving pattern of incidents, states of feeling, or images which the poet has constructed in the sequence of his words by analogy with some pattern of human experience such as men have either known or believed possible or at least thought of as something that ought to be. This is not, then, a theory of poetry as "representation," with life set over against art as "a constant external reality" or subject-matter which art must somehow approximate or do justice to if it is to be good;[61] poetry, for Aristotle, is a complement and analogue of life rather than a copy; and though it is true that the characters in a tragedy must be "like" ourselves, this is because, if they were not, the specific "pleasure" assumed for tragedy would be impossible. And it goes without saying that the same thing is true of the manner of imitation, as the technical principle which governs the particular way in which the object constructed by the poet is disclosed in his words.

There remains the final cause or intention, and this, too, is made in a fashion internal, since it is clear that although the specific "power" of a poem becomes actual only in the minds of readers or spectators and presupposes general human capacities for emotion, yet for the poet himself whose immediate end at least is assumed to be the making of an imitation, the problem of what is to be its *dynamis* is inseparable from the problem of what exactly, in terms of the moral qualities of the actions and characters, its imagined object is to be and by what selection of words and what contrivances of representation this object is best revealed. The catharsis through pity and fear which is the peculiar power of tragedy (or of the kind of "tragedy" Aristotle discusses) is thus a function primarily not of causes in the audience (as in the *Politics*) but of how the poet has constructed his tragic plot: it is what we experience—and this is the definition implied in Chapter 13—when a man like ourselves comes to undeserved misfortune through a completed sequence of probable or necessary actions. It is the formal cause of tragic structure in the most specific sense, and as such it necessarily effects a hierarchical ordering of the three material parts, the object of imitation being prior in causal importance to the means and the manner inasmuch as the emotional power of a tragedy—which is the first principle of its construction though not necessarily the first thing thought of—depends most completely and directly on its action, character, and thought and secondarily and indirectly, though often in highly significant ways, on its diction and music and its dramatic and theatrical technique.

It is about the construction of such wholes—at once artificial and possessed of determinate "natures" which permit scientific knowledge of their production—that Aristotle proposes to inquire; and his problem is twofold. On the one hand, he has to collect his definitions of particular species of poetry from the existing works in which the forms and their respective "powers" are clearly evident, taking care to distinguish their essential artistic principles from the conventions of material or technique through which the principles are realized at any given time;[62] and from the definitions thus attained—in which the conception of imitation is specified as narrowly as possible to fit the object imitated, the means and manner used, and the "power" discernible in each species—he has to reason *a posteriori* to the number and nature of the constituent parts of each form and to its various subspecies. On the other hand, since, as he says in the *Nicomachean Ethics*, "every art and every inquiry, and similarly every action and pursuit, is thought to aim at some good,"[63] he must make clear at the same time what are the conditions of artistic success and failure in the poetic forms he treats: he must say, to quote again his opening formula, "how plots ought to be constructed if the poetry is to be good."[64] I have referred to these as two problems; the truth is that the question of value in poetry, for Aristotle, is inseparable from the question of what are the various species of poetry as defined by their peculiar "powers," or rather it is the directing end and justification of the whole scientific enterprise.

But what is the "good" at which poetics aims? Or, since the good is an end, what is, for Aristotle, the end of poetry? Some interpreters of the *Poetics*, having in mind especially the ninth chapter, have thought that he looked upon poetry as ultimately a form of cognition—as a means by which we may penetrate through particulars to general truths, since he clearly says that the statements of poetry are universals. This, however, as the context shows, is to confuse what is an essential condition of probability and necessity in plots—a means, that is, of achieving completeness of form—with the end of poetry. The kinds of poetry Aristotle is considering are imitations, and poetic imitation, though it is something more serious and philosophical than history (since it necessarily gains its effects through exhibiting the causes of its actions in the characters of the agents), and though knowledge and truth are obviously involved in it, is not itself a mode of knowledge, as is evident from the reference to Empedocles in Chapter 1. We have also been frequently told, by critics who think it necessary to assert general ends for poetry and who conceive of no other possible ends than those comprised in the ancient distinction of instruction and delight, that the end of poetry, for Aristotle, is the giving of pleasure; and he has sometimes been praised and sometimes reproached for taking so low or so sensible a view of the question; this is the opinion, especially, of those who think, though without any textual evidence whatever so far as I can see, that the *Poetics* was intended as a reply to Plato's indictment of poetry in *The Republic*.[65] To interpret thus, however, is to read back into Aristotle the terms of later theories—like that of Johnson, for example—in which principles for judging poems are derived not from a specific consideration of the internal nature of poetic products but from a general analysis of the psychological factors which condition the responses of audiences to them; and the view clearly does violence to Aristotle's own conception of the relation between pleasure and its objects.

58

The main point of this conception is that pleasure is not a thing in itself that can be used to define adequately an end of human activity, but always something which goes with and completes activities when they are successful and is a sign of their success in the participant or beholder. The two are, as Aristotle says in the *Nicomachean Ethics*, "bound up together and [do] not . . . admit of separation, since without activity pleasure does not arise, and every activity is completed by the attendant pleasure"; and the pleasure is greatest (as, for instance, in reading clear handwriting with good eyes) when "both the sense is at its best and it is active in reference to an object which corresponds." Activities and objects, however, differ widely in kind and value; hence pleasures differ in the same ways; and to talk about pleasure except as the "proper pleasure" attendant upon a particular species of activities or objects and signifying by its intensity the quality of any of these, is to talk as little to the point as we do, according to Aristotle, when we attempt to define the "good" in morals or anything else in abstract and universal terms.[66]

It would be inconsistent with Aristotle's general view, then, to make pleasure as such the end or good of poetry; and the truth is that that is not his doctrine. He recognizes in *Poetics* 4 that men would never have written poetry or continued to read it except for the natural pleasure afforded by imitations and by ordered arrangements of sounds; and he speaks later of the "tragic pleasure" and the "pleasure proper to tragedy" and distinguishes this from the pleasure appropriate to comedy.[67] But it is one thing to speak thus and quite another thing to make the production of pleasure the general aim of the poet's activity. In Chapter 4 he is saying that poetry arose out of certain pleasurable activities common to all men, and in the later passages he is saying that the inferential and emotional activity of witnessing a tragedy is completed, when the tragedy is well made and the spectator is able to appreciate it, by the peculiar delight which goes with the catharsis through pity and fear of such feelings—in short, with the achievement by the poet of a complete action of the kind distinctive of tragic imitation, the catharsis being the pleasure which supervenes when an action

59

arousing in us painful emotions is brought by the poet's art to its necessary or probable end. The whole emphasis, that is to say, is on the nature of the poetic object to which the pleasure in question corresponds and of which it is the accompaniment and sign for whoever can contemplate the object with understanding and sensitivity; and the good which poetics aims at, and which the poet, in so far as he is an artist, pursues as his immediate end, is nothing other than the excellent making of poems, as poems, in their respective kinds.

Now the excellence of anything, for Aristotle, is the maximum actualization, within the necessary limits of its matter, of what its nature is capable of. The nature of the kinds of poems he is dealing with is to be imitations; and the excellence of imitations, in the sense of that which they can peculiarly become, is to be self-sufficient wholes possessed of all their necessary parts and of these rightly ordered and proportioned with respect to each other and the whole. Completeness, as implying unity and order, and magnitude, as implying appropriate size or fullness of development—these are the criteria of poetic beauty in general: that is why, in the definition of tragedy, its object of imitation, which is its chief determining part, is said to be a serious action which is complete as having magnitude. Completeness is a matter of the probable or necessary connections of the incidents or of whatever else the object consists of, and the sign of its achievement, as Aristotle says in *Poetics* 8, is such a close interrelation of the parts that "the transposal or withdrawal of any one of them will disjoin and dislocate the whole." Magnitude is a matter of the more or the less in anything the poet may do in a poem, and the right magnitude, as in any of the arts, lies in a mean between too little and too much. "In everything that is continuous and divisible," says Aristotle in the *Nicomachean Ethics*, "it is possible to take more, less, or an equal amount, and that either in terms of the thing itself or relatively to us; and the equal is an intermediate between excess and defect." It is thus that "every art does its work well—by looking to the intermediate and judging its works by this standard (so that we often say of good works of art that it is not possible either to take away or to add anything, implying that excess and defect destroy the goodness of works of art, while the mean preserves it; and good artists, as we say, look to this in their work). . . ."[68] The beauty or best state of poetry, in short, consists in the mutual adequation in poems of parts and whole, matter and form, the best poems being those in which the whole is such that it subsumes and governs all the parts and the parts are such that the intrinsic possibilities of none of them are sacrificed to the achievement of a clear but relatively empty whole.

This is the general standard, but it is obviously not a standard which a poet can easily use in practice except as a reminder of the direction his mind ought to take in considering his problems. These, as poetic problems, will always be particular to the special kind of structure and "power" he is trying to give to the concrete materials of his invention (whether this structure and "power" has a common name, such as tragedy, or not); and as his materials and poetic aims vary, so also will vary the precise practical meaning of all such concepts as excess and defect, unity, order, magnitude, and beauty: the beauty of tragedy is one thing and that of comedy quite another, and the correct mean between parts and whole in a full-length drama or novel will not be the same as the corresponding mean in a short story or a lyric. Hence the question of better and worse in poetry can never be answered in absolute terms; the answer is always relative, not to ourselves (as when dramas are judged to be good because they are "effective" for particular audiences), but, in Aristotle's phrase, to "the thing itself," that is, immediately to the part that is being constructed and ultimately to the form of the whole to which the part belongs and the peculiar "power" it is to have, the rule in any case being a specification of the general criterion already stated. As a consequence the theoretical discussions of better and worse in the *Poetics* tend to be of two kinds. The first of these is illustrated by the argument, in Chapters 13 and 14, from the special "pleasure" of tragedy to the nature of the plot and its crucial incidents which will yield this pleasure most completely and intensely; it is illustrated also by the final discussion, in Chapter 26, of the respects in which tragedy is superior, in general, to epic in its capacity for realizing the "power" common to these two species. Here the assumption is of an end to be

61

achieved, and the question concerns the means best adapted to its achievement. In the other discussions the inquiry is into the potentialities of particular parts, and the question concerns the kind of construction of these which, generally speaking, will actualize to the fullest degree their respective possibilities; as, for example, in the remarks on the probable unexpected in Chapter 9, on the superiority of complex to simple or episodic plots in Chapters 9, 10, and 13, on the best types of discovery in Chapters 11 and 16, on the relation of the *desis* to the *lysis* in Chapters 15 and 18, and on the chorus in Chapter 18: the criteria in all these instances derive from the general assumption that that poetry is best which is most complete and self-sufficient— that is, which has all its causes within itself rather than in the exigencies of the poet—and which produces most intensely its "proper pleasure." The conclusions in both cases are perforce general, and the problems of a poet, in writing an individual work, are always particular, inasmuch as his materials of story and character, imagery and mood, however he has come by them, impose limits on what he can do, so that the theoretically best thing may not always be within his power. The normative statements of poetics are thus not invariable rules but formulations of what are in general better and worse possibilities; and the practical decisions of poets, as well as our judgments of poems —since, like the moral choices of men in concrete situations, they depend on particular facts—must ultimately derive from perception rather than theoretical knowledge.[69] Such is necessarily the relation, in the productive arts, between the processes of making and reasoning; but this does not mean that theoretical understanding of the possibilities inherent in poetry or tragedy can safely be dispensed with in favour of mere instinct or taste: the poet will be all the better, on the whole, for having considered "scientifically" what he ought to aim at if he wishes to write poems that will be artistically excellent in their respective kinds.

It should be recognized, moreover, that the ends or criteria of excellence specified in poetics are not ends or criteria imposed on the poet from without, as in many systems of "abstract" criticism, but derive from an examination of the possibilities inherent in the arts poets practise as these are revealed in what poets have done. The discoveries of poetics are merely a reduction to principle of discoveries originally made by poets themselves as they have been led by genius or by chance to realize more of the potentialities of imitation than had been known before. The poetic theorist can generalize these discoveries and order them in terms of his knowledge of the nature of imitation in general; but if Aristotle can point out, for example, what is the better rather than the worse type of unity or magnitude in tragic and epic actions or what is the best way of imitating in narrative forms or how poetic illusion is most completely attained, this is because Homer had understood and actualized all these possibilities.[70] It is not a question merely of imitating Homer or any other poets who have similarly added to the resources of their art (as Sophocles, for instance, added the third actor[71]) but of taking advantage of the superior resources they have uncovered and of moving farther in similar directions. And we can know the superiority of anything thus discovered in two ways: partly by examining it in the light of the possibilities inherent in the nature of imitation or of (say) tragic imitation, and partly by observing how it has actually worked—by a deduction, that is to say, from general theory supplemented by an inference from signs. We can know, thus, by reasoning from the assumed end of tragedy, that the type of plot which best produces a catharsis through pity and fear is one in which the events move toward a catastrophic ending, and our reasoning is confirmed, as Aristotle remarks, by the fact that "on the stage, and in the public performances, such plays, properly worked out, are seen to be the most truly tragic; and Euripides, even if his execution be faulty in every other point, is seen to be nevertheless the most tragic certainly of the dramatists."[72]

It should be easy, in view of this, to understand the important place which the history of poetry occupies in the *Poetics*. The basis of the whole work, indeed, is historical, inasmuch as its definitions, being simply inductions of the universal traits exhibited by particular works, must rest upon a wide acquaintance with what poets have done; we could never know, for example, what the peculiar "power" of tragedy is without direct experience of poems in which this "power" is manifestly present—there being no way in which an actuality can be inferred from a general "abstract" principle. And what is true of the definitions of such forms as tragedy and epic is true also of the propositions about their parts and devices: hence the constant resort, throughout the *Poetics*, to historical examples of tragic or epic practice. But, more than this, the history of poetry, for Aristotle, is an essential means to the selection of those ends in poetry which give him the basis of his judgments of value. The ends are facts in the sense that they are reflected in the practice of poets when poetry, as imitation or as tragic or comic imitation, has attained a stage of development in which the forms, or some of them, "natural" to it exist in their fully differentiated state, even though they may be capable of further particular development. Hence the general history of poetry at the beginning of Chapter 4—a history in which poetry is shown to have originated in the universal and natural impulse of men to make and to enjoy imitations because of the pleasure that goes with learning and with melodies and rhythms; then to have divided into two general classes by virtue of the interest of some poets in representing men better than we are and of others in making satirical attacks on the bad, both in appropriate metres; and finally to have eventuated, with Homer, in self-contained works of art the final cause of which is the beauty rather than either the general pleasurableness or the moral utility of the imitations. What Homer did in effect was to take morally differentiated actions, both serious and comic, as the objects of his imitations and to treat these in his verses in such a way as not only to reveal more fully than his predecessors the nature and possibilities of dramatic representation but also, and most significantly, to show that the perfecting of the poetic whole itself, as a rendering in pleasurable words of universally intelligible and emotionally effective forms of human action, is a sufficient end alike for poets themselves and their readers. It is indeed a final end in two important senses—in the sense that it is an end peculiar to the poetic art rather than one imitative poetry shares with other arts or activities and also in the sense that it subsumes the other ends of pleasing and instructing, and goes beyond them. For it is distinctive of poetry such as Homer's that it utilizes the pleasure we all take in imitation and rhythm, and the vivid interest we have in other human beings and especially in the moral issues in which they can be involved, in

64

order to make objects which we can continue to appreciate, after our first curiosity is satisfied, for the sake of their intrinsic rightness and beauty. This therefore is where poetic theory, in its normative aspect, in general must begin; and a similar function, in defining a starting-point for judgments of value, is served by the brief histories of tragedy and comedy which follow in the second part of Chapter 4 and in Chapter 5.

To say that the foundations of the *Poetics* are in history is not, of course, to say that its propositions have only historical validity or that what it gives us is merely a generalized description of Greek practice in epic and tragedy. The *Poetics* is a statement, or at least an outline sketch, of a science, and as such it deals with principles and causes rather than with conventions or poetic traditions, with the artistic necessities and possibilities of particular forms rather than with accepted rules and models; and these, being universals, will always, once they are firmly established, continue to have validity and relevance as long as poets aspire to write successful poems of these kinds. They will not, indeed, hold good, in any strict or complete way, for poems with structures of other kinds—and the possibilities of formal differentiation in poetry, and hence of the continued discovery by poets of new forms and devices or of fresh potentialities in the old, are indefinite in number. Poetics, therefore, can never be thought of as something fixed and determined; it must aim, rather, to be a progressive science, always lagging somewhat behind poets but never, if it is to keep alive, remaining indifferent to what new poets are trying to do. There are signs in the *Poetics* that Aristotle was not unconcerned with the developments of his day,[73] and we may be sure that if he lived now, with all the advantages of an immensely fuller history, he would recognize, for example, that more can be learned about the possibilities of beauty in tragic plots from *King Lear* and *The Brothers Karamazov* than from *Oedipus Rex* and more about the possibilities of narrative imitation from James and Conrad than from Homer.

IV

The only type of poetic structure which Aristotle discusses systematically is tragedy, his account of the epic being largely

65

an analysis of the differences between it and tragedy that follow from its difference in imitative manner, on the assumption, apparently, that the specific "power" of the two forms is the same. I shall speak here, therefore, mainly of the analysis of tragedy.

The discussion begins with the definition in Chapter 6, and what follows turns on two principal questions, the first of which concerns the number and attributes of the parts or elements any tragedy must have. Now a tragedy, or any other kind of poem, is a whole in two senses—a quantitative sense and a qualitative sense—and its structure, accordingly, has two corresponding aspects, which have often been confused by later critics. The quantitative structure of a tragedy is the disposition of its matter in discrete sections: such in Greek tragedy, as Aristotle explains in Chapter 12, are the prologue, the exode, the episodes, and the choral portions distinguished into parode and stasimon; and these have analogues in modern drama in the traditional five-act structure of full-length plays and in Shakespeare's shifts from blank verse to prose. In a well-made tragedy these parts will serve to mark off and accentuate significant differences in the character of what is going on in the poem itself; but as structural devices they derive from convention rather than from specific necessities inherent in the art of tragedy, and hence they determine the form and effect of a tragedy only in a secondary way. What the poet or the theorist of poetry must be chiefly concerned with are those parts the conception and handling of which will directly determine the quality of the poetic whole itself in the sense both of the peculiar "power" it has and of the degree of its success in maximizing this "power." Of such qualitative parts tragedy has six, the first three—plot, character, and thought— deriving from the fact that tragedy imitates human actions and that the quality of human actions depends on two natural causes, namely, the moral habits of the agents and their mental processes and states; the next two—diction and melody—deriving from its medium of metrical language combined with music; and the last —the spectacle—deriving from its distinctive manner of imitating through the use of actors on a stage. These are necessary structural parts, and there can obviously be no others co-ordinate with them; all of them except melody and spectacle are also the essential qualitative parts of epic.

66

Only a few of these terms, I think, call for comment. By diction (*lexis*) Aristotle means simply the arrangement of words (or, in tragedy, of words metrically ordered) that expresses the thought of the dramatic agents. Thought (*dianoia*) is what the words most immediately signify; it is manifest whenever the persons in the action state a universal proposition or argue a particular point; it includes proof and refutation, the expression or arousal of emotion, and the characterizing of things as better or worse, important or unimportant. Character (*ethos*) is also something present in or inferable from the speeches, whether these are speeches merely or also acts; in its most formal sense, it is what reveals the moral purpose (*proairesis*) of the agents, that is, the sort of thing they distinctively seek or avoid, but the term can be broadened to include signs of other peculiarities of the speakers less directly related to the crises of the action.[74]

There remains plot (*mythos*), and concerning this there has been an extraordinary amount of confusion among commentators on the *Poetics*. When we examine the text,[75] we see that plot, for Aristotle, is that part of the poetic whole which represents, or rather constitutes in the poem, the object of imitation—in tragedy, a serious action; it is, he says, the synthesis of the things done or said in the play (*synthesis ton pragmaton*). But he also insists that plot is the end of tragedy, its first principle, its "soul," as it were; and he remarks later that a poet is a poet essentially by virtue of his ability to make plots, even though he may base his tragedies on historical persons and events. Now both of these last statements are patently meaningless or false if we conceive of plot in any of the several fashions which have become current in modern times: for example, as that we refer to when we paraphrase the story of a play or novel, or construct a scenario of what happens in its successive acts and scenes; or as that we think of when we say of Shakespeare, or any other writer, that although he took his "plots" from earlier works, he nevertheless showed great originality in filling them in; or when we oppose "plot" to "character" or "imaginative vision," or identify "plot" merely with the "argument" of the work or with the pattern of external actions in contrast to what "goes on in Mrs. Brown's head." But plot for Aristotle is none of these things. In the completest and most formal sense (as the end, principle, or "soul" of a work), the plot of a tragedy is nothing more or less than its whole object of imitation as this is imaginatively constructed, with its necessary specifications of moral character and states of mind, by the poet and embodied by him, in ways appropriate to his chosen manner of imitation, in the words of his poem; it is the total imitated action of the poem as qualified ethically in such a way as to produce the special "tragic pleasure." In this sense, we can speak of plots only specifically—as tragic plots, comic plots, and so on; and this is the meaning of plot in Chapters 13 and 14. But, abstracting from this, we can also speak of plot more generally as the special kind of artistic whole or structure which is the necessary material condition of any sort of poetic *dynamis* that depends on the imitation of a sequence of human actions; and this is the meaning of plot in Chapters 7 through 11. In both senses plot is clearly something the poet constructs, the difference being that, whereas in the second sense plot is conceived of as a part or substrate (though the most important one) of tragic form, in the first sense it is the tragic form itself in its completest actuality.

A completed tragedy is an organic whole in which everything, as I have said before, is contained in the words as its indispensable artistic matter, so that the formal parts of plot, character, and thought are, from this point of view, inseparable from the material part of diction. This does not mean, however, that the parts which Aristotle distinguishes are merely "abstractions," as has been asserted by several contemporary critics who have been interested, not in the productive conditions of poetry, but primarily in the responses to poems of readers or in the reflection in poems of the minds of their writers.[76] For the poet at any rate there is nothing unreal or "abstract" in these distinctions. They correspond, for one thing, to different basic types of poetic skill necessary to the construction of an excellent tragedy but not possessed in equal measure by all poets. Some poets thus can develop dramatically effective scenes without being able to synthesize them in a continuous action with sustained emotional power; others are able to write passages of dialogue of great interest for their thought who lack the capacity to make their speakers talk like human beings with distinctive personalities

68

and moral characters; others, again, are good at intimating character in appropriate words and thought but not at setting their personages in action; still others know how to write technically excellent verse but not how to make it sound like convincing speech or to express in it other than commonplace ideas; and there have always been would-be dramatists who have been able to write exciting or moving poems in dialogue form which could never be successfully performed on a stage. Or, again, a playwright might begin by sketching his tragic plot as a whole, with its constituent incidents and necessary discriminations of character and thought, in a continuous sequence of speeches, and then, in subsequent rewritings, reconsider each of the speeches to see how it would properly go if the characters of the speakers were particularized further in such and such ways, then work through the whole again for the sake of making the thought more varied or interesting, and then finally decide that it would be better to substitute verse for his original prose or prose for his original verse.

Nor is it true that these distinctions lack reality and importance for the reader or critic. We are being affected by the plot of a tragedy, or of any other poem that imitates human actions, whenever we feel any of its parts, however minute or apparently verbal, not as isolated beauties, but as moments in a continuous progression from one situation or state of mind or of moral character to another, to which we respond emotionally in a dynamic rather than simply static way, that is, with expectation or suspense appropriate to the form of the work. We are being affected by character, as distinguished from plot, whenever we respond to speeches or actions with feelings—whether of interest merely or of admiration, hate, contempt, or some mixture of approval and blame, or the like—that rest upon inferences as to what kind of human being the person is apart from the situation in which he is engaged. We are being affected by thought, as distinguished from both plot and character, whenever we have a sense of passing from ignorance to knowledge, or to more complete knowledge concerning what is going on in someone's mind, or whenever we judge that what is being said is interesting in itself or peculiarly appropriate to the character or the situation.

And we are being affected by the diction as such, in abstraction from its imitative functions, whenever we feel an immediate pleasure in the arrangement of the sounds and words or have an impression of unusual freshness, unexpectedness, vividness, concision, or force (or the contraries of these or other qualities) in the writer's expression. The total effect of any poetic work is of course a composite or synthesis of all such particular effects, but they can in fact be differentiated, without too great difficulty, by any attentive reader and be seen to depend, for their existence, on fundamentally distinct artistic principles.

The second of Aristotle's questions about tragedy, with which he deals in close conjunction with the first, concerns the causes of success or failure in the poet's handling of the tragic parts. Of these the plot, as we have seen, is most important: it is the first principle or architectonic part, to the beauty and emotional efficacy of which the other parts contribute—the character and the thought most directly, the diction, *qua* diction, less immediately, the music and the spectacle incidentally as supporting accessories. The best tragedy, indeed, is one in which the subordinate parts not only serve, in their various ways, the plot but possess, to the greatest extent compatible with the integrity of the whole, the independent excellences of which each is capable. The plot, however, is primary: there can be no good tragedy without a good plot since it is upon the plot that the tragic "power" most completely depends; but there can be effective tragedies with relatively poor character (in Aristotle's sense of character as a part), relatively undistinguished thought, and relatively mediocre diction, and a tragic plot does not cease to be tragic when the play is read rather than witnessed on a stage.[77]

It is therefore on the excellences possible in plot that Aristotle's main emphasis falls. In his general discussion of plot—that is, of plot not determined specifically to tragic ends—the starting-point is the first clause of his definition: that tragedy is an imitation of an action which, besides being serious, is a complete whole having magnitude. The warrant of this last phrase is ultimately in the history of poetry: it is precisely to such self-contained constructions that the efforts of imitative poets have tended, and those tragedies, or other poems, have been thought most beautiful of which these attributes of wholeness and a right magnitude can be predicated. The problem, therefore, is to discover the general conditions, in the making of tragic plots, of their existence; and this Aristotle does in his statements, in Chapters 7–9, about the nature of order in plots (as consisting in a continuous sequence from beginning through middle to end), about the proper magnitude of plots (as consisting in such a length as permits of a completed change of fortune by means of incidents following one another probably or necessarily), about the material basis of unity in plots (as more completely given by a single action than by a single hero), and about the kinds of connections that must be effected between the successive parts of plots if poetic wholeness is to be achieved (as dependent on showing not what merely happened or is possible but what is probable or necessary in terms of the universals implied in the character and the situation). This is followed, in Chapters 10 and 11, by a deduction of the major species of plots from the assumption that tragedy imitates actions: "Plots are either simple or complex, since the actions they represent are naturally of this twofold character." And the general superiority of complex to simple plots, it is implied though not explicitly argued, lies in two things: in their capacity to afford more of the "unexpected" and "wonderful," which, when it comes about in what we perceive to be a probable sequence of events, will necessarily enhance the tragic, or any other, pleasure; and in the fact that, through the device of "recognition," they permit wider extremes of emotion and thought.

These, however, are only necessary and not sufficient conditions of an excellent tragic plot, and this general discussion must therefore be completed by inferences from the peculiar *dynamis* of the imitations which Aristotle, relying again on history and general opinion, has selected as most distinctively and powerfully "serious"—the catharsis through pity and fear of such emotions. The pleasurable catharsis—the settling of the soul into its normal state of rest after painful disturbance—will come about if the action is properly complete, with its incidents following one another, not by chance or by the arbitrary manipulation of the poet,[78] but in an inherently probable or necessary order.

Hence, assuming such a construction in well-made tragedies, Aristotle concentrates on the question of what kind of plot will most successfully arouse the emotions of pity and fear, these being respectively what we feel when we contemplate undeserved misfortunes and what we feel when such a misfortune threatens one who is like ourselves in being neither wholly just and knowing nor wholly villainous.[79] The tragic hero, clearly, must be a man of this intermediate kind, but preferably one better rather than worse, since the events will then be more striking; and he must be moved in the plot from a state of good fortune to one of bad, and the more miserable the final state the more completely "serious" the action will be. The seriousness will also be proportionate to the human evil the action brings into play, and the extreme of human evil, Aristotle assumes, lies in the committing of unjust acts, and especially of unjust acts done against persons who ought to be protected and loved. Now these conditions could be satisfied by a plot in which an innocent protagonist of the kind described is brought to undeserved ruin by the villainous acts of a supposed friend, as in many eighteenth-century tragedies. And this would undoubtedly be "tragic" for Aristotle, but much less tragic than a plot in which the unjust act is done by the protagonist himself on one of his friends, but done in such a way that he, too, suffers the consequences in remorse and pain of mind and the audience, while lamenting the deed, can nevertheless hold him not entirely culpable; for it is this kind of unjust act—springing not from deliberate intention but from *hamartia* or action done in ignorance of the circumstances rather than of the moral principle at stake[80]—that we most fear in ourselves and pity most fully in others when it brings upon them misfortunes partly but not wholly deserved. Something like this, at any rate, seems to have been Aristotle's reasoning in Chapters 13 and 14, when he concludes that the most excellent type of tragic plot is one of which the material cause is a noble but intermediate kind of man; the formal cause, the passage of such a man, and of those associated with him, from good fortune to an appropriate extreme of bad fortune (with no "happy" reversal at the end); and the efficient cause, an unjust act, or sequence of unjust acts, committed by the hero on persons close to him, in consequence

72

not of unjust intent but of *hamartia* of some kind. And it may be added that, whether or not this is the most tragic plot-form absolutely (it is not precisely the form, for example, of *Macbeth*), it clearly offers greater possibilities to the poet than most of the other "tragic" plot-forms which Aristotle mentions or which have been attempted in later times.

The problem of "character" in tragedy—when character is viewed not as one of the determinants of plot (as in Chapter 13) but as a form to be achieved in the speeches out of the materials of diction and thought—is a problem primarily of what traits of moral purpose or personality the poet ought to select and embody in his words if the ethical element in his poem is to do its work most adequately. And he can go wrong in four ways: first, by making the *dramatis personae*, or any one of them, say or do things on particular occasions or habitually that are insufficiently serious or morally elevated or otherwise detrimental to his plot and its tragic effect; second, by not keeping vividly in mind the basic sort of human being a given person is intended to be so that the particular traits manifested in his speeches fail to fuse together into the impression of a single unified character; third, by neglecting to choose signs of the characteristics intended which will convey the effect that the person speaking or acting is a possible human being of a certain kind (i.e., by not making the imitated person "come alive"); and fourth, by failing to make such changes in character as the action may require seem necessary or probable. These are the negative bases of the four criteria of character-traits in tragedy which Aristotle sets forth in Chapter 15: that they be "good" or "useful" (*chresta*), "appropriate" (*harmottonta*), "like" (*homoion*), and "consistent" (*homalon*); and it is clear that, with some changes in the definitions of each, the list would serve for any other poetic species of which plot is the controlling form.

The material basis of "thought" in drama is the capacity of language, as the poet's medium, to be formed into arguments or into statements of fact or of general truth, to express and evoke emotions, and to discriminate the relative value of things. It appears in the speeches, and is, says Aristotle, the power of saying the "possible" (*enonta*) and the "appropriate" (*harmot-*

73

tonta); it falls, furthermore, under two distinct arts, that of politics and that of rhetoric, the older dramatists making their persons speak *politikos*, the modern dramatists *retorikos*. This statement, in Chapter 6, is not easy to interpret, but it can be read, I think, as an indication of two levels of potential achievement in the poet's handling of thought. To achieve the "possible" is clearly a minimum requirement: the persons in a plot can properly entertain only such thoughts as are possible in the sense of being permitted by their general characters and relevant to the general situation; they must at least speak pertinently and in keeping with the seriousness of the occasion—and this is what the earlier dramatists were mainly content to make them do, so that their speeches have the quality of political deliberations but little more. To achieve the "appropriate" is to go beyond this; it is to use the resources of rhetoric in order to achieve nuances of character and emotion and to adapt the speeches in a particularized way to what is going on, as well as to the universal issues involved in the action. And the implication, I take it, is that the best thought is that which achieves both the "possible" and the "appropriate" at the same time.[81]

There is perhaps nothing in the *Poetics* that seems more alien to the contemporary critical mind than the fashion in which Aristotle disposes of the problem of diction: in three chapters (20–22) the first two of which resolve it into its elements, including metaphors, and the third of which deals with the criterion of good diction—namely, that it be at once clear and not mean—and with the ways in which the diction of tragedy differs from that of epic and dithyramb. To critics who are disposed to identify poetry with a certain manner of using words and in whose systems the question of diction is consequently prior to, even if it does not altogether absorb, questions of plot, character, and thought, it has naturally seemed strange not only that Aristotle should relegate the words of tragedy to the last place in his list of its parts but should discuss them with so little evident sense of their high importance; there has even been talk of an "Aristotelian separation of plot and character from diction."[82] It is necessary, however, to bear in mind two things: first, that the distinctive problem of poetics for Aristotle, as we have seen, is not the appreciation but the construction of poetry; and, second, that if the question of diction seems unimportant for him, this is not because it is not, in one sense, all-important, but because much of it has already been dealt with. The poetic quality of a tragedy is its quality as a completed imitation in words; it is only as its object of imitation is constructed successively in the speeches that it has any existence or power; it is immediately to the words, moreover, that spectators or readers respond, and from these, as reinforced on the stage by the actors' voices and movements, that they infer the character and emotional significance of what is going on. Language is therefore of supreme importance, for if this fails in a poem, everything fails; but it is necessarily last in the order of qualitative parts for the simple reason that, given an adequate mastery of language by the poet, the question of what the actual words of a particular tragedy ought to be is one that can never be answered finally until the poet has found answers for all the complex questions involved in the detailed construction of its object. And the principles that serve him in answering these latter questions are also, in large measure, the principles that govern, in a good tragedy, the choice and arrangement of words. For the words, sentences, and rhythms spoken by the characters of a tragedy are as much parts of the imitated action as any of their non-verbal acts (such as stabbing Polonius or jumping into Ophelia's grave); and their selection and ordering in the speeches demands the same attention to considerations of necessity and probability and of appropriateness to the desired emotional effects as does the invention of the "things" themselves. The right solution of the problem of diction in a tragedy is consequently inseparable, in its most crucial aspects, from the right solution of the problems set for the poet by his desire to give to his intended matter of character, thought, and action a certain determinate structure and power; and the major part of the problem of diction can accordingly be subsumed under the discussion of these other problems, leaving over for special treatment merely the material elements that must be united to form the metre and language of the speeches and the general aims that ought to guide the poet if his choice of words and rhythms is to facilitate comprehension of his action and at the

75

same time be pleasurable in itself and appropriate to the tragic form.

The analysis of the internal parts of tragedy—music and spectacle being external in the sense of depending largely on other arts than the poetic—thus runs from plot, as the principal and architectonic part, through character and thought, to diction, in descending order of causal determination; and for each of these Aristotle inquires what in general is its best state. We may add one further point, though this will take us beyond anything explicitly developed in the *Poetics*. It would be false, in the language of Aristotle's criticism, to say that a tragedy or any other poem is essentially a "verbal structure" or that it exists primarily in a "verbal universe." We can, however, say that it *has* a verbal structure. For what a poet does, in writing a poem, is to set down sound after sound, word after word, sentence after sentence, until he has composed a continuous significant speech, or *logos*, which in the end is his poem, and which has a kind of unity, Aristotle remarks, by virtue not of signifying one thing, as in a definition, but of being itself one as a particular conjunction of many speeches.[83] A good poem can thus be said to have wholeness both as a *mythos* and as a *logos*; and although the primary problem of poetics is the excellent construction of the *mythos*— and it is with this that Aristotle mainly deals—the composition of the *logos*, as a coherent verbal whole, also presents problems to the poet that go beyond the finding of the right words and rhythms to body forth his plot. These are partly problems of preserving throughout the poem a certain more or less flexible norm of vocabulary and metre; but the most important of them are consequences of the general problem of poetic manner (as distinguished from the particular problem of dramatic spectacle), that is to say, of the most effective fitting of the *logos* as a whole to the *mythos*. They will obviously require different solutions, depending on different kinds of skill, according as the poem is, let us say, a drama intended for acting on a public stage, a dramatic poem meant to be recited or read, or an epic or novel, even though the essential plot-form and effect may be the same in all these cases. The ways in which they can be solved in particular works, moreover, will inevitably be affected by the ruling con-

76

ventions of their forms: even with the same plot-form, again, the structure of the poet's discourse will not be the same in a tragedy having the quantitative parts of Greek tragedy as it would be in a tragedy designed for the English stage of the early seventeenth century. And finally, and irrespective of these differences, the verbal structure of a tragedy or any imitative poem will be determined necessarily by a whole complex of particular decisions, inherent in the nature of the poet's art, as to how much of his object he will represent explicitly and how much he will leave to inference; as to what parts of the represented action he will exhibit dramatically and what parts by narrative report; as to what order he will follow in disclosing the elements of his story, and with what continuities and discontinuities, juxtapositions and contrasts in the arrangement of its scenes; and so on through other problems of a similar character the right solution of which, relatively to the intended "power" of the plot, is an essential if not sufficient condition of artistic success.

V

Such, in general, I believe, are the philosophic bases of the "line of inquiry" which constituted poetic science for Aristotle, and such the consequences for the problem of poetic structure of the very special critical language in which its questions and hypotheses are framed. I shall return in the final lecture to those features of Aristotle's language (in the construction here given to it) which I believe are permanently useful for the practical criticism of poetic works, but I would suggest in the meantime that, when the *Poetics* is read thus—as an attempt to deal not with poetry as a whole but with certain forms of imitative poetry in their aspect only as imitations—some of the common objections to the treatise lose most of their force. It is true enough that Aristotle "nowhere refers to the great problems that gave vitality to Greek tragedy, problems relating to man and his cosmic relations, to the workings of Fate, human destiny and the like";[84] it is true that he does not dwell explicitly on "the part played by the imagination in all poetic activity";[85] it is true

77

that he fails to deal with the Greek tragedians as "the Prophets of their age";[86] it is true that he leaves out of his account the survival of ritualistic forms in the classic drama. But it surely does not follow from this, if what I have been saying is correct, that he was "unaware," in his literal-minded concentration on poetic forms and devices, of the existence of such questions. He may have been aware or not, but in either case the special task he was undertaking would not have admitted them, for him or anyone else, as relevant questions; they belong rather, as he would say, to other inquiries than those of the productive science of poetics.

I must add a warning, however, which may well appear unnecessary, that the interpretation of the *Poetics* I have been attempting to develop in this lecture differs widely, and in several fundamental respects, from most of the versions of Aristotle's purposes and procedures in criticism that have been current from the Renaissance to our day, the version of Lessing being perhaps, at least on some important points, the chief exception. It is far from being the *Poetics* of Butcher; it has little in common with the *Poetics* which Mr. Ransom has subtly translated into the terms of his own theory;[87] it is not the *Poetics* to which Mr. Francis Fergusson appeals through the medium of the Cambridge school of classical anthropologists and Mr. Kenneth Burke;[88] it is not the *Poetics* that Mr. Blackmur would "marry" with Coleridge.[89] I would say for my version that it respects the order of Aristotle's text, that it takes account of the most important passages in his other works which might be expected to throw light on the meanings of the general terms he uses in discussing poetry and on the nature and implications of the method he is evidently employing, and that it attempts to consider what possible senses his statements could have when they are applied to the actual problems of poets engaged in the construction of poems. For all that, and with so much weight of authority against me, I should be inclined to doubt the accuracy of what I have been saying were it not that the principal divergences from my account in other interpretations can be fairly well explained when we consider the nature of the general assumptions concerning poetry and criticism by which the majority of these have been governed. This last, however, is a complicated story in itself, which I shall touch upon briefly at the beginning of the next lecture, as a prologue to what I wish to say about some of the very different conceptions of the language of criticism and the structure of poetry that have dominated critical writing in the English-speaking countries during the present century.

The languages of contemporary criticism

THE INFLUENCE of the *Poetics* on later criticism has taken two principal forms, both of them stemming from what are, I think, relatively external aspects of Aristotle's contribution. It has been an influence, in the first place, of and upon doctrine, mediated by the varying interpretations which commentators from the sixteenth century onward have put on Aristotle's pronouncements concerning poetry, tragedy, and epic, and especially on his statements about such topics as unity of action, probability, catharsis, the tragic hero, the place of the "marvellous" in tragedy and epic, and the relation of poetry to history and philosophy: whenever in any period the authority of the *Poetics* has been either invoked or repudiated, it has been of its supposed teachings on these and similar points that most people have tended to think. And along with this, in the second place, has gone an even more pervasive influence of Aristotle's special vocabulary on the words which critics of all persuasions have used in speaking of the parts and devices of poetry in most if not all of its kinds. In this sense we can say that his effect on criticism will have ceased only when critics no longer talk, in however un-Aristotelian a way, of medium, manner, representation, action, plot, character, thought, diction, probability, expectation, surprise, peripety, recognition, or the tragic flaw.

A critical language, however, is something more fundamental than the particular doctrinal conclusions it is used to express and the particular terminology in which its analysis is stated. These may easily persist when the language itself, as a set of basic concepts derived and defined in accordance with a distinctive method, has disappeared; and the history of "Aristotelian" interpretation and critical practice has been very largely, I think, a history of the survival of the content and vocabulary of the *Poetics* in abstraction from the characteristic framework of definitions and principles of inquiry which constituted poetic science as Aristotle understood it.

What above all have not survived are precisely the original assumptions on which, as I tried to indicate in the last lecture, his entire procedure is founded: first, that the objects of poetics are "concrete wholes" of various kinds, having in common the character of being imitations in words of human actions, passions, and characters, the essential differences among which are a function of their respective emotional "powers"; secondly, that the end of poetics is the perfecting of such wholes in their different species in so far as this depends on the poet's art; and thirdly, that the method of poetics consists in reasoning back from the inductively known nature of any such whole to the necessary and sufficient internal conditions, in the structure to be fashioned by the poet, of a maximum achievement of the specific form of beauty of which it is capable. The disappearance from later criticism of these first principles has been, it seems to me, the crucial change; and its consequences can be traced in most of the departures from the *Poetics* which have manifested themselves in the history of the "Aristotelian" tradition.

The term "imitation" has persisted, but never, as far as I am aware, has it been used in Aristotle's precise sense to signify the internal relationship of form and matter characteristic of the class of objects to which poems, or rather some of them, belong. Its meanings have varied widely in different critics, but whether poetry has been thought to be imitative in the special sense that it bodies forth imaginatively ideas or moral types (as in Sidney) or in the more general sense that it is discourse about nature (as in Johnson), the relationship the term denotes has been invariably an external relationship between poems and the ideal or empirical realities they call to mind; and one important result of this has been the loss or blurring of the distinction between poems that

81

are structurally "imitations" and poems that employ imitative devices of fictions, figures, and metres as means to didactic ends. And it has been much the same, too, with Aristotle's other key terms and principles. Poems have continued to be thought of as wholes possessed of powers to affect human minds in various ways; but they have been wholes, for these "Aristotelians," in some other sense than that implied by Aristotle's conception of *synolon*, and their powers have normally been defined, not as the "proper pleasures" that go with specific forms of poetry by virtue of their construction, but with the more general capacity of poetry to serve, though in different ways in different genres, the needs of readers or spectators for pleasure and instruction. It has been so, for example, with the cathartic power of tragedy: however variously this has been interpreted—whether in morally therapeutic terms or in terms that assimilate tragedy to primitive purification rites—the reference has consistently been to a practical rather than strictly poetic end. The good, consequently, at which poetics aims has been treated as a good that cannot be wholly identified with the intrinsic beauty of the poetic product but must be looked for in something beyond this, in the communication of truth or moral edification or in the provision of superior delights for common or superior minds or in some conjunction of these ends. The sharp line of distinction, in Aristotle, between poetry and the arts of rhetoric and teaching has thus been broken down, and it is not strange that the "Aristotelians" of the Renaissance and the Neoclassical period were able to mingle easily the precepts of the *Ars poetica* with those of the *Poetics* or to find statements of the ends and virtues of poetry quite as readily in Cicero and Quintilian as in Aristotle. With this shift of orientation, moreover, the analysis of the internal constitution of tragedies, comedies, and epics could hardly remain the same: not only has plot been separated from the *dynamis* that makes of it a first principle in these poetic species and confused with the materials of myth or story out of which it is formed, but few traces have remained of the causal hierarchy that relates plot and the other parts in the analysis of the *Poetics*: instead, though the names have survived, the parts themselves have usually been discussed as a series of discrete elements—

82

separately causative of pleasure or instruction—which for the poet are so many "beauties" to aim at and for the critic so many topics to use in organizing his remarks.[90] And finally, and perhaps most important, the method of "Aristotelian" poetics has ceased to be that of an inductive science based on hypothetical necessity and has become what for Aristotle would be a kind of dialectic— a discourse about poetry in general and its various species the first principles of which are sought, not where Aristotle sought his, in the being of the things included in his science by virtue of his hypothesis, but rather in the generally accepted opinions of men of taste and learning concerning what the pleasure and instruction of poetry ought to be.[91]

Now we may suspect that all this would not have happened— or happened with the same consistency throughout the tradition —but for the hidden presence, in the thinking of these critics, of presuppositions about poetry and criticism that impelled them, more or less unconsciously, and despite the pious regard many of them felt for Aristotle's authority, to distort his doctrines by restating them in terms of basic critical concepts of quite a different sort from his. The influence of a number of non-Aristotelian languages can be detected in the history of Aristotelian interpretation, but most of these can be viewed, I think, as variants of one fundamental mode of approach to poetry, the importance of which not merely for the reading of the *Poetics* but for criticism in general, including most of the criticism of our time, it seems to me hard to exaggerate.

II

So well accepted, in fact, has this other language become— so much a part of our habitual ways of thinking about literature— that it requires some effort to isolate it in our minds as a particular and by no means inevitable framework for the discussion of poetic structure. Its peculiar character will perhaps become evident, however, if we look at a few contemporary definitions of poetry constructed in its terms. I begin with one by Mr. Yvor Winters. "If rational communication about poetry is to take place," he says, "it is necessary first to determine what we mean by a poem"; and he goes on to answer this question in the following way:

A poem is first of all a statement in words.

But it differs from all such statements of a purely philosophical or theoretical nature, in that it has by intention a controlled content of feeling. In this respect, it does not differ from many works written in prose, however.

A poem differs from a work written in prose by virtue of its being composed in verse. The rhythm of verse permits the expression of more powerful feeling than is possible in prose when such feeling is needed, and it permits at all times the expression of finer shades of feeling.

A poem, then, is a statement in words in which special pains are taken with the expression of feeling. This description is merely intended to distinguish the poem from other kinds of writing; it is not offered as a complete description.[92]

The important thing here is not Winters' definition itself but the fact that it is presented without any preliminary specification of what "poems" or varieties of "poems" he has in mind and that it is a definition arrived at by first constituting a poem as "a statement in words" comparable to "other kinds of writing" and then distinguishing it from other kinds of "statement" in respect first to its content and then to its linguistic form.

These are also the basic terms in which poetry is defined by a good many other critics of our day, however greatly they may differ in their selections of defining traits. "Poetry," we are told in Cleanth Brooks' and Robert Penn Warren's *Understanding Poetry*, "is a form of speech, or discourse, written or spoken"; "like all discourse, [it] is a communication—the saying of something by one person to another person"; but it differs from scientific discourse in being a communication not of objective facts but of "attitudes, feelings, and interpretations" and from such practical discourse as deals with these things in aiming at a superior "clarity and precision of statement."[93] For Professor Pottle, similarly, poetry is "language" or a "kind of speech." It is, he says, "language that expresses the qualities of experience, as distinguished from language that indicates its uses." In this strict and theoretical sense, poetry is coextensive with language, but in the ordinary or popular sense of the term, poetry occurs

84

"when the concentration of the expressive element of speech becomes so great that we distinctly feel it to predominate over that other element which we have called the practical or scientific."[94] The general critical position of Mr. Ransom is rather different from that of either Professor Pottle or of Messrs. Brooks and Warren, and is explicitly set in opposition to the position of Mr. Winters, but he approaches the task of formulating the nature of poetry in essentially the same way. "A poem," he writes, "differentiates itself for us, very quickly and convincingly, from a prose discourse"—the difficulty, however, is to know precisely what the differentia is. It is not "moralism," he says, not "emotionalism, sensibility, or 'expression,'" and not "structure proper," since this is "the prose of the poem, being a logical discourse of almost any kind, and dealing with almost any content suited to a logical discourse"; it is rather the "order of content" which distinguishes the "irrelevant local texture" of the poem from its "logical structure"; and he concludes by suggesting that the differentia of poetry as discourse is "an ontological one." Poetry "treats an order of existence, a grade of objectivity, which cannot be treated in scientific discourse."[95] And much the same general assumption provides the point of departure for René Wellek and Austin Warren in their recent *Theory of Literature*, in which they characterize the literary work of art as "a whole system of signs, or structure of signs, serving a specific aesthetic purpose," and find that this structure is made up of "several strata, each implying its own subordinate group," from the basic "sound-stratum," through the individual and composite meanings of the words, to the objects represented in the poem and, finally, to its total "philosophical meaning."[96]

How different all this is from Aristotle can readily be seen. For him, as we have observed, the starting-point of poetics is the existence of certain distinctive classes of human productions, using language as their medium, to which the name "poetry" has become peculiarly attached; and the first question is what is their essential nature when we view them, not in all their possible aspects and relations, but in their aspect as concrete artistic wholes. The answer is that, when thus considered, they happen all to be "imitations," and hence can be differentiated and defined, for the purposes of poetic science, by considering what they imitate, in what they imitate, how they imitate, and with what special powers. As imitations they belong to a very large class of objects, some of which, like houses, differ from poems in having a utility beyond their forms, and others of which, such as paintings and dances, differ from poems in the character of the imitative means they employ; these latter are therefore excluded from the sphere of poetics except as bases for explanatory analogies (as in Chapters 1, 2, 6, and 15). As imitations, moreover, poems are sharply separated, at the beginning of the inquiry, from the other arts or faculties which use language as their instrument, such as scientific and philosophical writing, history, rhetoric, on the simple ground that these do not give us imitations in any strict sense of the word; thus it is that when history and philosophy are referred to in the *Poetics* (as in Chapters 9 and 23), it is merely for the sake of marking off more clearly the special nature of poetry. Rhetoric is in a different case, since the development of "thought" in poetry involves the use of devices which are obviously common to rhetoric and poetry; but imitative poetry, for all that, remains an art distinct from that of oratory in its ends, forms, and principles of construction; and it is also, as we have noted, an art distinct from that which produces the various kinds of "poems" which we have come to call didactic. For Aristotle, in short, the world of poetics is a world of concrete objects, natural and artificial, within which the term "poetry" delimits sharply and literally, for the poetic inquiry, those artificial wholes, of whatever species, that use a medium of words to body forth interesting and moving patterns of human experience, for the sake of the specific beauty of the imitation; and the definitions with which his scientific argument proper begins are definitions, not of poetry in general, but of the particular species of poetry, such as tragedy, of which he proposes to discuss the better and worse modes of construction.

For the modern critics from whom I have quoted, on the other hand, the world of poetic criticism is a world made up of, and bounded by, whatever characteristics can be attributed to human discourse of any kind in virtue of any of the causes of discourse, whether natural or artificial; the term "poetry" here designating, differently in different critics, some special selection and combination of the characteristics which such a view of discourse discloses. They have set out to define poetry in general, and they have taken as their genus what, in Aristotle, is the differentia separating poetry from other non-linguistic modes of artistic imitation, with the result that comparisons of poetry with other kinds of linguistic discourse, which for Aristotle are devices of explanation posterior to his delimitation of imitative poetry, become for them essential means of delimiting the nature of poetry. They are compelled, therefore, to get at their necessary differentiae by a process of dichotomous division within some general body of traits attributable to discourse as a whole. They tend accordingly to fix upon some such evident fact as that discourse (whether poetical, rhetorical, philosophical, scientific, historical, and so on) is statement, or communication, or expression, or embodiment of knowledge, or something else equally general, and then to look for significant extremes of difference within this basic idea. Thus discourse may be in prose or in verse; it may state concepts or feelings; it may communicate objective facts or "attitudes, feelings, and interpretations"; it may express the qualities of experience or indicate its uses; it may give us knowledge of logical relations among things merely or bring things before us in their whole concrete substance; it may or may not aim at a superior "clarity and precision" of utterance. In the table of contraries thus established, one column will be headed "poetry" and the other column "not-poetry" or something else more specific such as "science" or "logical discourse," and in this way a definition of poetry with a differentia signifying what is special to its language or content or both will be set up as a means of selecting the referents of the critic's propositions. Given the starting-point there can be no other way of proceeding, but the results stand in sharp contrast to those of Aristotle in several respects. The definitions, to begin with, are inevitably definitions applicable to the whole of whatever is taken to be poetry and hence they make of poetry—or of that which the word "poetry" properly names—one qualitatively homogeneous thing, however variously it may manifest itself in the different poetic genres. They are definitions, again, which, while thus unifying poetry

87

and setting it in opposition to all non-poetic discourse, nevertheless preserve the continuity of nature between it and the kinds of discourse from which it is distinguished, so that the differences tend to be differences of degree rather than of kind and poetry necessarily participates, in its peculiar way, in all the possibilities attributable to its genus (as is especially clear in the remarks of Messrs. Pottle and Ransom). And finally, whereas in Aristotle the identity of the concrete objects with which poetics deals is something known prior to the inquiry into their nature and kinds, and hence prior to the definitions of the science, on the basis simply of a common sense apprehension that what are called epics, tragedies, comedies, etc. appear to constitute a distinctive class of things, the determination, in these other critics, of what individual works or groups of works are really poems can take place only after the definition of "poetry" or "poem" has been established.

It is thus correct to say of these other critics, as not of Aristotle, that poetry exists for them primarily in a "verbal universe." And this fact has consequences of the greatest importance with respect both to the principles on which their criticism is based and to the method by which these principles are discovered and applied. The principles of poetics, for Aristotle, we have seen to be principles peculiar to the art of poetry, as the distinctive art of "making" or "imitating" human actions and other experiences in words, or to one or another of the various poetic species; they are identical with the necessary and sufficient internal causes, or principles of construction, that must operate in the writing of a given poem if it is to be a beautiful whole of the particular form desired; they vary accordingly from species to species; and they can be discovered only by reasoning *a posteriori* from the inductively known nature of any given kind of existing poems to the conditions of artistic success or failure in poems of that sort. For the critics in the second tradition, on the other hand, the principles of poetic criticism are necessarily specifications of principles operative throughout the field of writing as a whole. The basic principles of poetry are therefore identical with the principles basic to all varieties of verbal composition; and of these the most basic, as Quintilian long ago remarked, are the two elements without which purposive speech of any kind could not exist—*res* and *verba*, things and language, a subject and the words in which it is expressed, a content and a verbal form; after which the next most important, in any discourse that goes beyond a single utterance, is arrangement.[97] If poetry is to be studied in terms of its character *as discourse*, in a context of other modes of verbal statement, these are indeed the primary elements to which the critic must refer and upon which he must build—as the modern critics I have quoted clearly do—in his efforts to say what poetry is as a special mode of speech, to discriminate its possible kinds, or to determine the standards by which it is to be judged.

They are, it will be noted, the elements which Aristotle distinguished for rhetoric rather than for poetics,[98] and hence, as principles of poetry, they are essentially reductive, in the sense that, unlike the distinction of object, means, manner, and "power," which applies only to imitative poems, they tend to assimilate the structure of poetry to the structure of any discourse, however "unpoetic," in which we can discriminate aspects of content, language, and arrangement. It is necessary therefore to look for other principles through which the meanings of these basic terms (and especially of the first two) can be so specified as to give us a distinctive subject-matter for the criticism of poetry; and this is what the definitions of poetry I have quoted and the many others like them in this tradition are designed to do. They are based on the assumption that poetry has no intrinsic nature such as can be known sufficiently by an induction of the conditions essential to the production of poems as special kinds of wholes but is something that participates, with a difference, in the nature of discourse in general, or rather in what is taken, hypothetically, as the characteristic of discourse in general which appears to illuminate most satisfactorily for the critic the problems and values of poetry. This characteristic once selected, the next step is the determination of appropriate differentiae; and from the hypothesis thus formed the critic can then derive, by dialectical necessity of the kind illustrated in the first lecture,[99] all the more particular terms he needs for the discussion of poetry and poems.

Nothing can be more evident, however, than that discourse as such has an indefinite number of distinguishable aspects, uses, and relations, any one of which may be made the starting-point of a critical system. We have seen that it may be viewed as statement, as communication, or as expression, and correspondingly different definitions of poetry consequently achieved. The definitions will be different, too, according as poetry is thought to participate most fully in the cognitive functions of discourse, or in its functions of entertainment, or in its capacity to mould character, or to symbolize the unconscious desires and actions of the mind. And as these determinations and others vary, so the nature of poetry will be supposed to be most completely revealed when it is subsumed under rhetoric, or dialectic, or semantics, or psychology, or anthropology, or sociology—when it is treated, that is, differently in different systems, as a kind of persuasion in ornamented language, or as a mode of developed metaphor, or as a kind of argument or "exploration," or as an activity akin to dreams, folktales, myths, and rituals, or as an instrument of social action, and so on. All these, and other, possibilities have been exemplified in the history of this critical tradition, and the future will doubtless bring forth many fresh analogues and models of a similar sort.

And it is much the same with the bases which critics may choose for differentiating poetry from whatever are taken to be the non-poetic modes of discourse. Consider, for example, Coleridge's famous definition of a "poem" in Chapter 14 of the *Biographia Literaria*, in which, after saying that a poem "contains the same elements as a prose composition" and that the difference between them must therefore consist in a different combination of these elements, "in consequence of a different object being proposed," he proceeds to divide the possible "objects" or aims of composition into two kinds—theoretical or historical truth, and pleasure—and then to divide pleasure, in turn, into that afforded by the composition as a whole and that afforded by the elaboration of its parts; and he then concludes by describing a poem as "that species of composition, which is opposed to works of science, by proposing for its *immediate* object pleasure, not truth; and from all other species (having *this* object in common with it) it is discriminated by proposing to itself such delight from the *whole*, as is compatible with a distinct gratification from each component *part*."[100] Here the major distinction which provides the critic's principles is clearly one of ends, the assumption being that, although there can be no composition that does not seek to afford both pleasure and knowledge, compositions may yet differ fundamentally according as one or the other of these aims is their primary reason for being. The controlling differentia, however, can obviously be drawn from any one of several other causes of discourse: for example, from the faculties of the mind involved in its production, as when critics contrast poetry with science or prose in terms of an opposition of imagination to reason or of sensibility to intelligence; or, again, from the kinds of responses discourse may evoke in readers, as when poetry is set over against scientific, historical, or practical writing in terms of an opposition between an "aesthetic attitude" of "perceptual or contemplative enjoyment" and all other attitudes that involve a reference from the discourse itself to things or actions;[101] or, again, from a consideration of possible subject-matters, as when the essence of poetry is said to lie in its substitution of fiction for statements of fact, or as when the illumination of experience is taken as the highest function of writing, and poetry is contrasted with philosophy and science in terms of its concern not with "any abstraction or generalization of experience" but with the experience itself in all its particularity and ambiguity;[102] or, finally, from a division of the kinds or uses of language, as when symbols are divided into those that merely "indicate objects and instigate operations" and those that "depict or enact or evoke what they signify" and poetry is then identified as symbolic expression of the second type.[103]

It is not to be wondered at, therefore, that the basic terms for analysing poems available to critics in this tradition should take on widely different meanings, and be related to one another in widely different ways, as a consequence of the great variation possible in the critics' definitions. Depending upon these, "content" in the sense of the psychological and moral tendencies of the author may be viewed as an internal principle in relation to which the "form" is the external body (as in Louis Cazamian's history of English literature); or "form" may be thought of as

91

internal and "content" in the sense of the raw materials of experience as external (as in Walter Pater). Or "form" as semantic "structure" may be constituted the essence of poetry, with "content" as only its paraphrastic statement (as in Cleanth Brooks). Or the distinction may be reduced to one between "outer form" and "inner form" (as in Wellek's and Warren's *Theory of Literature*). Or "form" in poetry may be defined as what distinguishes poetry as synthetic from prose as analytic, and "content" identified as social attitude and thus as extra-literary (as in F. W. Bateson's *English Poetry*). Or "form" may be subordinated as concrete "presentment" to "content" as the moral preoccupations that characterize a writer's "peculiar interests in life" and hence be incapable of judgment apart from these (as in F. R. Leavis' *The Great Tradition*).

The great advantage of this mode of criticism, indeed, is that it encourages, collectively, the highly diversified approaches to poetry which these examples illustrate. It opposes no limits to the construction of any definition or hypothesis or the application to poetry of any theory of value a critic may think significant or illuminating for his purpose; and this freedom to explore dialectically all conceivable aspects and relations of poetry that are common to poetry and other uses of language has been responsible for a large share of the critical insights and observations we now possess.

We can see in poetry or in individual poems, however, only what our critical language permits us to see; and it is the inescapable limitation of the language I have been describing that it allows us to discriminate only those traits of content, medium, and structure in poetry that have analogues, positive or negative, in discourse of other kinds. For the essence of the method, once the critic's principles are determined in one of the ways I have mentioned, is comparison and contrast, and this is possible only on the assumption that the things compared have some fundamental nature in common which the critic can use as a continuum in his comparison. It is thus, for instance, that Mr. Ransom proceeds when he decides that a poem "is a loose logical structure with an irrelevant local texture": the continuum here is clearly the logical structure which all discourse has in common, and the differentiation of poetry from other discourse is achieved by identifying the "structure proper" of poems with their necessary "prose" element and finding the poetry in the "irrelevant and foreign matter" which this supports in the poet's words—in brief, by resolving poetry into characteristics which are either modifications (witness "loose logical structure") or polar opposites (witness "irrelevant local texture") of characteristics proper to scientific or technical prose.[104] It is the same logic also that leads Mr. Wimsatt, in one of his recent essays, to differentiate the "verbal style" peculiar to poetry from that common to most species of prose by setting up a sharp antithesis between the "counterlogical" and the "logical" uses of language.[105] And we find the same reasoning in most if not all of the criticism that looks for "total meanings" or "ultimate assertions" in tragedies like *King Lear*, while insisting that these works are still not strictly didactic; for if poems are kinds of discourse, they must obviously have meanings and make assertions, and the critic's business is to discover what it is that distinguishes the statement of meaning in poems such as *King Lear* from its statement in other varieties of poetic and non-poetic writing. It is easy to see, therefore, why the critic who uses this language is necessarily restricted, in his selection of attributes for poetry or individual poems, to such characteristics as have clear counterparts or logical contraries in the non-poetic discourse which he takes as the other term of his comparison. This is not to say that the method is incapable of differentiating poetry, as poetry, from other things or of serving as a basis for practical criticism of a highly particularized and perceptive sort. It is, however, to say that the discriminations it permits between poetry and other forms of writing or between the various kinds of poetry are such—and such alone—as can be arrived at by asking what characteristics among those possible in discourse are here present and in what special modifications and combinations. It is not a method, in other words, that allows the critic, as Aristotle's method does, to consider poems in their peculiar aspect as distinct kinds of concrete wholes, of which the special character, as poetic wholes, is determined by internal

93

principles of construction that have, at least as far as imitative poetry is concerned, no strict parallels in philosophy, science, rhetoric, or history.[106]

III

I shall not dwell on the long-continued monopoly which this simple but extremely flexible mode of approach to poetry has enjoyed in our critical tradition. It is certainly as old as, if not older than, Aristotle; but its monopoly was first clearly established in the context of the grammatical and rhetorical studies of literary texts and problems that flourished in the schools of Hellenistic Greece and later in Republican and Imperial Rome.[107] It was then that modern criticism had its true beginnings; and if it is now for most of us unthinkable that poetry can be viewed in any other light than as a kind of discourse, to be analysed in terms of content and form, the ultimate credit or blame, I think, must be given to that brilliant age of philology and eloquence and to the habit which then became deeply fixed in men's minds of considering poetry, as well as philosophy and history, in intimate companionship with the other verbal arts. The association thus formed persisted, as we all know, into and throughout the Middle Ages, manifesting itself variously in the twelfth- and thirteenth-century arts of poetry that drew upon the *Ad Herennium* and Cicero's *De Inventione*, in the long tradition of allegorizing exegesis which derived from the principle (stated by Augustine, among others) that not only the words but also the "things" of discourse are meaningful signs, and in the many theoretical debates as to whether poetry is primarily a branch of grammar, or a kind of argumentation or persuasion subordinate to logic or morals, or a form of composition using the figures and structural devices of rhetoric.[108] The Renaissance had its own problems and characteristic words for discussing them, and it had, too, the *Poetics*; but even in the new "Aristotelian" criticism which emerged in the middle of the sixteenth century, the influence of Aristotle was overshadowed by that of Cicero, Horace, and Quintilian; and it is clear that many of the distortions of Aristotle's analysis to be found in such commentators as Robor-

94

tello, Minturno, Scaliger, and Castelvetro, to say nothing of their successors during the next two centuries, were the result, directly or indirectly, of their inability to conceive of poetry except in terms of analogies between it and rhetoric, logic, moral philosophy, and history. Nor has the continuity of this tradition been decisively broken from the sixteenth century to the present. There is a clear line of descent, for example, from the conceptions of humane learning which the Renaissance drew from Cicero and Quintilian to the eighteenth-century systems of "rhetoric and belles-lettres" and from these to such contemporary theories of "literature" as those of Thomas Pollock[109] and Wellek and Warren. It is significant that in a number of recent critics "rhetoric" either is another name for "poetics" or is made to stand peculiarly for the structural analysis of poems as distinguished from such other insights into poetry as can be derived from grammar, dialectic, and the psychology and anthropology of symbolic expression.[110]

The "new" criticism of our day—by which I mean the criticism that has been thought by its practitioners and others to differ most completely from the criticism of the past—is thus, as far as its basic language goes, a very old thing indeed. That language, however, while remaining constant in essentials throughout the long period from Hellenistic Greece to the twentieth century, has admitted of many changes from time to time in secondary characteristics; and I think we can best appreciate the distinctive orientation of contemporary criticism by relating it to two major shifts in critical concepts that have taken place, within the general tradition, since 1700. The first of these is the shift that led from the relatively specific "Aristotelian-Horatian" criticism of the Renaissance to the relatively generic criticism that came increasingly into vogue during the eighteenth century and has largely flourished ever since: from a type of criticism, that is to say, which sought to mediate between universal poetry (as discourse that instructs through pleasing) and individual poems in terms of the distinguishing aims, structures, conventions, and models of the various recognized poetic genres, to a type of criticism in which distinctions of genre are subordinated to those large distinctions of poetic quality that can be identified in the

95

poet's handling of words and subjects irrespective of the particular "forms" his composition takes.[111] For most succeeding critics in the central line from the generalizing and philosophic critics of the eighteenth century, through Coleridge, Wordsworth, and Hazlitt, Arnold, Mill, and Pater, to Eliot, Richards, Empson, Leavis, and the American "new critics," the focus of consideration has been mainly poetry in its qualitative unity; and the structure of poetry they have been chiefly, though not exclusively, concerned with has been the common structure, however variously they have defined it, that underlies the many particular and, from this point of view, more superficial structures which had been the major object of attention for Renaissance and Neoclassical critics.

The second change that has helped to determine in a crucial way the language of contemporary criticism is of much more recent date. The rise of modern criticism, we are told by one of its best known representatives,

is part of a general intensification of the study of language and symbolism. The development of semantics, symbolic logic, cultural anthropology, and the psychology of Jung and Freud may all be taken as responses to the same general situation . . . they all bear upon the problem of symbolism (logical and extra-logical) and represent attempts to recover symbolic "languages" whose real importance has become evident to us only as the supporting cultural pattern breaks down.

It is no accident, therefore, that a great deal of modern criticism has occupied itself with the problem of how language actually works and specifically how it works in a piece of literature.[112]

We need not accept this statement as wholly adequate history, but it does point, as I think everybody will agree, to one respect in which the critical effort of the present generation has differed most significantly from the critical efforts of any earlier period since at least the Middle Ages.

It is not that contemporary critics have suddenly discovered, after centuries of neglect, that the language of poetry is a topic demanding the most serious kind of study, though they sometimes talk as if this were the case. The change has had to do rather with the nature and source of the first principles from which

96

modern critics—or the more advanced among them—have chosen to argue to the distinguishing characteristics of poems as compositions in words. Language has always indeed been an important problem, as several contemporary critics have recognized by their lively interest in recovering and bringing up to date the traditional analyses of tropes and figures developed in the rhetoric and criticism of antiquity and the Renaissance. Until the recent past, however, most discussions of the language as well as of the non-linguistic aspects of poems have been framed in terms that derived their meaning and relevance from some other cause of poetry than its verbal medium. In the formalistic criticism that flourished from the Renaissance into the eighteenth century, the typical starting-point for critical arguments was found in the possible effects of poetry upon audiences and readers; a sign of this is the great prominence in the critical vocabulary of that time of words like "instruction and pleasure," "delightful teaching," "invention and judgment," "the probable and the marvellous," "decorum," "correctness," "general nature," "novelty," and "taste," and the subordination to these distinctively rhetorical principles of terms relating to the character and powers of the poet or to the qualities of diction and subject-matter that ought to be aimed at in different kinds of poems. The shift to a more generalized kind of criticism that began in the eighteenth century was marked, in its initial phase, by the introduction of terms designating broad characteristics of poetic subject-matter, with the result that the discussion of language was controlled, during this period, by principles signified in such words as "true and false wit," "the sublime and the beautiful," "the terrible," "the tender," "the picturesque," "the ludicrous," and so on. And finally, with the criticism that developed in the Romantic period and persisted through the nineteenth century, principles of both of these sorts tended to give place to principles drawn primarily from the sources of poetry in the basic faculties and operations of the mind. Not the pleasures or needs of audiences, or the affective qualities of objects or actions, but the nature of the poet and of the psychological and moral causes upon which poetry depends now became, at least in the more influential critics of this age, from Coleridge and Wordsworth on, the con-

97

trolling points of reference for the discussion of poetic language and substance; and the key positions in the critical vocabulary were pre-empted by such terms, and their contraries, as "genius," "imagination," "emotion recollected in tranquillity," "imaginative reason," "high seriousness," "insight," "intuition," "sensibility." From the nineteenth century this tradition of psychological and moral criticism, with its centre of gravity in the qualities of feeling and intelligence which poetry reflects, has descended to our own time. It was not so much against this tradition itself that the pioneers of contemporary criticism in the second and third decades of the present century were in revolt as against some of its later manifestations; and it can be said of at least one important group of present-day critics—including writers as diverse in other respects as Middleton Murry, T. S. Eliot, and F. R. Leavis—that the language of their criticism, for all the new prominence some of them have given to questions of diction and symbols, is still in its essential constitution the "romantic" language of Coleridge, Wordsworth, and Arnold.

This is not quite the case, however, with the large and growing body of contemporary critical writing which Professor Brooks, in the passage I have quoted, appears to have especially in mind. It is true that for a good many devotees of that criticism— among them Brooks himself and, before him, I. A. Richards—the *Biographia Literaria* has been a kind of sacred book, more precious to them, indeed, than to critics like Eliot and Leavis. What they have valued in Coleridge, however, has not been the characteristic framework and method of his criticism but certain of his doctrines, and these they have tended to translate, in ways well exemplified by Richards' *Coleridge on Imagination*, into the terms of a very different conceptual scheme of their own. It is a scheme—as we see it operating not only in Richards and Brooks but in the large number of contemporaries who share their interest in "the problem of symbolism"—of which the first principles are neither formal, as in Aristotle, nor rhetorical, as in much Renaissance and Neoclassical criticism, nor psychological and moral, as in the "romantic" criticism of the nineteenth and early twentieth centuries, but, in the broad sense of the word, semantic. I mean by this that the fundamental relationships with which

98

this criticism is concerned are not the internal relations of parts and wholes in poems considered as objects of art or the relations either of poems to the characters and demands of audiences or of poetry to its origins in the imagination and sensibility of poets, but rather the relations of poems to the "realities" which they signify in the experience, internal or external, private or social, of their makers and readers. Words and meanings, images and concepts, symbols and referents—these are the axes on which, in this criticism, everything turns; by these poetry is constituted as a special kind of language for the expression or communication of special kinds of thought not fully compassable by the human mind in any other medium; and the business of the theorist of poetry is to make clear the nature of this language and of the significant structures it determines in order that readers may not either look for types of meaning in poetry which it is not fitted to give or fail to grasp the subtler or deeper meanings which only poems, or at least good poems, can yield. Among the typical slogans of the school are statements like the following (which I cull from a variety of sources): that "form" in poetry is "meaning," that "literature is ultimately metaphorical and symbolic,"[113] that any poem is "a system of signs"[114] or "a fabric of meaning,"[115] that any good poem necessarily bears "a total metaphoric relation" to "the reality or the many circles of reality to which it refers,"[116] and that to understand a poem critically is "to permit the varied components of its total meaning to take their rightful places within it."[117] And the exposition and application of these and other similar doctrines has brought into vogue a new critical vocabulary, the key elements of which—all related in one way or another to the central concept of meaning—are such words as "theme," "statement," "evocation," "vision," "total meaning," "tension," "attitude," "denotation," "connotation," "ambiguity," "metaphor," "paradox," "irony," "symbol," and "myth."

This semantic approach to poetry as a species of language—this latest version of the Hellenistic-Roman subjection of poetics to grammar and rhetoric—is everywhere now, as we all know, the dominant critical fashion, the mode of dealing with poetry and its structure that has given us the most influential books on

99

critical theory and practical criticism of the past three decades, is now securely enthroned in the critical quarterlies, and is rapidly making its way into the courses and dissertations of the universities and even into the hitherto unreceptive pages of the philological journals. Looked at broadly or from a distance, the movement exhibits a striking unity of spirit and method, as well as a remarkable tendency to mutual admiration on the part of its adherents. Considered more closely, however, the apparent homogeneity of the "new criticism" is seen to be less complete than is often thought; and it is not hard to discover, beneath the common preoccupation of these critics with "language," "symbol," and "meaning," at least two distinct ways, which are often associated in individual critics, of getting at the semantic nature of poetry and hence of defining the characteristic symbolic structures that condition its meanings and values.

IV

For the critics, such as I. A. Richards, William Empson, Wilson Knight, John Crowe Ransom, R. P. Blackmur, Allen Tate, Cleanth Brooks, Robert Penn Warren, and their many followers, who have taken the first of these two ways, the language of poetry, or the language which is poetry, is primarily language in the ordinary sense of statement in words. Their initial problem, therefore, has been the negative one of distinguishing this language, and of vindicating its claims as a medium for the expression of truths or "values" not otherwise accessible to us, in the relatively narrow context of other modes of verbal discourse. They have proceeded consequently, in the fashion described earlier in this lecture, by fixing upon some familiar type of verbal expression which is admittedly not poetry and then deriving the distinctive attributes and structural patterns of poetry by dialectical comparison and contrast with this. The non-poetic term of reference (without which the method will not work, since the whole procedure depends upon securing the agreement of readers that something is not poetry) has sometimes been prose in general, sometimes discursive or "rational" prose (excluding, that is, the imaginative use of prose in fiction and drama

100

as being at least partly "poetic"), sometimes, and most characteristically, the prose of technical science. And the emphasis in the comparison has been sometimes on the one and sometimes on the other of the two main axes, as I have called them, of this criticism: on the one hand, the character of the symbols by which "meanings" are expressed or determined in the two opposed spheres of discourse; on the other hand, the nature of the "meanings" themselves that appear to separate poetry most completely from science or prose. In the first case poetry emerges as a particular kind of meaningful expression, in the other as the expression of a particular kind of meaning; but in both cases the characteristics ascribed to poetry will be such, and only such, as the critic can discover by attending to those semantic traits of discourse in general which have analogues both in poetry and in the non-poetic writing he has taken as the other extreme of his comparison.

It has been discovered, thus, by different critics, that the words of poetry differ from those of plain prose or scientific statement in being primarily "emotive," or evocative of attitudes and feelings, rather than directly "referential";[118] that the essence of poetic speech is not clarity but ambiguity, in William Empson's sense of "any verbal nuance, however slight, which gives room for alternative reactions to the same piece of language";[119] that the symbols of poetry, unlike those of discursive prose, are untranslatable, the meanings being bound to the particular symbolic forms the poet has chosen;[120] that this form has a value in itself over and above its significative function, so .that the expressions in poetry tend to be "opaque" rather than "transparent"; that the statements of poetry aim at a "synthetic" unity achieved by fusing together or reconciling disparate or discordant elements of meaning, whereas the statements of prose are typically "analytic," more closely tied to grammar and to the step-by-step process of syllogistic inference;[121] that the meanings of words in poetry are not fixed by prior definition, as in science, but are determined immediately, in the poetic discourse itself, by the "contexts" in which they stand;[122] that poetic meanings arise out of a certain rich and paradoxical "tension" in poems between the "logical" and the "counterlogical" potentialities of speech and rhythm;[123]

101

and finally, and more generally still, that, in contrast to the direct and explicit method of prose, the method of poetry is characteristically suggestive and indirect, not stating its meanings but rendering them dramatically in images, metaphors, symbols, characters, and situations.[124]

There have been quite as many different formulae, in these critics, for the special kind of "meaning" which poetry embodies, or should embody, as for the distinctive character of poetic speech; and they have been arrived at by a similar process of reasoning *to* what the content of poetry is *from* what the content of science or "rational" prose admittedly is not. For some critics the crucial opposition separating the two kinds of language is between statements of fact and implications of "attitudes, feelings, and interpretations";[125] for others, between structures of meanings that assert or deny the existence of things and "hypothetical" structures that affirm only possibilities (so that poetry is somewhat akin to mathematics);[126] for others again, between the "rational," "logical," "paraphrasable" or "prose" meaning which poetry shares in some degree with science and the subtle qualifications of this or additions to it that constitute the "poetry" of any poem;[127] for still others, between simple and easily apprehensible meanings that can be expressed directly in the forms of logical discourse, and meanings of a more complex or difficult sort that admit only of indirect expression through metaphor, symbol, or myth; and so on through many other similar attempts to set poetry apart from ordinary or scientific language in terms of the kinds of things it can say.

The great problem for the critics of this school, however, has turned on the question of what kind of unity and structure poetry has in view of its constitution as a mode of discourse comparable to science and "rational" prose but sharply opposed to these in both the character of the meanings it conveys and its manner of conveying them. The answers given by different critics have taken rather different forms, but they have all been governed by the same two assumptions. It is taken for granted, in the first place, that, since form in poetry is meaning of some kind, the structural unity of any poem must be a unity of signification or "theme," to be detected, in the critic's analysis, by looking for

102

some particular dominant "attitude" or "interpretation" to which all the other thematic elements of the poem appear to be subordinated in a hierarchy which is the poem's "total meaning."[128] Poetry, however, is not science or prose, although it may embody prose or scientific meanings; hence the "theme" which unifies any genuine poem can never be a mere "abstraction" or anything that can be adequately stated in a simple paraphrase of what the poem seems to be saying; for the unity of a good poem is the unity, not of a rational argument, but of an organism, in which the theme, having found "its proper symbol, defined and refined by the participating metaphors . . . becomes a part of the reality in which we live—an insight, rooted in and growing out of concrete experience, many-sided, three-dimensional."[129] The structure of a poem, therefore, can be discovered only by examining all of its parts, however minute, in their interrelations or interactions one with another, so that the critic is "forced to talk about levels of meanings, symbolizations, clashes of connotations, paradoxes, ironies, etc."[130] None of these can be abstracted from the poem and remain poetry, as a proposition can be abstracted from a science and still preserve its truth; they must all be considered in their contexts as defined by the poem; but the form of a poem, it should be observed, is not a principle over and above its constituent connected elements but rather the sum total of these: it is they—"all the individual relationships, implications, and resolutions"—which together "make up" the poem's form.[131] It is not accidental that these critics are fond of talking about "total meanings," "total assertions," "total responses": whatever may be the structure of a poem, it is a structure of a sort that can be found fully manifested in any of its constituent passages or sequences of imagery, and it becomes the structure of the poem only by a kind of additive inclusion of all the qualitatively similar structures which comprise the totality of the text. Hence it is that in any poetic analysis exemplifying these principles the movement of the argument is likely to be a movement from particular part to particular part and through these eventually to statements about the poem as a whole.[132]

The second assumption is one we have already noted, namely, that the poetic structure these critics are concerned with is the

103

"essential" structure which emerges when poetry is viewed as one homogeneous kind of thing, whatever concrete varieties of works the term may be made to include. It may still be useful to classify poems as dramatic, epic, lyric, satirical, etc. and likewise to discriminate the different possible patterns—such as the logical, the narrative, the descriptive, the repetitive, etc.—that may predominate in the arrangement of their parts. These, however, are relatively superficial distinctions, pertaining rather to the material conventions and techniques of poetry than to its "structure" as such; and what is wanted is a principle of structure inclusive enough to allow us "to approach a poem by Donne in the same general terms through which we approach a poem by Keats; or a poem of Wordsworth's, through the same terms which will apply to a poem by Yeats," or to see that the *Odyssey* and *The Waste Land* are constructions of the same basic kind.[133] For if poetry is what it is here taken to be, it is clearly in this common structure rather than in the differentiating accidents of materials and techniques that the qualities which make of these works "poems" must of necessity reside.

But what is the "essential structure" of poetry? We can best understand the variant formulations of its principles given by these critics, I think, if we look first at the manner in which they have been derived. The method is the opposite of that which Aristotle thought best suited to inquiries into the structure of both animals and the productions of art—"to state what the definitive characters are that distinguish the [particular species of] animal as a whole; to explain what it is both in substance and in form, and to deal after the same fashion"—i.e., by hypothetical necessity—"with its several organs: in fact, to proceed in exactly the same way as we should do, were we giving a complete description of a couch."[134] Such a method is applicable in criticism, however, only when the critic is in a position to formulate inductively the definitive characteristics and ends of particular kinds of poems; and that is precisely what these contemporary critics, in their preoccupation with poetry as a kind of language, have been unable to do, or rather have consistently sought to avoid. The definitive characteristics of poetry, for them, are merely its differences from science or "rational" prose, and its end is merely

104

to be the kind of language and to have the kind of common structure which this assumption implies. They have therefore fallen back, in their reasonings from the nature of poetry to its "essential structure," upon a method strikingly like that which Aristotle attributed to the early Greek physiologers. "Now that with which the ancient writers, who first philosophized about Nature, busied themselves, was the material principle and the material cause. They inquired what this is, and what its character; how the universe is generated out of it, and by what motor influence, whether, for instance, by antagonism or friendship . . . , the substratum of matter being assumed to have certain inseparable properties. . . ."[135]

I do not wish to press the analogy too hard, but it is surely accurate to say of these modern critics, first, that they have tended to argue to what the structure of poetry is from an initial consideration of its material elements of language and meaning and the "inseparable properties" which (as in the definitions cited above) inhere in these, and, second, that they have introduced something comparable to the "motor influences" or natural forces by which Aristotle's ancients sought to account for the formal configuration of the universe and of the things it contains. Of both aspects of the procedure many examples could easily be given. If we ask, for instance, why it is that for Professor Brooks the structure of the best poems is a structure of "paradox," the answer is that "even the apparently simple and straightforward poet is forced into paradoxes by the nature of his instrument. . . . The method is an extension of the normal language of poetry, not a perversion of it."[136] The necessity, in short, is a necessity not of any particular end or effect a poet may be trying to achieve but of the nature of the matter he is using, as if we were to say that the structure of a house is what it is because of characteristics inherent in the builder's materials, and think that a sufficient account. It is not, of course, as simple as that, for the argument also presupposes—and this is the second aspect—a certain tendency in the poet's materials of non-scientific language and non-scientific thought to move of themselves, as it were, in the direction of form. Or rather, more exactly, in the direction of two possible forms, one of which is assumed to be superior to

105

the other. For there lurks in the arguments of most of these critics a moving principle of explanation that has startling affinities with the contrariety of antagonism and friendship ascribed by Aristotle to the early natural philosophers. The materials of a poem, we are often told, may be of such a sort that they tend naturally to harmonize with one another; and in that case we get a structure of a simple and rather uninteresting type. In the best poetry, however, the materials are such as tend naturally to generate oppositions and "tensions" of all kinds; and the structure in that case is the working out of these into a final "equilibrium." It is in these terms that I. A. Richards, in a familiar passage of his *Principles of Literary Criticism*, distinguishes two kinds of poems, in the first of which—represented by "Break, Break, Break," "Rose Aylmer," and "Love's Philosophy"—we have an ordered development of "comparatively special and limited experiences, with a definite emotion, for example, Sorrow, Joy, Pride, or a definite attitude, Love, Indignation, Admiration, Hope, or with a specific mood, Melancholy, Optimism or Longing," and in the second of which—represented by the "Ode to a Nightingale," "Proud Maisie," "Sir Patrick Spens," "The Definition of Love," and the "Nocturnall upon S. Lucie's Day"—we have structures characterized by "an equilibrium of opposed impulses." "The structures of these two kinds of experiences," Richards says, "are different, and the difference is not one of subject but of the relations *inter se* of the several impulses active in the experience. A poem of the first group is built out of sets of impulses which run parallel, which have the same direction. In a poem of the second group the most obvious feature is the extraordinary heterogeneity of the distinguishable impulses. But they are more than heterogeneous, they are opposed. . . . They [the poems of the first group] will not bear an ironical contemplation. . . . Irony in this sense consists in the bringing in of the opposite, the complementary impulses; that is why poetry which is exposed to it is not of the highest order, and why irony itself is so constantly a characteristic of poetry which is."[137]

The notion that the structure of the best poetry is a structure achieved through the resolution into some kind of equilibrium of naturally conflicting or opposed elements of language and thought undoubtedly owes something historically to the general conception of poetic unity formulated by Coleridge in his definition of the imagination as the power that "reveals itself in the balance or reconciliation of opposite or discordant qualities";[188] and its vogue in contemporary criticism is certainly in part a consequence of the great influence of Mr. Richards. I would suggest, however, that such a view—a view which identifies the principle of poetic structure with qualities describable as "tension," "synthesis," "complex of attitudes," "paradox," "irony," or the fusion of "logical argument" and "irrelevant texture"—is precisely what might be expected from critics whose method of reasoning is such as I have just described. A good poem is obviously a complex unity of some sort, but the only way they can account for the particular character of its structure—given their starting-point in the "inseparable qualities" of the poet's semantic materials—is by the assumption of a moving cause, apart from any specific formal ends the poet may have, that is capable of bringing order out of conflicting impulses, attitudes, or symbolic devices without sacrificing or suppressing the conflict itself. The assumption is clearly present, I think, in the following passage from Professor Brooks:

The essential structure of a poem (as distinguished from the rational or logical structure of the "statement" which we abstract from it) resembles that of architecture or painting: it is a pattern of resolved stresses. Or, to move closer still to poetry by considering the temporal arts, the structure of a poem resembles that of a ballet or musical composition. It is a pattern of resolutions and balances and harmonizations, developed through a temporal scheme.

Or, to move still closer to poetry, the structure of a poem resembles that of a play. This last example, of course, risks introducing once more the distracting element, since drama, like poetry, makes use of words. Yet, on the whole, most of us are less inclined to force the concept of "statement" on drama than on a lyric poem; for the very nature of drama is that of something "acted out"—something which arrives at its conclusion through conflict—something which builds conflict into its very being.[189]

And the point is perhaps even more explicit in the contention of Robert Penn Warren that poetic structure becomes good poetic structure by virtue precisely of the "resistances" to form inherent in its materials.

107

Can we [he asks] make any generalizations about the nature of the poetic structure? First, it involves resistances, at various levels. There is the tension between the rhythm of the poem and the rhythm of speech . . . ; between the formality of the rhythm and the informality of the language; between the particular and the general, the concrete and the abstract; between the elements of even the simplest metaphor; between the beautiful and the ugly; between ideas . . . ; between prosaisms and poeticisms. . . . This list is not intended to be exhaustive; it is intended to be merely suggestive. But it may be taken to imply that the poet is like the jiujitsu expert; he wins by utilizing the resistance of his opponent—the materials of the poem. In other words, a poem, to be good, must earn itself. It is a motion toward a point of rest, but if it is not a resisted motion, it is motion of no consequence. . . . And the good poem must, in some way, involve the resistance; it must carry something of the context of its own creation; it must come to terms with Mercutio. . . . And all this adds up to the fact that the structure is a dramatic structure, a movement through action toward rest, through complication toward simplicity of effect.[140]

There is no critical language, as I have said, that cannot be made to yield valuable observations and insights when it is applied, with skill and discretion, to individual works, and the fruitfulness, within its limits, of this semantic language has been exemplified on many occasions. It cannot be objected, either, that it has led to statements about poetic elements and poetic structures which are not easily verifiable in poems when we examine them in the light of its principles: who is there who, having looked intently for instances of "tension," "paradox," or "irony," has ever failed to find them? The real difficulty with the method, it seems to me, is twofold. Its controlling aim is the differentiation of poetry as poetry from other things, but in so far as it accomplishes this, it is at the cost of leaving us with a view of poetry itself from which all except the most general kind of formal distinctions have been excluded in the interest of preserving its essence as a homogeneous and uniquely valuable thing. It cannot but be that in the long run the universally felt differences among poetic forms and effects should have their revenge and that we should begin to ask whether there is indeed any general principle of poetic structure that can be applied significantly to lyric and drama, the *Odyssey* and *The Waste Land*. And then too, when we observe that the same type of

108

common structure which we are asked to think distinctive of poetry is to be found, by the same mode of analysis, in many works not included in poetry by these critics—in Plato's dialogues, for instance, or the *Religio Medici*, or the essays of Emerson and Carlyle—it cannot but be that we should presently wonder whether the differentiating essence of poetry, if there be such a thing, does not continue after all to elude us.[141]

V

The most obvious difference between this and the second contemporary approach to the semantic aspect of poetry lies in the scope of the context within which poetry is placed for the purpose of exploring its nature and structure as a kind of meaningful language. In the thought of all the writers, such as the late Professor Coomaraswamy, Maud Bodkin, Kenneth Burke, Edmund Wilson, Lionel Trilling, Richard Chase, Francis Fergusson, and Northrop Frye (to mention only a few conspicuous names), who have shown us the possibilities of this other approach, the opposition of poetry to scientific and "logical" discourse is still, indeed, fundamental; but the centre of interest in their theories has shifted from a preoccupation with the negative analogies between poetry, in its verbal aspects, and science, to a preoccupation with the positive analogies between poetry, viewed in terms of its content of meanings, and the various other modes —not all of them verbal strictly—of objectifying the conceptions and impulses of the mind, and hence of ordering experience symbolically, which have been set over against science and discursive logic, in the speculations of the past half-century, as so many pre-logical or extra-logical types of "language." The affinities between the two critical parties have indeed been close. "Words," as Professor Brooks tells us, "open out into the larger symbolizations on all levels—for example, into archetypal symbol, ritual, and myth. The critic's concern for 'language' need not be conceived narrowly, even if his concern leads to an intensive examination: it can be extended to the largest symbolizations possible."[142] We are still dealing, in short, with an essentially semantic approach, in which critics of the second school have

109

easily been able to utilize the theories and results of the first. The two schools, however, can be profitably distinguished with respect not only to their contexts and primary data but also to the characteristic directions of their reasoning: whereas the critics of the first group have tended to give us a "constructive" account of poetry (having first reduced poetry to its common properties), the critics of the second group have been largely intent on interpreting poetry "reductively," in terms of something assumed to be far more primitive and basic in human experience, and this even when they have insisted that poetry is not merely that into which it is resolved.

As everybody knows, the insights upon which this criticism has been founded are the achievement not of literary critics but of theorists and scholars in several other disciplines that have risen to prominence since the later years of the nineteenth century, and especially of two of these—the cultural anthropology of Sir James Frazer, Jane Harrison, Emile Durkheim, Lord Raglan, and many others, and the psychoanalysis or analytical psychology of Sigmund Freud and C. G. Jung and their innumerable disciples and deviationist followers.[143] Distinct as the two developments have been in their origins and basic concepts, the influences they have exerted on the general thought and particularly on the criticism of the last two generations have tended to converge, thanks in part to the interest of some of the psychologists—notably those of the Jungian school—in applying their explanations to the materials of the anthropologists and in part to the efforts of philosophers of knowledge like A. N. Whitehead, Ernst Cassirer, Susanne Langer, and others, to construct general theories of symbolism capable of subsuming the contributions of both groups.

The responses of literary critics to this complex and dynamic movement have taken several forms, the most fundamental of which can be seen in the general assumptions about poetry and criticism that underlie the procedures of most of the critics in our second semantic school. Whether they have been influenced mainly by the psychologists or mainly by the anthropologists or, as has become most usual, by both in varying proportions, they have been of one mind, to begin with, in thinking of poetry as a

110

"symbolic language" having close affinities both of nature and of origin with dreams and other primary psychic manifestations, with folktales and oracles, rituals and myths, and in defining "symbolic language" broadly as any mode of activity in which inner experiences, feelings, and thoughts, either individual or collective, are expressed "as if they were sensory experiences, events in the outer world."[144] They have conceived of this language, moreover, not only as quite distinct in its grammar and logic from any of the conventional languages we use in science or everyday intercourse, but as the one natural and universal language of the human race, common alike to civilized men and savages, but easily obscured unless we penetrate beneath the surface of what men say or do to the underlying nature of the experiences which their symbols serve to express. The important meanings, in short, are the hidden meanings; it is in these that the highest values of poetry lie, since they are closest to what is basic and most determinative in our inner lives. "Every relation to the archetype," says Jung, "whether through experience or the mere spoken word, is 'stirring,' i.e. it is impressive, it calls up a stronger voice than our own. The man who speaks with primordial images speaks with a thousand tongues; he entrances and overpowers, while at the same time he raises the idea he is trying to express above the occasional and the transitory into the sphere of the ever-existing. He transmutes personal destiny into the destiny of mankind, thus evoking all those beneficient forces that have enabled mankind to find a rescue from every hazard and to outlive the longest night. That is the secret of effective art. The creative process, in so far as we are able to follow it at all, consists in an unconscious animation of the archetype, and in a development and shaping of this image till the work is completed."[145] Poetry, indeed, becomes impoverished and superficial in proportion as it cuts itself off from its sources in the myths and other "symbolizations" which most completely embody the universal meanings of mankind. "Later on," writes A. K. Coomaraswamy, "all these motifs fall into the hands of the writers of 'romances,' litterateurs and in the end historians, and are no longer understood. That these formulae have been employed in the same way all over the world in the telling of

111

variants and fragments of the one Urmythos of humanity implies the presence, in certain kinds of literature, of imaginative (iconographic) values far exceeding those of the belle-lettrist's fantasies, or the kinds of literature that are based on 'observation.' "[146] It is essential for criticism, therefore, to be able to read the "symbolic language" in which at least the greatest poetry is written; and this language, it is obvious, can be best known by studying it in its least sophisticated manifestations in the unconscious operations of the individual psyche and in the symbolic acts and imaginations—the folktales, rituals, and myths—of precivilized peoples.

The starting-point of this criticism, accordingly, is not the nature of poetry but the nature of the universal symbolic processes out of which, it is assumed, poetry has somehow arisen and in which, in varying degrees, poetry, together with our responses to poetry, necessarily participates. Its general hypotheses, as a result, are of two kinds. The first thing that has to be posited, if the criticism is to proceed, is the identity and the "inseparable attributes" of the non-poetic substrate, whether psychological or cultural, which the critic has chosen as his base. If this is primarily psychological, what is the psychology to be—that of Freud or of Jung or of somebody else? Or, if it is cultural primarily, what view is to be taken, among the conflicting possible views, of such things as rituals and myths?[147] How, for example, are these related, and are we to suppose that there are many myths or really only one basic myth with many variant transformations?[148] The critic will naturally be eager to associate himself with the most plausible or at least the most recent and fashionable of the many available theories in either field that might serve his needs. But he will also have to make up his mind at the outset about another matter: the nature of the causes through which the archetypes of poetry come to be present in poems; and here too he has a fairly wide range of choice, from Jung's hypothesis of a collective unconscious or racial memory[149] or Coomaraswamy's notion of a "Philosophia perennis"[150] to the more literal types of explanation that suppose either a continuing response to continuing fundamental experiences[151] or simple historical transmission.[152]

112

Whatever the critic's hypothesis in these two respects may be, it will function in the criticism as a general "abstract" principle (in Hume's sense), the consequences of which will be related by dialectical rather than hypothetical necessity to the poems or poetic forms to which it is applied. The nature of tragedy and comedy will thus be a deduction from the nature of the underlying and original myth of which, by hypothesis, they are taken to represent two contrary derivatives;[153] and the structural parts of tragedy will be distinguished and defined by correspondence with the structural parts of the ritual or the psychic process which has been selected as their archetype.[154] The method, in short, is of the same general order as that we have attributed to the other contemporary school.

The chief preoccupation of the critics who have made these assumptions has been with the semantic structures of particular works, from the Greek epics and dramas which were the objects of the pioneer researches of Jane Harrison, Gilbert Murray, F. M. Cornford, and other members of the Cambridge school of classical anthropologists to the innumerable medieval and modern romances, novels, dramas, and lyrics to which the same method of archetypal interpretation in either psychological or anthropological terms or a combination of both has been applied more recently.[155] The supposition governing all these studies has been the same; namely, that the true meaning of a poem, no more than of a myth or a religious rite or a dream, is to be looked for on the surface which it presents to the reader, or indeed in anything that its writer can be supposed to have deliberately contrived. Its true meaning is what it stands for or objectifies in the underlying experience, individual or collective, of the poet himself and of such of his readers as can be led to penetrate below its merely particular and historically determined patterns of imagery and theme. The structure of a poem is like the structure of a dream, as the psychoanalysts have taught us to understand this; it is a structure with at least two levels, corresponding to its manifest and its latent content respectively; and it is the business of the critic-interpreter to direct our attention away from what the poet, on the surface of his work, seems to be saying, or from what earlier criticism would have been content to allow him to say, to what is really going on in the depths of his mind or personality, however unaware he may be; and that will always be something more general and deeply human than at first appears, and often contradictory to the surface meaning. It is no accident that some of these critics, in casting about for devices of interpretation adequate to this view of poetry, have found a model for contemporary criticism in the long-neglected medieval schematism of the four levels of meaning as described, among others, by Thomas Aquinas and Dante. "What is possibly most in order at the moment," says one of them, "is a thorough-going refurbishment of the medieval four-fold method of interpretation, which was first developed . . . for just such a purpose—to make at least partially available to the reason that complex of human problems which are embedded, deep and imponderable, in the Myth."[156]

Finally, although the archetypes of poems are in poems, they can never be known from an examination only of poems. Hence the necessary reliance of these critics not only on the general theories of the anthropologists and psychologists but also, and even more exclusively, on their particular formulae and findings, as is abundantly evident in their constant use of such analytical devices as the Oedipus complex of Freud, the progression-and-retrogression pattern of Jung, and the lists which these and other psychologists have given of symbolic tropes, and likewise in their no less frequent adaptation to critical purposes of what they have read in Frazer and others about fertility and initiation rites, scapegoats, heroes, the Adonis myth, and the killing of the god-king.

All this, however, should become much clearer in the next lecture, in which I shall deal with what has happened to the structures of a certain number of generally familiar poems and other literary works when they are discussed in the two related semantic languages which now make up, as we have seen, the chief resources of contemporary criticism in its more advanced forms.

Conceptions of poetic structure in contemporary criticism

THE FINAL TEST of any critical language is what its particular scheme of concepts permits or encourages us to say, in practical criticism, about individual works. And in the light of this test, it would seem that the critical revolution of the past three decades—the revolution that has given us the semantically oriented theories of poetry discussed in the last lecture—has been extraordinarily fruitful in concrete results. That at least has been the verdict of many of the writers who have committed themselves, more or less exclusively, to the new methods of interpreting literary works which the semantic movement has made available. "Critical writing like this," says Mr. Ransom, commenting on a page of subtle verbal analysis by R. P. Blackmur, "is done in our time. In depth and precision at once it is beyond all earlier criticism in our language."[157] The "only profitable approach to Shakespeare," Mr. Knights assures us, "is a consideration of his plays as dramatic poems" with close attention to the thematic structure most completely expressed in their imagery and diction; and of this approach it has remained for our generation, he says, after three centuries of criticism directed to less important things, to discover the proper technique.[158] "Our age," we are told in a recent essay on the movement as a whole, "is indeed an age of criticism. The structure of critical ideas and the practical criticism that British critics—Leavis, Turnell, Empson, Read—and American critics—Ransom, Tate, Brooks, Warren, Blackmur, Winters—have contrived upon the foundations of Eliot and Richards constitute an achievement in criticism the like of which has not been equaled in any previous period of our literary history."[159] And there would appear to be ample warrant for such enthusiasm not only in the many examples of "close readings" of texts but also in the large number of thorough-going "revaluations" of the great works and writers in our literary tradition which this school of critics has given us. The criticism of lyric poetry has been transformed; the criticism of the drama and the novel is in process of transformation; we now have a Shakespeare, or rather several Shakespeares, the existence of whom has been one of the startling discoveries of our time.

Let us suppose, at least for the duration of this lecture, that we have been convinced by these claims and these apparent evidences of progress in criticism and have resolved to deal with the problem of the structure of particular poetic works in the terms provided by the current view of poetic form as "meaning" and of literature as "ultimately metaphorical and symbolic." We should then have, as I suggested in the last lecture, the choice of two rather distinct approaches to the question, with the possibility that these might nevertheless be combined in a single more comprehensive view. In the first approach our concern would be with poetry considered as a special kind of language for the expression of meanings that cannot be expressed, or so accurately expressed, in other modes of discourse, and hence with the structures of meaning which poets themselves have devised; in the second approach, our emphasis would fall predominantly on the participation of poetry, certainly of great poetry, in the common symbolic operations of the human mind, and hence on the structures of meaning which, because they are basic and universal in man's experience, are in a sense given to poets rather than created by them. The first would be a kind of "Aristotelian" approach (though without Aristotle's devices for differentiating poetic forms) that would lead to a concentration on "symbolic structure"; the second would be a kind of "Platonic" approach (though with a dialectic moving in the opposite direction from Plato's) that would issue typically in a concentration on "archetypal patterns."

116

II

Let us imagine, to begin with, that we are critics of the first of these two types, for whom lyric poems, dramas, and works of fiction are semantic structures of a distinctive kind communicating, by symbolic devices peculiar to poetic or imaginative literature, a "total meaning" that is primarily of the poet's own making, however universally significant it may also be. Given such a work to be interpreted and judged in these terms, how can we proceed and what sort of results can we expect to get?

Our problem will be the same, let us remember, whether the work is a lyric like *Lycidas*, a tragedy like *King Lear*, a comedy like *Much Ado about Nothing*, a tragicomedy like *Cymbeline*, a serious novel like *The Brothers Karamazov*, an allegory like *The Faerie Queene*, or a satire like *The Dunciad*. As poetic or imaginative works we shall not confuse these, in our readings, with scientific, philosophical, or rhetorical statements; but we shall not forget that poetic meaning or expression of meaning, wherever we find it, is one homogeneous kind of thing, in relation to which the formal or technical differences among poems are either irrelevant or have only a subordinate importance, as determining only the particular artistic means through which the writer's expressive intention or his insight into spiritual reality is made evident. The basic terms we shall use in our discussion will consequently be—and they can only be—the two terms that differentiate the elements present in all such works no matter of what specific kind. A poem, considered in this generalized way, in abstraction from the peculiar formal ends and effects at which different poems aim, is a composite of "meanings" or "themes" (in the sense of the ideas or attitudes or resolutions of opposed impulses which it symbolizes) and of the verbal and technical devices by which these are given concrete "poetic" embodiment in the poet's words. The "themes" will vary from poem to poem, and we shall see later how they may be identified or defined. All poems, novels, and dramas, we must insist, either have organizing themes or else are mere entertainments and hence not worthy of serious consideration; we must remember, as one of our contemporaries has insisted, that any poem, in so far as it is truly the poet's, "involves his own view of the world, his own values," and hence it will, "for better or worse, have relevance, by implication at least, to the world outside the poem" and be "not merely a device for creating an illusion."[160] And if it should be pointed out to us that to say this is to blur the old distinction between imitative and didactic works of literary art, or rather to make all good poems, in the sense of all poems that have "relevance to life," essentially didactic productions, our reply must be simply that we are not cutting our cake that way—that for our purposes the difference that matters is the difference between works in which we can find "themes" and works in which we cannot, and that there are no works, among those possessed of genuine poetic value, that do not fall in the first of these classes.

We shall accordingly not be content until we have discovered, for example, that the ballad of "The Three Ravens," through its contrasting symbols of the ravens and of the knight's hawks, hound, and "fallow doe," represents two opposite ways of looking at life, the one in purely materialistic terms, the other in terms that find "an importance in life beyond mere material circumstance";[161] or that Wordsworth's "Intimations" ode, through its imagery of light and darkness, explores "with some sensitiveness the relation between the two modes of perception, that of the analytic reason and that of the synthesizing imagination";[162] or that the central conflict in Joseph Conrad's *Victory* is between the forces of Life, with their positive values of goodness, love, and faith, represented by Lena, and the forces of Death, with their negative values of evil, hate, and scepticism, represented by Mr. Jones and his companions, the contest centring upon Heyst, "who manifests the pull of these two opposite poles of being."[163]

We must not give the impression, however, that such structures of meaning are explicitly stated by the works in which we find them or that they can ever be grasped, in their full emotional significance, except by sensitive study of the indirect poetic means through which they are achieved. We shall need terms to discriminate and to talk about these; and we cannot do better, in this respect, than to use the traditional names which older critics invented for very different rhetorical or poetic purposes: continuing to speak, thus, with Aristotle and the later critics in his line, about plot and characters, but treating these as "carriers"

118

of meaning rather than as structural parts; reviving, as Mr. Wimsatt and others have done,[164] the ancient and Renaissance rhetoric of tropes and figures, but giving a special importance—and an enlarged definition—to such "figures of thought" as image, symbol, metaphor, paradox, irony, antithesis, synecdoche, allegory, pun, and the like.

Such will be our not very complicated analytical apparatus for reading poems of all kinds, and we can use it in two different but complementary ways. We may want to put the emphasis, in our writing or teaching, on the peculiar manner in which, in poetry as distinct from other kinds of writing, meanings are apprehended and expressed. We shall start, in that case, with the "theme," assuming that this is easily knowable and anyway, in our abstract statement of it, not a primary cause of the poem's value, and our attention will be concentrated on discriminating the various elements of rhythm, diction, statement, imagery, symbol, character, narrative, and so on, that co-operate, in a successful lyric, drama, or novel, to give body, precision, and emotional force to what the poet is trying to say, our criteria being relative to the "form" rather than to the ideas of the poem and turning on such general qualities as concreteness, intensity, "organic unity," and dramatic rendering. The result will be the so-called "formal" criticism which has been made widely familiar, on this continent at least, in Brooks' and Warren's *Understanding Poetry*, and is practised, with notable minuteness and ingenuity, by Mr. Blackmur.

We may prefer, however, to throw the emphasis on the meanings of poems rather than on their technique of meaningful expression; and in that case we shall tend to follow the more radical line taken by Brooks and Warren themselves in some of their later writings and by the many "new" critics of Shakespeare, from Wilson Knight to Harold Goddard and Robert Heilman, who have studied the plays for their poetic "meanings" rather than for their representations of characters and actions. We shall go in, that is to say, for what are called "interpretations," and more particularly for "interpretations" that will uncover deeper significances in well-known poems than they have usually been thought to contain. Our general procedure will consist, accord-

119

ingly, in reducing the concrete elements of poems, plays, or novels to the underlying themes and interrelated patterns of themes which they embody, and our criteria of value, being relative to these rather than to the expression itself, will require statement in terms like "profundity," "maturity," "complexity," "universality," or "imaginative vision."

Let us follow, then, this second line and consider what equipment we need and what we have to do in order to reveal the "symbolic structures" or "thematic frameworks" that lie, as our method must suppose, beneath the surface of all serious poetic works, as the primary end of poets in writing or at any rate as our chief reward in contemplating their productions. What we shall want to be able to do can be gathered from what some of the critics whose example we are emulating have already done. It has been shown by one of them, for instance, that when Coleridge introduces the associated images of the Albatross, the moon, and the wind into *The Rime of the Ancient Mariner*, he means to tell us that the imagination, of which the moon is the symbol, can be friendly to man but also inimical to him when its claims as a source of knowledge are denied.[165] Another critic has brought together in a similar fashion all the recurrent images in *Macbeth* that relate to clothes on the one hand and to young and innocent children on the other and, finding in these "the inner symbolism of the play," has generalized from them a pervasive opposition between "the over-brittle rationalism on which Macbeth founds his career" and the "irrational" forces in life which Macbeth and Lady Macbeth have left out of account in their conspiracy to capture "the future" for themselves.[166] Another critic has applied the same method, in a much more elaborate way, to *King Lear* and has shown us how the many distinct "patterns" of imagery which run through that play can be made to signify the terms of a complicated dialectic turning on the ways in which man must, and must not, understand and assess the world of human experience if he is to attain intellectual salvation: the play, in its ultimate assertion, we are told, is "about" this problem, in all its many ramifications, rather than about the tragic consequences, in a personal and merely human sense, of Lear's initial mistake.[167]

120

In all these instances, symbolic structure has been derived from a consideration chiefly of imagery and diction, with the result that dramas and novels are more or less completely assimilated to lyric poems.[168] The more obvious structural elements of dramas and novels, however—their characters and plots—may also be interpreted so as to yield meanings of the same sort. Thus the murder of Duncan, for one critic of *Macbeth*, symbolizes both the intrusion of political evil into the divinely ordered state and the operation of evil desires in the individual soul;[169] and another critic of the same play has seen in Macbeth's course of action after Duncan's murder, and especially in the killing of Banquo and the incidents of the feast in Act III, a parable of the failure—the inevitable failure—of any one who attempts to restore the "natural order" of society by "unnatural" means.[170] And similarly, in a recent book by a critic who holds that the "symbolic content" of Shakespeare's plays finds "its most controlled expression in the characters as people," the "ground-plan" of *King Lear* is reduced to a scheme in which Edmund and Goneril and Regan represent the Flesh, Cordelia the Spirit, and Lear himself the Soul, which, because it occupies a middle place between the extremes of the Spirit and the Flesh, is capable of rejecting the Spirit but also "of being recalled and of turning again."[171] We need not assume that the characters and actions of drama and fiction are "symbolic" merely, as in allegory of the stricter type; we shall therefore find it convenient to make a distinction between the "symbolic" and the "realistic" in action and character, and to recognize that both modes of treatment may coexist in any work, the mark of the "symbolic" being that the character or action, however "realistically" handled, can be brought into significant relation, not merely with the plot, but also with the "theme" or "total meaning" we have attributed to the work as a whole; in that case it will be proper to speak of Othello, Desdemona, and Iago, for instance, not as persons simply, but, in the manner of Wilson Knight, as "the Othello, Desdemona and Iago conceptions."[172]

The general nature of our problem should be clear from these illustrations of the method in practice, as well as from those I mentioned earlier; and it really makes little difference, so far as

121

our essential procedure is concerned, whether we seek the crucial meanings of poems in the subtleties of their verbal and imagistic expression, or in the "larger symbolisms" of their characters and plots, or in some combination of the two. For, irrespective of such distinctions, what we are committed to, if we want to write criticism of this kind at all, is the discovery of conceptual equivalents for the concrete relationships of elements discernible in poems—their contrasts of rhythmical movement, verbal tone, and imagery, their oppositions of characters, their conflicts of motives and actions. We want to be able to move—to give one more example —from a perception of the dramatic particularity of Lear's abdication as Shakespeare renders it in Act I of the play to a recognition that this decision of Lear's is something more than appears on the surface—that it really stands for "a kind of refusal of responsibility, a withdrawal from a necessary involvement in the world of action"; and having found in the scene this "meaning," we want to be able to relate it to the other particular "meanings" in this and later scenes and ultimately to the "total meaning" which constitutes the structure of the tragedy when viewed in these terms.[173] But how is this to be done? Not, certainly, by any such immediate grasp of meaning as gives us the import of any plain prose statement, or even of any ironical utterance in the usual sense, in a language we know, nor yet by the kind of quick inference from generally intelligible signs that allows us, when we witness a drama or read a novel, to gather what the characters are either doing or intending. It does not follow, because Lear abdicates, that he is refusing responsibility or disengaging himself from "a necessary involvement in the world of action"; it is indeed quite clear from the text that neither he nor anyone else in the play ever thinks of his action in any such abstract existentialist terms. Nor is there any natural or even conventionally constant connection between images of children and the idea of "the future" or between the moon and the imagination. Yet it is just such apparently arbitrary equivalences between poetic particulars (which in most poems have always been read as such) and general concepts that we have to assert if we are to pursue successfully this critical line.

Our problem bears this much resemblance to the problem of

the scholarly interpretation of allegories like *Everyman* or *The Faerie Queene*, that the meanings we propose to attribute to poems must in some sense be better known to us than the poems themselves. It differs, however, in one all-important respect, namely, that whereas the most convincing interpretations of allegories have always started from a definite body of doctrinal propositions that can be shown to have been in the poet's mind when he wrote,[174] we, who have taken all serious imaginative literature as our province and are concerned besides with universal and poetic rather than with particular and historical meanings, have no such resource. Our problem is not to explain the allegories in allegorical poems, but to assert something akin to allegory of all "poetic" works that seem to us to have "relevance to life." We must attempt, therefore, to find a substitute for the historically known doctrines which have served the interpreters of Spenser and Dante; and this we can do only by providing ourselves with a set of reduction terms, as I shall call them, suitable for use in all cases—with a collection, that is, of preferred general distinctions such as will enable us, when we come to read particular works, to formulate and unify the complex oppositions and resolutions of "themes" in which, as embodied concretely in the patterns of words, images, characters, or actions, we must suppose that their "total meanings" consist.

These, along with a predisposition to look for symbolic relations everywhere and a certain facility in seeing affinities and contrasts among the verbal and imaginative components of texts, will form our essential equipment. And the distinctions we shall need are not particularly hard to come by. The most useful distinctions, indeed, will be the most commonplace, in the double sense of not being peculiar to any given science or system of thought and of being applicable to the largest variety of contexts in both literature and life; and it is noteworthy that the contemporary writers who have given us our most highly praised models of this kind of interpretation have invariably used as reduction terms such familiar and all-embracing dichotomies as life and death (or positive values and negative values), good and evil, love and hate, harmony and strife, order and disorder, eternity and time, reality and appearance, truth and falsity, certainty and doubt, true insight and false opinion, imagination and intellect (as either sources of knowledge or guides in action), emotion and reason, complexity and simplicity, nature and art, the natural and the supernatural, nature as benignant and nature as malignant, man as spirit and man as beast, the needs of society and individual desires, internal states and outward acts, engagement and withdrawal. Of such universal contraries, not restricted in their applicability to any kind of work, whether lyric, narrative, or dramatic, it will be easy enough for us to acquire an adequate supply, and once we have them, or some selection of them, in our minds as principles of interpretation, it will seldom be hard to discover their presence in poems as organizing principles of symbolic content. It requires no great insight to find an inner dialectic of order and disorder or a struggle of good and evil forces in any serious plot; or a profound dialectic of appearance and reality in any plot in which the action turns on ignorance or deception and discovery; or an intention to inculcate poetically "the wholeness and complexity of things, in contrast with a partial and simple view" (to quote a recent formula for *Romeo and Juliet*[175]) in any plot in which the characters become progressively aware that their enemies are not as bad or their friends as good as they had thought. And what is true of plots and characters is true also of language and imagery: perhaps the most striking thing about the essays on Shakespeare of Mr. Wilson Knight is the facility with which he has been able to subsume the wonderfully varied images of the plays under his favourite simple oppositions of "death themes" and "life themes," conflict and order, war and love, "tempests" and "music."

It would not, of course, be fair to say that our task of interpretation consists merely in imposing our preferred reduction terms arbitrarily on poems. The structure of meaning we are concerned to exhibit is one that we must suppose to be objectively in the poem by virtue of the poet's act of expression. It will be there, however, only indirectly, as what is symbolized by the totality of particular relationships and "tensions" observable in all the parts of the poem and on all the levels—from metaphors to plot or central image—on which meaning can be found; and in the best poems it will be identical with the one "theme" or

124

"pattern of resolved stresses" which appears to harmonize most completely the many other "themes" or oppositions of values of which the poem consists. All of these, moreover, will be ambiguous, in the sense that they are embodied in symbols which permit, both in themselves and in correlation with other symbols, of a wide range of variant interpretations—at any rate when they are viewed as we have chosen to view them. Our problem, therefore, will be dual: to make sense, in the fashion already described, of all the particulars of the poem—to say, for instance, what, out of various possibilities, Cordelia stands for, or which of several possible meanings we ought to ascribe to the contrast of the sun and moon in *The Rime of the Ancient Mariner*—and, above all, to fix upon the one equally ambiguous opposition, among the many evident in the imagery or events of the work, which we are to regard as the "carrier" of the central meaning. The problem in both of its aspects is clearly insoluble unless we bring to it minds already prepared to look for one order of central meaning in the works we examine rather than any of many other possible orders; and that this is precisely what the critics whose procedure we are following have in fact done is shown by the numerous incompatible semantic structures they have attributed, for example, to plays like *Macbeth* or to lyrics like the "Ode on a Grecian Urn." They are all selective interpretations, and the selection is governed in each case, though not always crudely, by the favourite reduction terms the critic has been able to find exemplified in the poem.

We shall have to be content, then, with a method of which the essentially rhetorical character is perhaps evident from what I have said. For the principles we must employ are not principles of poetry as such, and still less of any of its kinds; they are rather "topics" or "commonplaces" in the technical sense of the ancient, medieval, and Renaissance writers on rhetoric—that is to say, convenient general distinctions or heads of interpretation that can be made to fit without too much difficulty almost any poem we have in hand, as the orator can use the *topoi* of honour and dishonour, praise and blame, to supply himself with predicates which he will then attempt to make his hearers think are appropriate to a given man. Or if they are not merely that, they will be at best the contraries of a dialectic which is of our own making and to which we are bent on assimilating the poetically expressed thought or "vision" of the writers we are trying to interpret.

In either case we shall be engaged in imputing to our writers a structure of meanings that is very different from the apparent or (as we will prefer to say) superficial structures of any of their poems; a structure, besides, that has hitherto escaped the notice of readers and critics—or there would be no point in our discovering it now. We cannot expect, therefore, that what we say will at once command assent without a good deal of extra-critical, and hence rhetorical, assistance on our part. Of the various lines of persuasion open to us, I shall mention only a few of those which have been most commonly used by critics of this school. It can be urged that the interpretation we are proposing for (say) *Macbeth*, though likely to seem radically disturbing to traditional notions, does in fact succeed, as Roy Walker says of his peculiarly ingenious interpretation of that play, in "illuminating the play in its entirety," that is, in subsuming all the details under the construction we have put upon them.[176] And this will have considerable force so long as our readers fail to observe that the kind of construction placed on the details has already been determined, as in Mr. Walker's book, by the hypothesis which the details are said to support, or so long as they do not compare our account, as a scholar might do, point by point with alternative accounts by other critics that make similar claims to internal coherence and adequacy, and especially so long as they, or we, avoid bringing into the discussion the subversive principle of Occam's razor. Or we may concede that other formulae than our own have perhaps equal validity in their own terms, and then defend the validity of our own formula, as Mr. J. I. M. Stewart defends his version of Prince Hal's break with Falstaff, by insisting that on the deeper level poems may have multiple meanings, so that any plausible interpretation is correct.[177] Or, again, we may appeal to history: either in defence of a particular interpretation, as when Mr. Duthie supports his contention that the theme of Order and Disorder is a central organizing principle in most of Shakespeare by

126

pointing to the very frequent occurrence of this antithesis in Elizabethan non-dramatic writing;[178] or else in defence of the method of interpretation itself, as when Mr. Danby, presenting us with a highly allegorized *King Lear*, proceeds to urge the plausibility of this by reminding us that Shakespeare was a contemporary of Spenser and "stands closer than we do" to the morality plays and to the mental habits and the artistic attitudes of the Middle Ages, when "allegory-hunting was as exciting as motive-hunting is for us."[179] There is of course an unfortunate *non sequitur* in both of these historical arguments; and once we perceive this, we may well prefer to fall back, as many critics of this school have done, on still another topic of persuasion, and one excellently calculated to put both logic and history out of court. We can simply appeal to the doctrine—which has been explicitly stated, among others, by Wilson Knight and Harold Goddard[180]—that in poetic interpretation the ultimate authority is not historical fact or ordinary inference but the imagination or intuition of the critic himself, when he submits himself "with utmost passivity to the poet's work" undisturbed by analytical reason or historical method.[181] It is a truly powerful device, for of critical statements thus guaranteed the only possible refutation is one that convicts the objector in advance either of lacking the necessary spiritual equipment for reading poetry or of being misled by irrelevant intellectualism. And lastly, if this is not sufficient, there is always available to us the admirable topic which the older rhetoricians called "amplification." We can attempt to write so glowingly about the symbolic structures we find in poems that any literal-minded or sceptical reader will be made at least temporarily ashamed of his doubts (this is one of the great resources of Wilson Knight); or, short of this, we can advance our more difficult or novel points in sentences beginning with such phrases as "It is clear that" or "It is obvious that," etc., or, having stated a particularly daring interpretation, we can insist on its obviousness in the manner exemplified in Mr. Goddard's extremely original pages on the allegory in *Cymbeline*: "Does not the parabolic quality of all this," he asks, "fairly shout aloud and demand that we think of Imogen as the True England wedded secretly to the poor but genuinely gentle Posthumus

127

Leonatus, English Manhood and Valor? . . . The moment we take the leading characters of the play in this way, numberless details rush forth to fit into what we can scarcely help calling the allegorical design."[182]

These, then, are the possibilities open to us, and the limits within which we must work, if we take the first of the two approaches to poetry as semantic structure: an approach in which we will tend to view poetry in all its varieties as a kind of dramatized dialectic, a form of discourse that uses "poetic" devices of imagery, metaphor, symbol, parable, and allegory as means of stating or resolving problems, exploring or bringing unity into large and complicated areas of experience, adjusting competing values, or reducing the chaos of life to a unified imaginative vision—and all this on the initial assumption that the significant patterns of meaning to be sought in poems, general as these will be in our statement of them, are patterns which poets themselves have constructed and which therefore have no existence or value apart from the "poetry" in which they inhere.

III

Our initial assumption, if we prefer to take the second of the two contemporary approaches, will be almost the reverse of this. We shall tend to look upon the kind of "structural analysis" of poems in restricted poetic or rhetorical terms which I have been describing, as merely a first stage in criticism, beyond which, if we are to do justice to the profounder significances of poems, we must move on to a consideration of the extra-personal and extra-poetic sources of poetic themes and patterns in the larger symbolic activities of the poet's culture or of the human race in general. "Moby Dick," it has been said by one of the leading critics in this second school, "cannot remain within Melville's novel: he is bound to be incorporated into our total verbal experience of leviathans and dragons of the deep from the Old Testament onward";[183] and it is equally true, for any poet, that he must work with materials of imagery, character, and action and employ schemes of construction that are, to a lesser or greater extent, not of his invention, but are given to him, already formed

128

and charged with independent meanings and emotional associations, in the past experience of mankind. Our primary interest will be in such antecedents or substrates of poetry or of our responses to poetry. We shall consider them, however, not merely as antecedents or substrates in a historical sense but as present and living elements—more important ultimately than anything the poet himself can contrive by his art—in the "total meaning" of any great poem. In our study of them we shall make use of what philologists and literary historians have learned or conjectured about the "sources and analogues" of poetic works and about the origins of poetic forms; but we shall be much more interested in the newer sciences of cultural anthropology and psychoanalysis than in literary scholarship in the usual sense; and among scholars, we shall prefer those who, like Gilbert Murray and F. M. Cornford, have gone in for explanations of poetry that can be assimilated, without too great trouble, to the findings of Frazer, Freud, and Jung. We shall use these scholarly authorities, moreover, not for the sake of reconstructing the probable genesis of poems or poetic forms in literal terms, but with a view to the discovery, in poems, of the "real" structures and "deeper" meanings that derive from the reflection in poetry of pre-existing and more general ways of ordering human experience symbolically, in particular those ways which have been disclosed to us in modern studies of primitive myths and rituals and of the unconscious operations of the soul. Our distinctive subject-matter, that is to say, will be the participation of poems, through either their writers or the responses of their readers, in the underlying and basic forms of human thought and meaningful action; and our method will be typically an argument *to* poems, considered as composites of both individual and collective meanings, *from* what it has been fashionable to call, especially since the publication of Maud Bodkin's book in 1934, their "archetypal patterns"— a term that has sometimes been taken in the psychological sense, borrowed by her from Jung, of "that within us which, in Gilbert Murray's phrase, leaps in response to the effective presentation in poetry of an ancient theme," but more often in the objective sense of the ancient theme or pattern itself, to which our "archetypal" emotions correspond.[184]

129

What we may hope to accomplish by taking this critical line can again be inferred from what our contemporaries have been able to do. We may confine ourselves, if we choose, to those archetypes of poems to which we can give a more or less particularized historical status as the underlying forms, with their characteristic emotional associations, of a given period of culture. One such form has been discovered, for the English Renaissance, in the pattern of content common to the full-scale morality plays of the sixteenth century: these can all be reduced, it has been observed, to the image of a central figure, symbolic of humanity and hence "born with an ultimately irresistible compulsion to sin," who is tempted by Satan or his emissaries "to leave the path of righteousness and follow a course or career of wickedness at the end of which he is convicted of sin and becomes a manifest candidate for damnation," whereupon he is saved "by the intercession of Christ, the Blessed Virgin Mary, or some kindly saint and is taken without merit of his own into the bosom of God." Here, in this lowest common denominator of many morality plots, is clearly a pattern of profound cultural significance; and it requires but a simple step in "archetypal" criticism, as Mr. Hardin Craig has recently shown, to discover the same pattern, "amplified but not changed," with its religious implications still operative, in the basic action of *Macbeth*, which can likewise be reduced, if only we disregard enough of the plot Shakespeare constructed, to "the aberration of a hero, under delusion of the powers of evil," who pursues "a career of crime and wickedness, violent to the last degree . . . until such time as his course of evil [is] arrested," in fulfilment of our faith and Shakespeare's, "by outraged man acting as the punitive agent of God."[185] Both the historical archetype and the poetry, however, may be generalized much farther than this, to yield such insights as Wilson Knight gives us at the end of his essay on "Myth and Miracle":

For what [he asks] is the sequence of the *Divina Commedia*, *L'Inferno*, *Il Purgatorio*, *Il Paradiso*, but another manifestation, in the spatialized forms of medieval eschatology, of the essential qualities of the three groups of the greater plays of Shakespeare, the Problems, Tragedies and Myths? And what are both but reflections in the work of the two greatest minds of modern Europe—children respectively

130

of the Middle Ages and the Renaissance—of that mystic truth from which are born the dogmas of the Catholic Church—the incarnation in actuality of the Divine Logos of Poetry: the temptation in the desert, the tragic ministry and death, and the resurrection of the Christ? We should centre our attention always not on the poetic forms alone, which are things of time and history, but on the spirit which burns through them and is eternal in its rhythm of pain, endurance, and joy.[186]

But we need not stop with such relatively limited correspondences, and indeed there seems to be a kind of inner necessity in the dialectic of this criticism to push the quest for archetypes farther and farther back into the evolutionary antecedents of the poetic structures and themes with which it is concerned. Beyond history, or rather the schematized history of the cultural historians, lies the now equally schematized simpler age of primitive ritual and myth, the unity of which lies ultimately—as we have learned from Frazer and others—in man's first responses to the succession of the seasons, the rhythm of the earth's dying and reviving fertility, the cycle of youth, maturity, and decay, the obligation to prepare new generations for the collective life of the tribe. It is inevitable that we should seek in this world of social origins for the true prototypes and "real" significances of the ancient themes and formulae of construction that still determine, or should determine, what modern poets do when they succeed in affecting modern readers most deeply—and be guided, perhaps, in our search, by the Platonic faith expressed in Robert Graves's "To Juan at the Winter Solstice":

> There is one story and one story only
> That will prove worth your telling,
> Whether as learned bard or gifted child;
> To it all lines or lesser gauds belong
> That startle with their shining
> Such common stories as they stray into. . . .
>
> Much snow is falling, winds roar hollowly,
> The owl hoots from the elder,
> Fear in your heart cries to the loving-cup:
> Sorrow to sorrow as the sparks fly upward.
> The log groans and confesses
> There is one story and one story only.[187]

131

How rewarding the quest can be has been demonstrated again and again in the criticism of recent years. We may now know, thanks to the pioneer work of Mr. Colin Still, how wrong we were to think of *The Tempest* as a mere product of Shakespeare's imagination. It is no such thing, but rather a deliberately allegorical statement of the universal theme which appears most clearly in the early Greek mysteries of the Lesser and Greater Initiation—the double theme of purgation from sin and of rebirth and upward spiritual movement after sorrow and death.[188] We can learn similarly from Mr. Francis Fergusson to look upon Sophocles' *Oedipus Rex* no longer as a tragic imitation in Aristotle's sense but rather as "both myth and ritual," a dramatic reproduction, for an audience that still retained obscure feelings of "ritual expectancy," of the ancient rite of the spring-god as constructed by Jane Harrison and Gilbert Murray, the figure of Oedipus himself fulfilling "all the requirements of the scapegoat, the dismembered king or god-figure" of the older religion.[189] We can perhaps be persuaded, too, by Mr. J. I. M. Stewart, to see in the rejection of Falstaff by Prince Hal one of "the simpler rôles of archetypal drama." For anthropologists, he says,

are always telling us of countries gone waste and barren under the rule of an old, impotent and guilty king, who must be ritually slain and supplanted by his son or another before the saving rains can come bringing purification and regeneration to the land. Is not Henry IV in precisely the situation of this king? . . . Perhaps, then, we glimpse here a further reason why the rejection of Falstaff is inevitable—not merely traditionally and moralistically inevitable but symbolically inevitable as well. . . . I suggest that Hal, by a displacement common enough in the evolution of ritual, kills Falstaff instead of killing the king, his father. In a sense Falstaff *is* his father; certainly is a 'father-substitute' in the psychologist's word. . . . And Falstaff, in standing for the old king, symbolises all the accumulated sin of the reign, all the consequent sterility of the land. But the young king draws his knife at the altar—and the heart of that grey iniquity, that father ruffian, is as fracted and corroborate as Pistol avers. Falstaff's rejection and death are very sad, but Sir James Frazer would have classed them with the Periodic Expulsion of Evils in a Material Vehicle, and discerned beneath the skin of Shakespeare's audience true brothers of the people of Leti, Moa, and Lakor.[190]

This doubtless owes something to the imaginative powers of

132

"Michael Innes," but not too much, as we can see when we turn to the many other books and essays in which critics of the same school have shown us, for example, that Heyst in Conrad's *Victory* figures at the end of the story as "a sacrificial god-king," his committing himself to the flames being "a form of purification and expiation ritual . . . patterned after the killing of the god-king in primitive tribal ceremonies";[191] that *Lycidas* is not about Edward King but "about his archetype, Adonis, the dying and rising god, called Lycidas in Milton's poem";[192] that Ophelia is a "Fertility ghost"—"the little Spring-ghost, the fertility daemon, the vegetation spirit."[193]

But even this is only a half-way station on the road to the ultimate archetype—the Platonic One in reverse, so to speak—toward which this criticism ineluctably moves. Below the communal world of myth and ritual is the still more primitive and hence meaningful world of the individual psyche; and it too is a world of simple patterns, constantly repeated in the subrational experience of all men in every age, in the light of which we may expect to make deeper sense out of the more complicated structures of developed art. Our models here are many, though they naturally differ in form according to the particular school of psychology from which they draw their hypotheses and terms. What critics have borrowed from Freud is chiefly, perhaps, a new technique, or rather terminology, for uncovering the subsurface probabilities and necessities in poetic actions; as when Dr. Ernest Jones, and after him many literary amateurs in psychiatry, reduce the tragic motivation of Hamlet to the formula of the Oedipus complex; or as when Mr. Stewart, assuming that the poetic drama is necessarily concerned with unconscious volitions, argues from the authority of Freud to the presence of both "projected" and "delusional" jealousy in the behaviour of Leontes in Act I of *The Winter's Tale*: Shakespeare, he tells us, is here "penetrating to nature, and once more giving his fable something of the demonic quality of myth or folk-story, which is commonly nearer to the radical workings of the human mind than are later and rationalised versions of the same material."[194]

The hypotheses of Jung, on the other hand, have lent themselves characteristically to the identification of fundamental struc-

133

tural patterns, common to dream, myth, ritual, fairy tale, and poetry, which are but the objective counterparts or symbols, differing materially but not structurally in different cultures, of universal tendencies in the human psyche, and derive from this their persistent power to stir our emotions. Jung himself has given us a number of models of the procedure, as, for example, in his discussion of how the principle of progression and regression is symbolized in the myth of the whale-dragon:

The hero is the symbolical representative of the libido movement. The entrance into the dragon is the regressive course, while the journey towards the east (the night journey under the sea) with its attendant events symbolizes the effort towards adaptation to the conditions of the psychic inner world. The complete swallowing up and disappearance of the hero in the belly of the dragon represents the complete withdrawal of interest from the outer world. The overcoming of the monster from within is the achievement of adaptation to the conditions of the inner world; and finally, the escape with the help of a bird from the monster's body, which happens at the moment of sunrise, is the renewal of progression. It is characteristic that while the hero is within its belly the monster begins the night sea journey towards the east, that is to say, towards the sunrise. This seems to me to point to the fact that the regression is not necessarily a backward step in the sense of involution or degeneration, but rather represents a necessary phase in development. The individual has, however, no awareness of this development; he feels himself to be in a state of compulsion that resembles an early infantile state, or even an embryonic condition within the womb. If he lingers on in this condition, then only can we speak of involution or degeneration.[195]

How widely applicable such a formula is to the interpretation of artistic literature has been shown with special clarity by Miss Bodkin, in the many illustrations of psychic patterns, in writings ranging from Homer to D. H. Lawrence, which she has collected in her *Archetypal Patterns in Poetry*. The "tragic pattern," the "rebirth archetype," the "archetype of Paradise-Hades," the "image of woman," the "images of the Devil, the Hero, and of God": all these are finally reducible, she argues, to the basic Jungian motions of "progression and regression," "frustration and transcendence."[196] It is partly at least from Miss Bodkin, and hence ultimately from Jung, that Professor Tillyard has drawn

134

the conception of tragedy as a pattern of "destruction followed by regeneration"—in short, as the "rebirth archetype"—which he employs in his book on *Shakespeare's Last Plays* in order to demonstrate the underlying structural unity of *Cymbeline*, *The Winter's Tale*, and *The Tempest*, and to exhibit this unity as the necessary completion of a theme to which Shakespeare had already committed himself in *Richard II*, *Henry IV*, and *Henry V*.[197]

From these examples of the possibilities open to us in "archetypal" criticism, we may gather some idea of the nature of the results to which such criticism leads and of the equipment we must have if we are to practise it successfully. Our end is accomplished, at all three of the levels I have distinguished, when we have established the presence in poems of patterns of action, character, and imagery concerning which we can say that they are patterns originating not in the artistic purposes and inventions of the poets but in antecedent history or prehistory or in human nature itself, our assumption being that the profounder meanings of poems are a function always of the original meanings of the archetypes which they embody. We have, consequently, two problems: to discover the archetypes and to show that they are in the poems. And the first problem should cause us little trouble, at least if we may judge from what most of the practitioners of the method have done. We have only to be well read in the more authoritative, or celebrated, books in which the basic patterns of cultural history, of prehistoric myth and ritual, and of the operations of the unconscious have already been reduced to plausible and usable statement: our necessary and sufficient guides will be Freud and Jung, Frazer and Malinowski, Jane Harrison, F. M. Cornford, and Gilbert Murray, to mention the names that recur most often in the footnotes of critics belonging to this school. From such authorities—or from some particular selection or combination of them—we can get all the data we need by methods of reading which presuppose no specialized expertness in the sciences they treat. It will be better, indeed, if we ourselves are not technically trained in these subjects; else we might be led to wonder sometimes how we can perform a valid psychoanalysis of a patient with whom, because he is dead, we cannot

135

talk; or we might discover, to our embarrassment, that there perhaps never was in Greece any such elaborate religious rite as that from which Gilbert Murray, relying on the speculations of Miss Harrison, deduced the six ritual parts of Greek tragedy;[198] or we might even come to suspect that what Sir James Frazer tells us about primitive customs and myths is possibly determined quite as much by the distinctive conceptual framework and method of *The Golden Bough* as by the masses of information which that great book sought to interpret. It is true at any rate that there are few critics of the "archetypal" school who have felt the need of more than a second-hand knowledge of the history, anthropology, or psychology upon which they have based their interpretations of poems.

Our second problem is also easy enough to solve, provided we are clear as to just what we are trying to do. We want to be able to persuade our readers, for example, that "the form and meaning" of *Oedipus Rex* is that of the much older winter-spring ritual; or that the conflict between Antigone and Creon in the *Antigone* represents the resistance of the older matriarchal principle of society to the newer patriarchal principle;[199] or that Ahab in *Moby Dick* is, among many other things, "the *shaman*, that is, the religious leader (common among certain tribes of American Indians) who cuts himself off from society to undergo his private ordeal, through which he attains some of the knowledge and power of the gods";[200] or that in the development of Shakespeare's Prince Hal we can see "the classic struggle of the ego to come to normal adjustment, beginning with the rebellion against the father, going on to the conquest of the super-ego (Hotspur, with his rigid notions of honor and glory), then to the conquests of the *id* (Falstaff, with his anarchic self-indulgence), then to the identification with the father (the crown scene) and the assumption of mature responsibility";[201] or, again, that the imagery and action of *The Rime of the Ancient Mariner* symbolizes the two-fold movement of the soul, first "toward severed relation with the outer world, and . . . toward disintegration and death," then, "in an expansion or outburst of activity," upward and outward "toward redintegration and life-renewal."[202] And our arguments in all such cases will turn on an identification, in the concrete

136

materials and sequences of the poems, of whatever subpoetic patterns our preferred commonplaces and sources of interpretation, as applied to the details of the poems, encourage us to find there. But once we have made this identification, what will the resulting propositions mean, and what will be the guarantees of their truth?

I think it is clear, to begin with, that they are not propositions of the same order, or susceptible of the same kind of proof, as the common assertions of literary scholars that such-and-such poems derived their materials or their structural patterns from such-and-such earlier sources. They are not the kind of statements, either, that we have to make when we attempt to relate the *Prophetic Books* of William Blake or the operas of Richard Wagner or the poems of William Butler Yeats to the myths which these compositions were clearly designed to embody. Nor are they statements of the sort that can be made, quite legitimately, about certain modern poems, such as *The Waste Land*, in which ritual or mythic elements are deliberately used as artistic devices for objectifying or universalizing lyric thought. All such statements presuppose relationships of cause and effect, and depend for their probability, in any given case, upon literal historical evidence. Now there can be little doubt, I think, that "archetypal" criticism does in fact rest on the assumption of some kind of genetic relation, however remote or hard to trace, between poetry and whatever antecedents the critic takes as the source of his archetypes. It is difficult, indeed, to see how this criticism could have arisen without such causal hypotheses as that of the mythical or ritualistic origin of poetry or the Jungian notion of racial memory. These, however, have usually been taken merely as validating principles for the method in general rather than as premises to be invoked in support of particular interpretations; and Professor Frye is correctly describing the common practice of the school when he remarks that the critic "does not need to establish a solid historical tradition all the way from prehistoric fertility rites to the nature myth in the *Winter's Tale*, or take sides in the quarrel of Classical scholars over the ritual origin of Greek drama: he is concerned only with the ritual and mythical patterns which are actually in the plays, however they got

137

there."[203] This seems to me, moreover, to be a thoroughly sound position; for it does not commit us to arguing the presence of a nature myth in *The Winter's Tale* or a ritualistic form and meaning in *Oedipus* on the literal ground that they are there because these works are products of a tradition that began in ritual and myth. That would indeed be an instance of the grossest of fallacies in history and criticism, the supposition that the form or import of any developed thing can be inferred from its matter or evolutionary substrate—that since the adult man was once an embryo, his distinctive nature as an adult can be sufficiently explained in terms of the science of embryology.[204]

But what, then, are we saying when we assert, for instance, that the death of Heyst "is a form of purification and expiation ritual"? I think the answer is now evident: we are saying simply that when we apply to this incident in Conrad's novel the set of terms which Sir James Frazer or another has used to define the structure and meaning of the ritual in question, a striking resemblance between the two patterns emerges, especially if we are careful to attend to only the most general outline of the incident as Conrad presents it. We are stating, in short, not a relationship of effect to cause, but of like to like—that is, of analogy merely; our proposition is a kind of proportional metaphor in which, because of the parity of relations we perceive between the parts of the incident in *Victory* and the parts of the ritual, we transfer to the incident the words, and their connotations, which anthropologists have employed to state the significance of the ritual, thus conferring at once upon Heyst's act the quality of something religious and ancient, something more profound and human than any modern novelist, however great, could be expected to invent. That is all we shall really be saying, I am convinced, in any instance of "archetypal" interpretation, so that in a very genuine sense, in this approach, not only literature but criticism itself can be said to be "ultimately metaphorical and symbolic." And there are great advantages in so conceiving it; for we shall then not need to worry either about the conflicting interpretations which different critics of this school have placed upon the same works—inasmuch as an indefinite number of significant analogies is always possible for the same thing—or about the problem of inventing arguments to support our particular findings. The patterns we are concerned with are actually *in* the poems (on the assumptions of our method) if they can be seen there; and they will be seen, and thought important indices of latent meanings, by all such readers, at least, as have been conditioned by temperament or the contagion of current literary thought to look upon poetry as necessarily an imitation or reflection, in its greatest moments, of those deeper human realities that have been disclosed to us most clearly, after long neglect, by the psychologists and cultural anthropologists of the early twentieth century.

These, then, are the principal ways in which the structure of poetic works has been defined and investigated by those critics of our time for whom the question of the structure of poetry has been the central problem of criticism. Whatever we may think of the results we are able to achieve in practical criticism by using the methods of these critics, the results are inevitably conditioned by, and hence are relative to, the basic conceptual language that has been developed in recent years out of the very old tradition of criticism in which poetry is thought of as a mode of discourse and in which theories of poetry, of a necessarily "abstract" sort, have been derived by a dialectic of negative and positive analogies from a consideration of the nature of discourse in its non-poetic varieties. It is less important, therefore, for our purposes, to dwell on the individual successes and failures of these contemporaries than to raise the question of the general adequacy of the critical language they have employed for the study of poetic structures in comparison with the one major alternative to this language which the history of criticism has so far given us but which has as yet been little used in the analysis and criticism of particular works. And to that I shall turn in the concluding lecture.

Toward a more adequate criticism of poetic structure

WE CAN JUDGE of the adequacy of any procedure in practical criticism only by considering the concepts and the methods of reasoning which it presupposes and asking ourselves what important aspects, if any, of the objects we are examining they force us to leave out of account. And when this test is applied not merely to the two contemporary schools of criticism discussed in the last lecture but to the long tradition of critical language from which they have emerged, it becomes apparent, I think, that there are nowhere present in this tradition any means for dealing precisely and particularly with what I shall call the forming principle or immediate shaping cause of structure in individual poems.

The principle I speak of is one that operates in much the same way in all the arts; and there is nothing mysterious about it—nothing which any one who has ever written anything, however unpoetic, cannot verify for himself by reflecting a little upon his own experience. The process of literary composition has often been rather crudely divided, especially by authors of textbooks on English writing, into two stages: a stage of preparatory reading, thinking, planning, incubation, and a stage of putting the materials thus assembled into words; and what happens in the second stage has usually been represented as a direct transference to paper of the ideas or imaginations which the writer has come into possession of in the first stage—as a simple matter, that is, of giving to an acquired content an appropriate verbal form. I have myself taught this easy doctrine to students; but never, I believe, since I began to meditate on the disturbing fact that all too frequently, when I have attempted to write an essay after a long and interested concentration on the subject, and the noting of many exciting ideas and patterns of key terms, and the construction of what looked like a perfect outline, I have found myself unable to compose the first sentence, or even to know what it ought to be about, or, having forced myself to go on, to bring the thing to a satisfying conclusion, whereas, on other occasions, with no more complete preparation, no greater desire to write, and no better state of nerves, I have discovered, to my delight, that nearly everything fell speedily into place, the right words came (or at any rate words which I couldn't change later on), and the sentences and paragraphs followed one another with scarcely a hitch and in an order that still seemed to me the inevitable one when I came to reread the essay in cold blood.

I have had so many more experiences of the first sort than of the second that I have tried to isolate the reason for the difference. And the best way I can explain it is to say that what I failed to attain in the former cases and did attain somehow, at one moment or another of the total process, in the latter was a kind of intuitive glimpse of a possible subsuming form for the materials, or at least those I attached most importance to, which I had assembled in my mind and notes—a form sufficiently coherent and intelligible, as a form in my mind, so that I could know at once what I must or could do, and what I need not or ought not to do, in what order and with what emphasis in the various parts, in developing my arguments and putting them into words. I have never been able to write anything which seemed to me, in retrospect, to possess any quality of organic wholeness, however uninteresting or thin, except in response to such a synthesizing idea. It is more than a general intention, more than a "theme," and more than an outline in the usual sense of that word; it is, as I have said, a shaping or directing cause, involving at the same time, and in some sort of correlation, the particular conceptual form my subject is to take in my essay, the particular mode of argument or of rhetoric I am to use in discussing it, and the particular end my discussion is to serve: I must know, in some fashion, at least these three things before I can proceed with any ease or success. As a conception my idea may be tight or loose, complex or simple; I call it a shaping cause for the very good reason that, once such a principle has come to me for a particular essay, it generates consequences and problems in the detailed working out of my subject which I cannot well escape so long as I remain committed to writing the essay as I see it ought to be written. It exerts, that is, a kind of impersonal and objective power, which is at once compulsive and suggestive, over everything I attempt to do, until in the end I come out with a composition which, if my execution has been adequate, is quite distinct, as an ordered whole, from anything I myself completely intended or foresaw when I began to write, so that afterwards I sometimes wonder, even when I applaud, how I could ever have come to say what I have said.

I do not believe that this experience of mine is unique among writers of prose, and I have been told by friends who are novelists, playwrights, or lyric poets that something like this is a true description of what happens also to them whenever they are successfully creative. The point indeed has often been hinted at by artists in the too infrequent moments when they talk in practical terms, undistorted by *a priori* critical doctrines, about their own or others' work. Most of the published criticism of T. S. Eliot has been more concerned with the qualities of poets than with the construction of poems; but what I have been saying about the all-importance and compulsive power of formal causes in writing is at least adumbrated in his famous "Impersonal theory of poetry" and more than adumbrated in his remark, in an early essay, that "No artist produces great art by a deliberate attempt to express his personality. He expresses his personality indirectly through concentrating upon a task which is a task in the same sense as the making of an efficient engine or the turning of a jug or a table-leg."[205] There is interesting testimony to the same effect, too, in some observations by Mr. Joyce Cary on the writing of novels. "Every professional artist," he says, "has met the questioner who asks of some detail: 'Why did you do it so

142

clumsily like that, when you could have done it so neatly like this?' And smiles, as on a poor dreamer without logic or understanding, when he gets the answer: 'It might have been better your way, but I couldn't do it because it wouldn't have belonged.'" This is well understood, he adds, by critics like Horace and Boileau, who, being also artists, had "learned in practice that there are rules of construction, mysterious relations in technique, which exist apparently in the nature of the art itself"—or, as I should say, in the nature of the particular work of art in hand— "and which oblige the artist to respect them," though these are by no means the same as the abstract notions of literary kinds which most critics insist upon when they discuss, for instance, the novel.[206]

Here then—in the artist's intuition of a form capable of directing whatever he does with his materials in a particular work—is an essential cause of poetic structure, the most decisive, indeed, of all the causes of structure in poetry because it controls in an immediate way the act of construction itself. Without it, no poetic whole; with it, a poetic whole of a certain kind and emotional quality, which will be excellent in proportion to the intrinsic possibilities of the form the poet has conceived and to his success in doing with his materials in his medium all that it requires or permits him to do if its full possibilities, as a form of a certain kind, are to be realized.

If form, however, in this constructive sense of the word, is thus an indispensable first principle for writers, it would seem that it might also be taken, with fruitful results, as a first principle in the practical criticism of their works. I do not find, unfortunately, although I have looked widely in the applied criticism of the past and present, that this has ever been knowingly and systematically done by any of the critics, in the tradition I have been speaking of in the last two lectures, who have thought the problem of structure in poetry to be an important concern. And there are at least two major reasons why this has been the case.

In the first place, as should be clear from my example, the shaping cause of any given literary work—the principle which determines for its writer the necessities and opportunities he must consider in composing it—is something over and above and, as a

143

principle, causally distinct from any of the potentialities he or anyone else can attribute in advance to either the materials he has assembled in his mind or the technical devices at his disposal. He can know what he can do, in fact, only after he has done it; and the doing is an act of synthesis which, if it is successful, inevitably imposes a new character on the materials and devices out of which it is effected. If we are to talk, therefore, about formal principles in poetry and be able to trace their consequences in the structures of particular poems, we must have terms in our criticism for more than the materials of subject-matter and language which poets use and the technical procedures possible in their art. Yet it is almost wholly on the basis of assumptions limited to these non-formal aspects of poetry that the critics in the tradition we have been discussing have undertaken to deal with problems of structure in poems. Some of them, as a consequence, have confined their attention entirely or mainly to questions of technique in the sense either of devices of prosody or diction (the rest of poetry being thought of as a matter of inspiration, invention, or subject-matter) or of representational devices in the drama and the novel (the problem of what is represented or why being thought of either as the business of particular writers or as not amenable to art): a good example of both the virtues and limitations of this latter approach is Percy Lubbock's *The Craft of Fiction*, in which the problem of structure or "form" in the novel is reduced to the problem of the different possible ways—some of them assumed to be intrinsically better than others—in which stories may be shaped in the telling.

For the many other critics in the modern tradition whose preoccupations have been not so much technical as aesthetic, the approach to poetic structure has been by way of a dialectic in which, as we have seen,[207] the "inseparable properties" of poetic thought and poetic expression have been derived by negative and positive analogies from the known or assumed characteristics of other modes of discourse, with the result that these critics have been able to distinguish only such attributes of form in poetry as can be discovered by asking how the elements of any discourse can be or have been related to one another in a com-

144

position. They have given us in this way many approximations to poetic form, which fail nevertheless, since they necessarily consist merely in possible or observed configurations of the poetic matter, to constitute in any complete sense shaping principles of structure. Some of the approximations have been very general indeed; as when structure, or the best structure, in poetry is identified with abstract relations of symmetry or balance (or their artful avoidance), of repetition with variation, or of oppositions reconciled, and the structural analysis of particular poems is directed to the subsumption of their details of content and diction under one or another of these schemes; or as when some figure of speech, such as metaphor, synecdoche, or irony, is fixed upon as the basic model of poetic structure and the analysis of poems determined accordingly. The approximations, however, can easily be more specific than these. A good many poetic patterns, thus, have been derived by deduction from the known possibilities of grammatical or rhetorical arrangement in discourse of whatever kind; such is Mr. Yvor Winters' resolution of possible modes of organization in poetry into seven major types: the method of repetition, the logical method, the narrative method, pseudo-reference, qualitative progression, alternation of method, and double mood;[208] the significant thing about these and other similar classifications[209] is their equal applicability to writings which the critics who make them would undoubtedly hold to be non-poetic. And other relatively particularized formulae have been arrived at by finding correspondences between the arrangement of parts in poems and the arrangement of parts in paintings or musical compositions; by analogizing poetic organization to the simpler and more evident structures of rituals or myths; and very often, especially among the historical critics, by imputing to poems, as structural principles, whatever conventions of design can be attributed to the earlier works which served their writers as models. Whether general or particular, however, what these expedients give us are merely signs or manifestations or qualities of order in poems rather than the causes from which, in individual poems, the order springs; they call attention to "patterns" in poems of often great intrinsic interest, but they provide no means, since none are available in the critical language

145

these critics are using, for helping us to understand why the "patterns" are there or what their precise function is. For this we require something more than any method can supply that is content to infer conceptions of form solely from the characteristics and possibilities of poetic materials.

In the second place, as my initial example also perhaps suggests, the question of shaping principles in poetry is a question not of deductive theory but of empirical fact; the problem, in any given poem, is what actually was, for its poet, the primary intuition of form which enabled him to synthesize his materials into an ordered whole. Until we have some idea of that we cannot proceed to inquire into its consequences in the poet's invention and rendering of details; and this means that the first principle of our analysis must be an induction of which the only warrant is the evidence of the poem itself. We may be assisted in making this by our knowledge of other poems, and we need general concepts, moreover, to guide us, since it is only through concepts that we are ever able to understand particular things. But what we are looking for is, first of all, a fact—possibly a fact of a kind that has no complete parallel in the earlier or later history of poetry, inasmuch as it is the mark of good poets that they try to avoid repeating too often the inventions of others. It is fatal therefore to think that we can know the shaping principle of any poem in advance or, what amounts to the same thing in practice, that we can get at it in terms of any predetermined conception or model of what structure in poetry or in this or that special branch of poetry in general either is or ought to be. Yet this is exactly what most of the critics who have concerned themselves with questions of structure in practical criticism have attempted to do. They have come to poems equipped, so to speak, with paradigms of poetry, or of epic, tragedy, lyric, and so on, and hence with more or less definite specifications concerning the nature of the structural patterns they ought to look for; and they have as a consequence been unable to see any structural principles in poems except those already contained in their preferred definitions and models.

Let me give one more example of this paradigm method in operation; I take it from a recent essay on *Othello* by Professor

146

Robert Heilman.[210] Now the question of the structure of *Othello* could surely be approached inductively through a comparison of the material data of action, character, and motive supplied to Shakespeare by Cinthio's *novella* with what happened to these in the completed play. We could then ask what particular shaping principle, among principles possible in serious dramas, we must suppose to have governed Shakespeare's construction of the tragedy if we are to account with a maximum completeness and economy both for the new uses to which he put his borrowed materials and for the differences between the succession of our expectations and desires when we read the *novella* and when we witness or read *Othello*. This is not, however, where Mr. Heilman starts. His problem is not to develop a hypothesis which will adequately explain the structural peculiarities of this play but to read the play in the light of a hypothesis (of the "abstract" sort) already formed in his mind and previously used as the basis of his interpretation of *King Lear*. *Othello* he knows is a "poetic drama" (since it is a dramatic representation in which the verse and diction are obviously important parts); it must therefore have the characteristic structure of "poetic drama," which is to say, according to Mr. Heilman, a structure composed of two elements—"drama" and "poetry"—which operate in "collusion," as two "languages" or "bearers of meaning," to the end of expressing symbolically a "total meaning" relative to a given subject or "theme." The argument of his essay is accordingly a simple application of this paradigm to the facts of the text which it enables him to select as significant data. "The most obvious approach to the structure of drama," he remarks in the beginning, "is to equate structure with plot and then to describe plot in terms of those familiar and yet somewhat elusive elements sometimes called rising action, climax, dénouement, etc." This would give us a number of observations, or guesses, about the stages of the action, the location of the climax, and so on, which might be true enough but which would yield at best, as he says, "only superficial information." Such information, we can agree, might well be superficial for any critic; what makes it seem superficial to Mr. Heilman is of course the hypothesis he is engaged in applying. For if *Othello* is not merely a drama but a "poetic

147

drama," then its structure must be "equated" with something else than plot—namely, the interaction of its "drama" and its "poetry." The subject of the dramatic action, he says, is primarily not jealousy (as many have supposed) but love; the advantage of this view is that it not only names the dominant theme but indicates "the forces which give the play a composition of a certain kind," inasmuch as the "central tension is between the love of Othello and the hate of Iago, the specific forms taken in this play"—and here we meet the familiar reduction terms—"by good and evil." This "dramatic structure," however, is constantly modified in the course of the play by the parallel and (in Mr. Heilman's sense) strictly "poetic" structure constituted, in the speeches, by the many patterns of imagery that turn on symbolic oppositions of black and white, darkness and light, hell and heaven, foul and fair, chaos and order. These, we are told, are not so many static antitheses merely, but form a kind of dialectical action, corresponding to and enriching the dramatic action, through the successive permutations and shifts which the basic pairs of terms, at least in Mr. Heilman's exposition, are made to undergo. Much of this is illuminating and provocative; one would not care to embark upon a discussion of the structure of *Othello* without first taking account of Mr. Heilman's observations. I do not think, however, that he comes very close to defining any principle of structure for *Othello* that could conceivably have guided Shakespeare in constructing the poetic whole which arouses in us such poignant tragic emotions. What he exhibits are rather some of the material antecedents of the tragic structure in the conceptions of love and jealousy which the writing of the play presupposed and some of the consequences of the structure in the imagery and thought by which it is made effective in the words; and his only warrant for "equating" the combination of these aspects with the structure of the play is his prior assumption, which controls his examination of the text, that the structure of *Othello* must be of this sort.

These, then, are the main reasons why the dominant languages of modern criticism, for all the many insights into poetry which those who use them have attained, are inadequate means for dealing with the causes and aspects of structure in particular

148

poems that have their bases in the productive acts of poets. We need for this purpose, if the question happens to interest or seem important to us, a language in which we can envisage our questions as questions of fact rather than of relations of ideas (such as "drama" and "poetry" or "poetry" and "prose"); in which we can talk about the internal necessities and possibilities in poems and the problems these posed for their poets rather than merely about the necessities and problems defined for us by our special choice of dialectical premises; in which we can develop terms for distinguishing the formal causes of poems from their material constituents and technical mechanisms; and in which, finally, we can achieve a precision of differentiation in speaking of the structures of different poems which is not glaringly incommensurate with the formal inventiveness of poets. The only near approach to such a critical language, however, is that made long ago by Aristotle; it would be foolish not to avail ourselves of his contribution, in its methodological aspects, so far as possible; and we have therefore to consider to what extent we can still profit, in practical criticism, by attempting to adapt to our current needs the principles and analytical devices which he was the first and almost the last to use.

II

It is not a question of regarding the *Poetics*, in Mr. Blackmur's phrase, as a "sacred book"[211] and certainly not of looking upon ourselves, in any exclusive sense, as forming an "Aristotelian" or "Neo-Aristotelian" school. It would be a desirable thing, indeed, if we could do away with "schools" in criticism as they have been done away with in most of the disciplines in which learning as distinguished from doctrine has been advanced. But our loyalty at any rate should be to problems rather than to ancient masters; and if it happens that we have problems for which Aristotle can give us the means, or some of the means, of solution, we should be prepared to benefit from his initiative in precisely the same way as many of our contemporaries have benefited from the more recent initiatives of Coleridge, Richards, Frazer, and Freud without necessarily becoming disciples of any of these men. And

149

it is not difficult to see what there is in Aristotle, or what we can develop out of him, that is immediately pertinent to the problem of poetic structure in the particular form in which I have defined it at the beginning of this lecture.

I should put first in the list the conception of poetic works as "concrete wholes."[212] Now anything is a concrete whole, as I have said before, the unity of which can be adequately stated only by saying that it "is such and such a form embodied in this or that matter, or such and such a matter with this or that form; so that its shape and structure must be included in our description" as well as that out of which it is constituted or made. And of the two natures which must join in any such whole, or in our account of it, "the formal nature is of greater importance than the material nature" inasmuch as the "form" of any individual object, such as a man or a couch, is the principle or cause "by reason of which the matter is some definite thing."[213] In spite of the now somewhat unfamiliar language in which the conception is stated in Aristotle, the underlying insight is one that we can easily translate into the terms of common experience. I take, for instance, a piece of modelling clay. There are many things which I cannot do with it—of which, as Aristotle would say, it cannot be the matter; but on the other hand the potentialities it does hold out, within these limits, are indefinite in number: I can make of it, if I wish, a geographical globe, with all its continents indicated, or the model of a house, or the bust of a sinister-looking man, and so on through a vast range of similar possibilities that is bounded only by my invention and skill. In any of these realizations the thing I make remains a thing of clay, having all the permanent characteristics of such a thing; but it remains this only in a partial sense; in itself, as a particular object to which we may respond practically or aesthetically, it is at the same time something else—a globe, a house, a sinister-looking man; and any description we may give of it, though it must obviously specify its clayness—that is, its material nature—would be of no use to anybody unless it also specified the definite kind of thing into which the clay has been shaped—that is, its formal nature. And the latter is clearly more important than the former since it is what accounts, in any particular case, for the clay being

150

handled thus and not otherwise and for our response being of such and such a quality rather than any other.

It is not difficult to see how the conception fits the work of the poet or of any other writer. Here is a speech in a famous novel:

"Ah, my poor dear child, the truth is, that in London it is always a sickly season. Nobody is healthy in London—nobody can be. It is a dreadful thing to have you forced to live there; so far off! and the air so bad!"²¹⁴

Taken in isolation, this may be described simply as an expression of regret that the person addressed has to live in London, based on the commonplace thought that the air of London, as compared with the air of the country, is far from healthy. The speech, we may say, is made out of this matter; but it is a matter, obviously, that permits of a variety of particular uses: it might be a speech in an idyll, or in a satire, or in a moral epistle in the manner of Cowper; and in each case its formal nature and hence our response would be different. It is actually, of course, a speech by Mr. Woodhouse in *Emma*; and when it is so read, in its position in the dialogue of Chapter 12 and in the light of what we have already seen of Emma's father, it assumes the nature of a characteristic comic act, wherein the most important thing is not the commonplace thought itself, but the excessive and inappropriate emotion, at the prospect of Isabella's coming departure for home, which this is made to express, and which is the formal principle shaping the matter of the speech into a definite, though not self-contained, artistic unit capable of directing our thoughts in a particular way.

Or here again is a whole poem, the material nature of which is comprised of the following sequence of happenings:

A young Italian duke, influenced by his idle companions, dismisses the wise counsellor his father had recommended to him, refuses the advice of his fiancée, and devotes himself to a life of private pleasure and neglect of public duty. A Turkish corsair takes advantage of this situation to storm the Duke's castle and to reduce him and all his court to slavery; and the Duke falls into despair when he learns that his fiancée is destined for the conqueror's harem. She, however, deceives the corsair into giving her a delay of three days and a chance to speak to her lover. She uses this time to rouse the Duke to repentance for

151

his past errors and to work out with him a plan whereby he and his father's counsellor will attempt a rescue before the three days are up. The plan succeeds; the Duke and his friends overcome the corsair's troops and make him prisoner. The Duke's false companions then demand that the Turk be executed; but the Duke, grateful for the lesson his captivity has taught him, responds by banishing them and allowing the corsair to depart unharmed; whereupon he marries his fiancée and resolves to rule more wisely in the future.

As an action this is clearly not without some form, being a coherent and complete chain of possible events, to which we are likely to respond by taking sides with the Duke and the girl against their captors. I am sure, however, that anyone who reads *The Duke of Benevento* for the first time after hearing my summary will think that I have given a very indefinite account of what happens in Sir John Henry Moore's poem and hence misled him completely as to the poem's distinctive nature and effect. He will probably be prepared to read a vaguely tragicomic romance or drama of a kind common enough in the 1770's; what he will actually find is a short piece of 204 lines beginning as follows:

> I hate the prologue to a story
> Worse than the tuning of a fiddle,
>   Squeaking and dinning;
> Hang order and connection,
> I love to dash into the middle;
>   Exclusive of the fame and glory,
> There is a comfort on reflection
>   To think you've done with the beginning.
>
> And so at supper one fine night,
>   Hearing a cry of Alla, Alla,
> The Prince was damnably confounded,
>   And in a fright,
> But more so when he saw himself surrounded
> By fifty Turks; and at their head the fierce Abdalla,
>
> And then he look'd a little grave
> To find himself become a slave, ...

And so on consistently to the end, in a rapidly narrated episode of which the formal nature is the kind of anti-romantic comedy clearly foreshadowed in these lines—a form that is only potentially in the story of the poem (since this could yield several other forms) and is created out of it, partly indeed by Moore's pre-Byronic language and manner of narration, but also, as a reading of the whole poem will show, by the notably unheroic qualities of character and thought which he gives to his hero and heroine, with the result that we are unable to take their predicament any more tragically than they themselves do.

It can be seen from these illustrations how different is such a conception of the internal relations of form and matter in a "concrete whole" from the later and much commoner analytic in which form or art is set over against content or subject-matter in one or another of the many ways we have already illustrated.[215] A poem, on the view of its structure suggested by Aristotle, is not a composite of *res* and *verba* but a certain matter formed in a certain way or a certain form imposed upon or wrought out of a certain matter. The two are inseparable aspects of the same individual thing, though they are clearly distinct analytically as principles or causes, and though, of the two, the formal nature is necessarily the more important as long as our concern is with the poem as a concrete object. On the one hand, we do not cease to talk about the matter of a poem when we examine its formal structure, and, on the other hand, there is a sense in which nothing in a completed poem, or any distinguishable part thereof, is matter or content merely, in relation to which something else is form. In a well-made poem, everything is formed, and hence rendered poetic (whatever it may have been in itself), by virtue simply of being made to do something definite in the poem or to produce a definitely definable effect, however local, which the same materials of language, thought, character-traits, or actions would be incapable of in abstraction from the poem, or the context in the poem, in which they appear. We are not speaking poetically but only materially of anything in a poem, therefore, when we abstract it from its function or effect in the poem; we speak poetically, or formally, only when we add to a description of the thing in terms of its constituent elements (for example, the content of a metaphor or the events of a plót) an indication of the definite quality it possesses or of that in the poem for the sake of which it is there. In an absolute sense, then, nothing in a successful poem is non-formal or non-poetic; but it is also true that structure of any kind necessarily implies a subordination of some parts to others; and in this relative sense we may intelligibly say of one formed element of a poem that it is material to something else in the same poem, the existence and specific effectiveness of which it makes possible. We may thus speak of the words of a poem as the material basis of the thought they express, although the words also have form as being ordered in sentences and rhythms; and similarly we may speak of thought as the matter of character, of character and thought in words as the matter of action or emotion, and so on up to but not including the over-all form which synthesizes all these subordinate elements, formally effective in themselves, into a continuous poetic whole. Or we can reverse the order of consideration, and ask what matter of action, character, and thought a poem requires if its plot or lyric structure is to be formally of a certain kind, or what kind of character a speech ought to suggest if it is to serve adequately its function in a scene, or what selection and arrangement of words will render best or most economically a given state of mind.

Here then is an intelligible, universally applicable, and ana-lytically powerful conception of the basic structural relations in poems which we can take over from Aristotle without committing ourselves to the total philosophy in which it was evolved. We can also take over, in the second place, the method of investigation and reasoning which he found appropriate to structures of this kind.[216] The conception and the method, indeed, can hardly be divorced. For if we are to consider poetic works, in practical criticism, from the point of view of their concrete wholeness, then our central problem is to make their elements and subordinate structures causally intelligible in the light of their respective organizing forms. This can be done, however, only by means of general concepts embodying answers to two major questions relative to such kinds of poetry as we may be interested in: first, what different forms can go with what different matters, and, second, what parts, and what constructions of each of them, are necessary to the achievement of any given form. But these, it is obvious, are questions of fact, the answers to which can never be given by any "abstract" method but must depend upon in-

154

quiries of an *a posteriori* type which move inductively (in Aristotle's sense of induction) from particulars to the universals they embody and from ends or forms thus defined, by hypothetical necessity to the essential conditions of their realization in poetic matter. The method, of course, is not Aristotelian in any unique sense, but no one has shown as fully as he did how it may be applied to poetics or how completely it depends, in this application, upon an adequate knowledge of literary history.

The method is factual, but it is not indifferent to values; and the third thing we can learn from Aristotle is a manner of considering questions of better and worse in poetry which is likewise appropriate to the conception of poems as concrete wholes organized by formal principles.[217] As things made by and for men, poems, as I have said before, can have a great variety of uses and be judged not improperly in terms of many different criteria, moral, political, intellectual, grammatical, rhetorical, historical. To judge them as poems, however, is to judge them in their distinctive aspect as wholes of certain kinds, in the light of the assumption that the poet's end—the end which makes him a poet—is simply the perfecting of the poem as a beautiful or intrinsically excellent thing. I do not mean by this that poems are ever perfected in an absolute sense. We need not quarrel with R. G. Collingwood when he remarks, in his *Autobiography*, that as a boy living in a household of artists he "learned to think of a picture not as a finished product exposed for the admiration of virtuosi, but as the visible record, lying about the house, of an attempt to solve a definite problem in painting, so far as the attempt has gone." "I learned," he adds, "what some critics and aestheticians never know to the end of their lives, that no 'work of art' is ever finished, so that in that sense of the phrase there is no such thing as a 'work of art' at all. Work ceases upon the picture or manuscript, not because it is finished, but because sending-in day is at hand, or because the printer is clamorous for copy, or because 'I am sick of working at this thing' or 'I can't see what more I can do to it.' "[218] This is sound sense, which critics and aestheticians ought to learn if they do not know it; but it is clearly not incompatible with the assumption that what a poet seeks to do, as a poet, is to make as good a work poetically

155

speaking as he can; and this goodness, we can surely agree with Aristotle, must always consist in a mean between doing too much and not doing enough in his invention and handling of all its parts. The criterion, again, is not an absolute one; the mean in art, as in morals, is a relative mean, which has to be determined in adjustment to the particular necessities and possibilities of the form the artist is trying to achieve. And just as the poet can know these only by trial and error plus reflection upon the general conditions of his art and on what other poets have been able to do, so the critic can know them, and the ends to which they are relative, only by similar *ex post facto* means. He must therefore leave to other critics with less strictly "poetic" pre-occupations the task of formulating criteria for poetry on the basis of general "abstract" principles; his business is to take the point of view of the poet and his problems and to judge what he has done, as sympathetically as possible, in terms of what must and what might be done *given* the distinctive form, new or old, which the poet is trying to work out of his materials.[219] And here, once more, the procedure of Aristotle can be of use.

We can still profit, moreover, not merely from these general features of his approach—all of them relevant also to other than critical problems—but likewise from many of the more particular applications of his method in the *Poetics*, including, first of all, the fundamental distinction, on which the whole treatise is based, between poetry which is "imitation" and poetry which is not.[220] The former, for Aristotle, is poetry in the most distinctive sense, since its principles are not the principles of any other art; but to insist on this is not to question the possibility of discussing as "poetry" other kinds of works of which the materials and devices, though not the forms, are those of poems in the stricter meaning of the word; the difference is not one of relative dignity or value but purely of constructive principle, and hence of the kinds of hypotheses and terms that are required, respectively, for the analysis and judgment of works belonging to each. The distinction, as Aristotle understood it, has played no important part in the subsequent history of criticism. A class of "didactic" poems has, it is true, been more or less constantly recognized, but the differentiation between these and other poems has most often been made in terms of purpose, content, and technique rather than of matter and form, a "didactic" poem being distinguished sometimes as one in which the end of instruction is more prominent than that of delight, sometimes as one that uses or springs from or appeals to the reason rather than the imagination, sometimes as one that relies mainly on precepts instead of fictions and images or that uses direct rather than indirect means of expression. This breakdown of the original distinction was natural enough in the periods of criticism in which the ends of poetry were defined broadly as instruction and pleasure, and it is still natural in a period, such as our own, when the great preoccupation is with "meaning" and with poetry as a special kind of language for expressing special modes of signification. In both periods, although some classes of poems have been set apart as "didactic" in a peculiar and frequently pejorative sense, all poetry, or all poetry except that which can be described as "entertainment" merely, has tended to assume an essentially didactic character and function. The prevalence nowadays of "thematic analysis" as a method of discussion applicable to all poetic works that can be taken seriously at all is a clear sign of this, as is also the currency of "archetypal" analogies. The result, however, has been to banish from criticism, or to confuse beyond clear recognition, a distinction which has as much validity now as when it was first made and which has not been supplanted by any of the later distinctions, since these all rest on quite different bases of principle. The distinction is simply between works, on the one hand, in which the formal nature is constituted of some particular human activity or state of feeling qualified morally and emotionally in a certain way, the beautiful rendering of this in words being the sufficient end of the poet's effort, and works, on the other hand (like the *Divine Comedy, Absalom and Achitophel, Don Juan, 1984,* etc.), in which the material nature is "poetic" in the sense that it is made up of parts similar to those of imitative poems and the formal nature is constituted of some particular thesis, intellectual or practical, relative to some general human interest, the artful elaboration and enforcement of this by whatever means are available and appropriate being the sufficient end of the poet's effort. Great and serious works can be and have

157

been written on either of these basic principles of construction, but the principles themselves, it must be evident, are sharply distinct, and the difference is bound to be reflected, in innumerable subtle as well as obvious ways, in everything that poets have to do or can do in the two major kinds. To continue to neglect the distinction, therefore, is merely to deprive ourselves unnecessarily of an analytical device—however hard to apply in particular cases—which can only serve, when intelligently used, to introduce greater exactness into our critical descriptions and greater fairness into our critical judgments.

Of the many other distinctions and concepts in the *Poetics* which are still valid and useful—at least for the kind of discussion of poetic structure we now have in mind—nearly all are limited, in their strict applicability, to imitative works. For any inquiry into such forms we cannot neglect, to begin with, the all-important distinctions of object, means, manner, and *dynamis* upon which the definition of tragedy in Chapter 6 is based. They are, as I have tried to show in the second lecture, the essential and basic determinants of the structure of any species of imitative works when these are viewed as concrete wholes,[221] for we can conceive adequately of such a whole only when we consider as precisely as possible what kind of human experience is being imitated, by the use of what possibilities of the poetic medium, through what mode of representation, and for the sake of evoking and resolving what particular sequence of expectations and emotions relative to the successive parts of the imitated object. It is always some definite combination of these four things that defines, for the imitative writer, the necessities and possibilities of any work he may have in hand; for what he must and can do at any point will differ widely according as he is imitating a character, a state of passion, or an action, and if an action (with character, thought, and passion inevitably involved), whether one of which the central figures are men and women morally better than we are, or like ourselves, or in some sense worse; and according as he is doing this in verse of a certain kind or in prose or in some joining of the two; and according as he is doing it in a narrative or a dramatic or a mixed manner; and according, finally, as he is shaping his incidents and characters and their

158

thoughts and feelings, his language, and his technique of representation (whatever it may be) so as to give us, let us say, the peculiar kind of comic pleasure we get from *Tom Jones* or that we get from *The Alchemist* or, to add still another possible nuance of comic effect, from *Volpone*. These, then, are indispensable distinctions for the critic who wishes to grasp the principles of construction and the consequences thereof in any imitative work; and he will be sacrificing some of the precision of analysis possible to him if he fails to take them all into consideration as independent variables—if he talks, for instance, about the plot of a novel or the pattern of images in a lyric poem without specifying the emotional "working or power" which is its controlling form,[222] or if, in dealing with any kind of imitative work, he neglects to distinguish clearly between the "things" being imitated, upon which the *dynamis* primarily depends, and the expedients of representational manner by which the writer has sought to clarify or maximize their peculiar effect.[223]

There remains, lastly, the detailed analytic of imitative forms which is represented in the *Poetics* by the chapters on tragedy and epic. I need not repeat what I have said in the second lecture about Aristotle's distinctive conceptions—which have largely vanished from later criticism—of plot, character, thought, and diction—or about the relationships of causal subordination in which these "parts" are made to stand to one another in the tragic and epic structures, so that the last three (together with music and spectacle in tragedy), while being capable of form themselves, have the status of necessary material conditions of the plot, which, in the most specific sense of the synthesis of things done and said in a work as determined to a certain "working or power," is the principal part or controlling form of the whole.[224] I have said why this analysis seems to me sound, given the assumptions on which it is based and its limited applicability to works of which the subjects are actions of the more or less extended sort Aristotle here had in mind. We can therefore still use it, and the many constituent definitions and distinctions it involves, in the criticism of the larger poetic forms; and we can profit particularly, I think, from the discussion of tragic plot-form in Chapter 13, not only because it gives us a clue to the

159

structure of many later "tragic" works (this plot-form is clearly the formula, for example, of *Othello*, though not quite of *Macbeth*, and certainly not of *Richard III*) but also, and chiefly, because it suggests the four general questions we have to ask ourselves about any work having a plot as its principle of construction if we are to see clearly what problems its writer faced in composing it: as to precisely what the change is, from what it starts and to what it moves; in what kind of man it takes place; by reason of what causes in the man's thoughts and actions or outside him; and with what succession of emotional effects in the representation.

III

We should be merely "Aristotelians," however, rather than independent scholars were we to remain content with what we can thus extract from Aristotle for present-day critical use; and we should be able to deal only crudely and inadequately with a great many of the most interesting structural problems raised by modern works. We need therefore to push the Aristotelian type of theoretical analysis far beyond the point where Aristotle himself left off, and this in several different directions.

There are, to begin with, the many non-imitative species of poetry or imaginative literature with which the *Poetics* does not deal at all. A large number of these have been roughly distinguished in the nomenclature and theories of subsequent criticism under such heads as: philosophical poems, moral essays, epigrams, treatises in verse, occasional poems; Horatian satires, Juvenalian satires, Varronian or Menippean satires; allegories, apologues, fables, parables, exempla, thesis or propaganda dramas and novels. But though a vast deal of critical and historical discussion has been devoted to these forms, we have as yet only fragments and beginnings of a usable inductive analytic of their structural principles as distinguished from their material conventions.[225]

Again, there are all the shorter imitative forms, most of them later in origin or artistic development than Aristotle, which we commonly group together as lyric poems; much of the best criti-

160

cism of these has been concerned either with their techniques and fixed conventional patterns or with a dialectical search for the qualities of subject-matter and expression which are thought to differentiate lyric poetry, as a homogeneous type, from other poetic kinds.[226] What we need to have, therefore, is a comprehensive study, free from "abstract" assumptions, of the existing species of such poems in terms both of the different "proper pleasures" achievable in them and of the widely variant material structures in which the pleasures may inhere. Lyrics, it is plain, do not have plots, but any successful lyric obviously has something analogous to a plot in the sense of a specific form which synthesizes into a definite emotional whole what is said or done in the poem and conditions the necessities and probabilities which the poet must embody somehow in his lines; and the nature of this formal principle—whether it is, for example, a man in an evolving state of passion interpreted for him by his thought (as in the "Ode to a Nightingale") or a man adjusting himself voluntarily to an emotionally significant discovery about his life (as in the "Ode on Intimations of Immortality")—has to be grasped with some precision if we are to be able to speak appropriately and adequately about the poem's construction in all its parts and the degree of its artistic success. And here too most of the necessary analytical work still remains to be done.[227]

We are much better off, thanks to Aristotle, with respect to the full-length imitative forms of narrative and drama; but even in this field of theory there are many important outstanding questions. Except for one suggestive paragraph in Chapter 5 on the general nature of the ridiculous, the *Poetics* as we have it is silent on comedy; and although there is much to be learned from the innumerable later discussions, especially since the eighteenth century, the insights these make available still have to be translated out of the rhetorical and psychological languages in which they are, for the most part, embodied into the more consistently "poetic" language we are committed to using. That there are a good many distinguishable comic plot-forms, both in drama and in narrative, must be evident to every one; but as to what they are, and what different artistic necessities and possibilities each of them involves, we have as yet, I think, only rather vague

161

general notions; and the problem has not been greatly advanced by the traditional classifications into comedy of intrigue, comedy of manners, comedy of character, and so on.[228] The same thing is true of the many intermediate forms between comedy in the stricter sense and tragedy proper: of tragicomedy, for example, or the "serious" and "tender" comedy which emerged in the eighteenth century, or the kind of domestic novel which Jane Austen wrote in *Pride and Prejudice, Mansfield Park*, and *Persuasion*, or the adventure romance in its earlier as well as its contemporary forms, or even the detective novel, much as has been written about the "poetics" of that. Nor is tragedy itself in much better case. What the *Poetics* gives us is an analytic of only one among the many plot-forms which the critical opinion as well as the common sense of later times has thought proper to call "tragic"; and it is one of the unfortunate results of the respect which Aristotle has always commanded that critics have tended to blur the distinctive principles of construction and effect, or to impair the artistic integrity, of these "non-Aristotelian" tragic forms in their eagerness to bring them in some fashion under his definition. We need therefore a fresh attempt at analysis, by the same method but in more appropriate terms, for such plot-forms, among others, as are represented severally by *Richard III* and *The Duchess of Malfi*,[229] by *The Orphan*, by *The Brothers Karamazov*, and by *A Passage to India*.

It is not merely of the forms of drama and narrative, however, that we require a better theory but also of many of their characteristic structural devices. We still tend to think of plot in its material aspects in the limited terms in which it is treated in the *Poetics* on the basis of the somewhat elementary practice of the Greeks, with the result that when we have to deal with works that combine in various ways two or many lines of action or concern themselves primarily not with external actions but with changes in thought and feeling or with the slow development or degeneration of moral character or with the fortunes of groups rather than of individuals, we often fall into the confusion which has led many modern critics to reject the concept of plot altogether. This is clearly no solution, but the remedy can be only a more comprehensive and discriminating induction of

162

possible dramatic and narrative structures than Aristotle was able to provide. And there is also the complex question of how plots of whatever kind, or their equivalents in other forms, have to be or can be represented in the words—the question, in short, of imitative manner in a sense that goes beyond, while still depending upon, Aristotle's distinction of the three manners in his third chapter. Of all the topics I have mentioned, this is perhaps the one on which the largest body of precise and useful observation has been accumulated, by all those critics from the Renaissance to our day who have devoted themselves to the "techniques" first of the drama and epic and then of the novel, short-story, and lyric. Even here, however, much remains to be done; and one of the chief requisites, I think, is a clearer posing of the whole problem in such a way as to correlate the many devices of manner which these critics have discriminated, as well as others that have escaped them, with the distinguishable functions which manner has to serve with respect to form. I have touched upon some of these functions in the second lecture,[230] and I will add only the suggestion that there are likely to be, in all richly developed imitative works, incidents, characters, speeches, and images which are not parts of the plot-form but must be viewed by the critic as elements of "thought" in a sense akin to but distinct from that intended by Aristotle in Chapters 6 and 19. We may treat as "thought" of this kind anything permitting of inference in a poetic work, over and above the direct working of the imitated object, that functions as a device, vis-à-vis the audience, for disclosing or hinting at relevant traits of character or situation, awakening or directing expectations, conditioning states of mind, emphasizing essential issues, suggesting in what light something is to be viewed, or, more broadly still, setting the action or some part of it in a larger context of ideas or analogies so that it may come to seem, in its universal implications for human beings, not simply the particular and untypical action it might otherwise be taken to be. Every novelist or dramatist—or lyric poet, for that matter—who reflects on his own work will understand what this means; but the conception has still to become widely recognized among critics, or it surely would have been applied long since to such things as the apparently superfluous episodes and characters and the recurrent general words and patterns of images in Shakespeare—the dialectic of "Nature" in *King Lear*, for instance—concerning which most recent writers have thought it necessary to offer much more profound explanations.[231]

It would be well, finally, if we could carry our method of inductive and causal analysis into some of the larger questions of theory—common to both imitative and non-imitative poetry— to which these writers and other contemporary critics have given special prominence: we could profit greatly, for example, from a re-examination, in our distinctive language, of poetic images, of the elements and functions of diction in poetry, of the various modes and uses of symbols, and of the structural characteristics of myths.[232]

We need not wait, however, for the completion of these possible studies before beginning to use such theory of poetic forms as we now possess in the service of practical criticism. There is after all a close mutual interdependence, in the method we are considering, between theoretical analysis and the investigation of particular works; and as our attempts at application become more numerous and more varied in their objects, so will our grasp of the necessary general distinctions and principles tend to improve.

IV

In these attempts, as should be clear from what I have said, we shall be making a pretty complete break with the tradition of practical criticism discussed in the last two lectures—a tradition in which it has always been necessary, before individual works of poetic art can be analysed or judged, to conceive of poetry as a homogeneous whole and to define its nature in some kind of dialectical relation to other modes of discourse and thought. We shall not need, for our purposes, to commit ourselves to any of the numerous and apparently inconsistent theories of poetry, tragedy, lyric, or the like, based on such a presupposition, which this tradition has developed. We shall not need to worry, as so many contemporaries have done, about how poetry differs from

164

science or prose, or about what its mission is in the modern world. We shall not need to decide in advance of our studies of poems whether poetry in general is best defined as a kind of language or a kind of subject-matter; whether its end is pleasure or some species of knowledge or practical good; whether its proper domain includes all the kinds of imaginative writing or only some of these; whether it is most closely akin to rhetoric and dialectic or to ritual, myth, or dream; or whether it is or is not a separable element in prose fiction and drama. Nor shall we need to assume that all good poems have "themes" or that poetic expression is always indirect, metaphorical, and symbolic. Not merely would such speculative commitments be useless to us, given our empirical starting-point, but they would be fatal, in proportion as we allowed our analyses to be directed by them, to our very effort, since they would inevitably blind us to all those aspects of our problem which our particular doctrine of poetry failed to take into account.

I do not mean that we shall not have to make some assumptions of our own, but only that these need not and ought not to be particularized assumptions about the intrinsic nature and necessary structure of our objects considered as a unitary class of things. We shall have to assume that any poetic work, like any other production of human art, has, or rather is, a definite structure of some kind which is determined immediately by its writer's intuition of a form to be achieved in its materials by the right use of his medium, and, furthermore, that we can arrive at some understanding of what this form actually is and use our understanding as a principle in the analysis and criticism of the work. We shall have to come to some agreement, moreover, as to what we will mean by "poetic works"; but here again the fewer specifications we impose on ourselves in advance the better. It will be sufficient for all our purposes if we begin, simply, by taking as "poems" or "works of literary art" all those kinds of productions which have been commonly called such at different times, but without any supposition that, because these have the same name, they are all "poems" or "works of literary art" in the same fundamental structural sense—that the art necessary to write *The Divine Comedy* or *The Faerie Queene* is the same art, when viewed in terms of its peculiar principles of form, as the art which enabled Shakespeare to write *King Lear* and *Othello*. And for such productions we shall need to assume, in addition, only one common characteristic: that they are all works which, in one degree or another, justify critical consideration primarily for their own sake, as artistic structures, rather than merely for the sake of the knowledge or wisdom they express or the practical utility we may derive from them, though either or both of these other values may be importantly involved in any particular case.

The problem of structure, for any individual work of this kind, is the problem—to give it its most general statement—of how the material nature of the work is related to its formal nature, when we understand by form that principle, or complex of principles, which gives to the subject-matter the power it has to affect our opinions and emotions in a certain definite way such as would not have been possible had the synthesizing principle been of a different kind. The question, as I have said, is primarily one of fact and cause; and it is answered, for a given work, when we have made as intelligible as we can the fashion in which its material elements of whatever kind—words, images, symbols, thoughts, character-traits, incidents, devices of representation— are made to function in relation to a formal whole which we can warrantably assert was the actual final cause of its composition. By "actual final cause" I mean simply a cause without the assumption of which, as somehow effective in the writing, the observable characteristics of the parts, their presence in the poem, their arrangement and proportioning, and their interconnections cannot be adequately understood. In discovering what this shaping principle is in any work we must make use of such evidence as there may be concerning the history of its conception and writing, including any statements the writer may have made about his intentions. Our task, however, is not to explain the writer's activity but the result thereof; our problem is not psychological but artistic; and hence the causes that centrally concern us are the internal causes of which the only sufficient evidence is the work itself as a completed product. What we want to know is not the actual process but the actual rationale of the poem's construction in terms of the poetic problems the writer faced and the reasons which determined his solutions. And in looking for these we shall assume that if the poem holds together as an intelligibly effective whole, in which a certain form is realized in a certain matter which never before had this form, the result can be understood fully only by supposing that such and such problems were involved and were solved by the writer in accordance with reasons which, in part at least, we can state; and this clearly does not commit us to holding that the problems and reasons we uncover in our analysis, as necessarily implied by the completed poem, must have presented themselves to the writer explicitly as such in a continuous movement of self-conscious deliberation; it will be sufficient if we can show that the poem could hardly have been written as it is or have the effect it does on our minds had the writer not done, somehow or at some time, what these particular problems and reasons dictate.

We can never, of course, know such things directly, but only by inference from the consequences of the conceived form, whether of the whole or of any of its parts, in the details of the completed work; and there can be no such inference except by way of hypotheses which both imply and are implied by the observable traits of the work. There are, however, hypotheses and hypotheses, and the character of those we shall have to make is determined by the nature of our problem. We propose to consider poems as unique existent things the structural principles of which are to be discovered, rather than as embodiments of general truths about the structure of poetry already adequately known. Hence our procedure must be the reverse of that procedure by way of preferred paradigms or models of structure which we have seen to be so characteristic of contemporary practical criticism. Our task is not to show the reflection in poems of complex or "ironical" attitudes, interactions of prose and poetry or of logical structure and irrelevant texture, patterns of ritual drama, or basic mythical themes, on the assumption that if the poem is a good poem it will inevitably have whichever of these or other similarly derived general structures we happen to be interested in finding examples of; it is rather the task of making formal sense out of any poetic work before us on the assumption that it may in fact be a work for whose peculiar principles of structure there are nowhere any usable parallels either in literary theory or in our experience of other works. The hypotheses we have to make, therefore, will not be of the fixed and accredited kind which scientists employ only when their problem is not to find out something still unknown but to "demonstrate" a classic experiment to beginners, but rather of the tentative kind—to be modified or rejected altogether at the dictation of the facts—which are the proper means to any serious inductive inquiry. They will be particular working hypotheses for the investigation of the structures of individual poems, not general hypotheses about such things as poetry or "poetic drama" in which the specific nature of the individual structures to be examined is already assumed.

We must also distinguish between critical hypotheses in the strict sense and interpretative hypotheses concerning the details of literary works in their material aspects. It is not one of our presuppositions that "form" in poetry is "meaning"; we should hold, rather, that meaning is something involved in poems as a necessary, but not sufficient, condition of the existence in them of poetic form, and hence that the recovery of meaning is an essential prerequisite to the discovery of form though not in itself such a discovery. Before we can understand a poem as an artistic structure we must understand it as a grammatical structure made up of successive words, sentences, paragraphs, and speeches which give us both meanings in the ordinary sense of that term and signs from which we may infer what the speakers, whether characters or narrators, are like and what they are thinking, feeling, or doing. The great temptation for critics who are not trained and practising scholars is to take this understanding for granted or to think that it may easily be obtained at second hand by consulting the works of scholars. This is an illusion, just as it is an illusion in scholars to suppose that they can see, without training in criticism, all the problems which their distinctive methods are fitted to solve. The ideal would be that all critics should be scholars and all scholars critics; but, although there ought to be the closest correlation of the two functions in practice, they are nevertheless distinct in nature and

168

in the kinds of hypotheses to which they lead. The hypotheses of interpretation are concerned with the meanings and implications in texts that result from their writers' expressive intentions in setting down particular words and constructions and arranging these in particular sequences. Such meanings and implications, indeed, are forms, of which words and sentences are the matter; but they are forms of a kind that can appear in any sort of discourse, however unpoetic. They are to be interpreted by resolving the forms into the elements which poems share with the common speech or writing and the common thought and experience of the times when they were written; and this requires the use of techniques and principles quite different from any that poetic theory can afford: the techniques and principles of historical grammar, of the analysis and history of ideas, of the history of literary conventions, manners, and so on, and the still more general techniques and principles, seldom methodized, by which we construe characters and actions in everyday life.

The hypotheses of criticism, on the contrary, are concerned with the shaping principles, peculiar to the poetic arts, which account in any work for the power of its grammatical materials, in the particular ordering given to these, to move our opinions and feelings in such-and-such a way. They will be of two sorts according as the questions to which they are answers relate to the principles by which poetic works have been constructed as wholes of certain definite kinds or to the reasons which connect a particular part of a given work, directly or indirectly, with such a principle by way of the poetic problems it set for the writer at this point. And there can be no good practical criticism in this mode in which both sorts are not present; for although the primary business of the critic is with the particulars of any work he studies down to its minuter details of diction and rhythm, he can never exhibit the artistic problems involved in these or find other than extra-poetic reasons for their solutions without the guidance of an explicit definition of the formal whole which they have made possible.

A single work will suffice to illustrate both kinds of critical hypotheses as well as the relation between them, and I will begin by considering what idea of the governing form of *Macbeth*

169

appears to accord best with the facts of that play and the sequence of emotions it arouses in us. I need not say again why it seems to me futile to look for an adequate structural formula for *Macbeth* in any of the more "imaginative" directions commonly taken by recent criticism; I shall assume, therefore, without argument, that we have to do, not with a lyric "statement of evil" or an allegory of the workings of sin in the soul and the state or a metaphysical myth of destruction followed by re-creation or a morality play with individualized characters rather than types,[233] but simply with an imitative tragic drama based on historical materials. To call it an imitative tragic drama, however, does not carry us very far; it merely limits roughly the range of possible forms we have to consider. Among these are the contrasting plot-forms embodied respectively in *Othello* and in *Richard III*: the first a tragic plot-form in the classic sense of Aristotle's analysis in *Poetics* 13; the second a plot-form which Aristotle rejected as non-tragic but which appealed strongly to tragic poets in the Renaissance—a form of serious action designed to arouse moral indignation for the deliberately unjust and seemingly prospering acts of the protagonist and moral satisfaction at his subsequent ruin. The plot-form of *Macbeth* clearly involves elements which assimilate it now to the one and now to the other of both these kinds. The action of the play is twofold, and one of its aspects is the punitive action of Malcolm, Macduff, and their friends which in the end brings about the protagonist's downfall and death. The characters here are all good men, whom Macbeth has unforgivably wronged, and their cause is the unqualifiedly just cause of freeing Scotland from a bloody tyrant and restoring the rightful line of kings. All this is made clear in the representation not only directly through the speeches and acts of the avengers but indirectly by those wonderfully vivid devices of imagery and general thought in which modern critics have found the central value and meaning of the play as a whole; and our responses, when this part of the action is before us, are such as are clearly dictated by the immediate events and the poetic commentary: we desire, that is, the complete success of the counter-action and this as speedily as possible before Macbeth can commit further horrors. We desire this,

170

however—and that is what at once takes the plot-form out of the merely retributive class—not only for the sake of humanity and Scotland but also for the sake of Macbeth himself. For what most sharply distinguishes our view of Macbeth from that of his victims and enemies is that, whereas they see him from the outside only, we see him also, throughout the other action of the play—the major action—from the inside, as he sees himself; and what we see thus is a moral spectacle the emotional quality of which, for the impartial observer, is not too far removed from the tragic *dynamis* specified in the *Poetics*. This is not to say that the main action of *Macbeth* is not significantly different, in several respects, from the kind of tragic action which Aristotle envisages. The change is not merely from good to bad fortune, but from a good state of character to a state in which the hero is almost, but not quite, transformed into a monster; and the tragic act which initiates the change, and still more the subsequent unjust acts which this entails, are acts done—unlike Othello's killing of Desdemona—in full knowledge of their moral character. We cannot, therefore, state the form of this action in strictly Aristotelian terms, but the form is none the less one that involves, like tragedy in Aristotle's sense, the arousal and catharsis of painful emotions for, and not merely with respect to, the protagonist—emotions for which the terms pity and fear are not entirely inapplicable.

Any adequate hypothesis about the structure of *Macbeth*, then, would have to take both of these sets of facts into account. For both of the views we are given of the hero are true: he is in fact, in terms of the nature and objective consequences of his deeds, what Macduff and Malcolm say he is throughout Acts IV and V, but he is also—and the form of the play is really the interaction of the two views in our opinions and emotions—what we ourselves see him to be as we witness the workings of his mind before the murder of Duncan, then after the murder, and finally when, at the end, all his illusions and hopes gone, he faces Macduff. He is one who commits monstrous deeds without becoming wholly a monster, since his knowledge of the right principle is never altogether obscured, though it is almost so in Act IV. We can understand such a person and hence feel fear and

171

pity of a kind for him because he is only doing upon a grander scale and with deeper guilt and more terrifying consequences for himself and others what we can, without too much difficulty, imagine ourselves doing, however less extremely, in circumstances generally similar. For the essential story of *Macbeth* is that of a man, not naturally depraved, who has fallen under the compulsive power of an imagined better state for himself which he can attain only by acting contrary to his normal habits and feelings; who attains this state and then finds that he must continue to act thus, and even worse, in order to hold on to what he has got; who persists and becomes progressively hardened morally in the process; and who then, ultimately, when the once alluring good is about to be taken away from him, faces the loss in terms of what is left of his original character. It is something like this moral universal that underlies, I think, and gives emotional form to the main action of *Macbeth*. It is a form that turns upon the difference between what seemingly advantageous crime appears to be in advance to a basically good but incontinent man and what its moral consequences for such a man inevitably are; and the catharsis is effected not merely by the man's deserved overthrow but by his own inner suffering and by his discovery, before it is too late, of what he had not known before he began to act. If we are normal human beings we must abhor his crimes; yet we cannot completely abhor but must rather pity the man himself, and even when he seems most the monster (as Macbeth does in Act IV) we must still wish for such an outcome as will be best, under the circumstances, not merely for Scotland but for him.

But if this, or something close to it, is indeed the complex emotional structure intended in *Macbeth*, then we have a basis for defining with some precision the various problems of incident, character, thought, imagery, diction, and representation which confronted Shakespeare in writing the play, and hence a starting-point for discussing, in detail, the rationale of its parts.[234] Consider—to take only one instance—the final scene. In the light of the obvious consequences of the form I have attributed to the play as a whole, it is not difficult to state what the main problems at this point are. If the catharsis of the tragedy is to be complete,

172

we must be made to feel both that Macbeth is being killed in a just cause and that his state of mind and the circumstances of his death are such as befit a man who, for all his crimes, has not altogether lost our pity and goodwill. We are of course prepared for this double response by all that has gone before, and, most immediately, in the earlier scenes of Act V, by the fresh glimpses we are given of the motivation of the avengers and by Macbeth's soliloquies. But it will clearly be better if the dual effect can be sustained until the very end; and this requires, on the one hand, that we should be vividly reminded once more of Macbeth's crimes and the justified hatred they have caused and of the prospect of a new and better time which his death holds out for Scotland, and, on the other hand, that we should be allowed to take satisfaction, at last, in the manner in which Macbeth himself behaves. The artistic triumph of the scene lies in the completeness with which both problems are solved: the first in the words and actions of Macduff, the speeches about young Siward, and Malcolm's closing address; the second by a variety of devices, both of invention and of representation, the appropriateness of which to the needed effect can be seen if we ask what we would not want Macbeth to do at this moment. We want him to be killed, as I have said, for his sake no less than that of Scotland; but we would not want him either to seek out Macduff or to flee the encounter when it comes or to "play the Roman fool"; we would not want him to show no recognition of the wrongs he has done Macduff or, when his last trust in the witches has gone, to continue to show fear or to yield or to fight with savage animosity; and he is made to do none of these things, but rather the contraries of all of them, so that he acts in the end as the Macbeth whose praises we have heard in the second scene of the play. And I would suggest that the cathartic effect of these words and acts is reinforced indirectly, in the representation, by the analogy we can hardly help drawing between his conduct now and the earlier conduct of young Siward, for of Macbeth too it can be said that "he parted well and paid his score"; the implication of this analogy is surely one of the functions, though not the only one, which the lines about Siward are intended to serve.

173

Such are the kinds of hypotheses we shall need to make if we are to have critical knowledge of the shaping principles of poetic works or of the artistic reasons governing the character and interrelation of their parts. They are working suppositions which, as I have said, both imply and are implied by the particulars of the works for which they are constructed; and they can never be made well by any critic who is not naturally sensitive to such particulars and in the habit of observing them closely. These, however, though indispensable, are not sufficient conditions. It never happens in any inquiry into matters of fact that the particulars we observe determine their own meaning automatically; the concrete or the individual is never intelligible except through the general and the abstract; and if we are to allow the facts to speak for themselves, we must in some fashion supply them with a language in which to talk. Hypotheses, in short, are not made out of nothing, but presuppose on the part of the inquirer who forms them a systematic body of concepts relative to the subject-matter with which he is dealing. The critic who proposes to explore hypothetically the structures of individual poems is in the same predicament; he must bring to his task, inescapably, general ideas about poetic structure, or he can never construct a workable hypothesis about the structure of any poem.

Hence the crucial importance for the practical critic of poetic forms, in the sense we are now giving to this term, of the kind of analytic of poetry which was outlined earlier in this lecture. From the point of view of the criticism of individual poems, the concepts and distinctions involved in that analytic differ from those which most contemporary critics have been content to use: they supply, not a unified set of terms for constituting structural patterns in poems (like Mr. Heilman's formula for "poetic drama" or the theories that make all good poetry a species of "ironical" or "paradoxical" structure), but a great variety of terms designating distinct and alternative principles, devices, and functions in poetry from which the critic need select only such combinations as appear to be relevant to the poems he is examining. What he thus acquires are not hypotheses ready formed but elements out of which he may form such hypotheses as the

174

facts of his poems seem to warrant—in short, knowledge of structural possibilities only, resting on inductive inquiry into the principles poets have actually used in building poems and hence expanding with the development and progressive differentiation of poetry itself, so that he brings to the discussion of individual poems merely conceptual materials for framing pertinent questions about them without any predetermination of the substance of his answers, much as a physician uses the alternatives given him by medical theory in diagnosing symptoms in one of his patients. In the other mode of criticism the relation of theory to a particular poem is the relation of a previously selected idea or pattern of structure to its embodiment or reflection in a given work; here the relation is one of many known possibilities of structural patterning in poetry to the actualization in the poem examined of some one or more of these.

A critic using the first type of theory might argue somewhat as follows, for example, about the structure of Gray's *Elegy*. We must assume, he might say, the language of poetry being what it is, that the principle of structure in any good poem is a principle of balancing and harmonizing discrepant connotations, attitudes, and meanings; we must look therefore for a structure of this kind in Gray's poem or be content to relegate it to an inferior class of poetry; and our quest, indeed, is not in vain, for when we examine the text in the light of our general hypothesis of "ironical" structure, we quickly find that all the details of the *Elegy* can be subsumed under the theme of a continuous contrast of two modes of burial—in the church itself and in the churchyard—in which, as in all good poetry, opposing meanings are finally resolved.[235] A critic, however, whose theory was of the second type, would proceed in an altogether different way. He would have no favourite hypothesis of structure as such, but would know merely that among short poems which, like the *Elegy*, evoke in us serious emotions, the shaping principle may be of several essentially distinct types, each of them generating distinct artistic problems for the poet; and he would use this knowledge as a basis for asking himself some such questions as these: Is what happens in the *Elegy* best explained by supposing, as the other critic has clearly done, that the poem is intended to

175

be read as an emotionalized argument in verse (whether about modes of burial or something else), the personal qualities of the speaker and the setting of his meditation being simply devices for enforcing the unifying dialectic? Or is the poem better read— better, that is, with respect to the actual shaping principle of its construction—as an imitative lyric? And if it is this latter kind of structure, is the form one in which the speaker is conceived as being merely moved in a certain way by his situation (as in Gray's "Ode on a Distant Prospect of Eton College"), or as acting in a certain manner in relation to it (as in Marvell's "To His Coy Mistress"), or as deliberating morally in a certain state of mind on what is for him a serious issue in life? Weighing these possibilities (which give us perhaps the major forms which short serious imitative poems can have), our second critic would probably conclude that it is the last possibility which best explains both the constructed matter and the arrangement of the *Elegy* and the peculiar quality of the emotions which Gray's words and rhythms arouse in us. He might then describe the *Elegy* as an imitative lyric of moral choice rather than of action or of mood, representing a situation in which a virtuous, sensitive, and ambitious young man of undistinguished birth confronts the possibility of his death while still to "Fortune and to Fame unknown," and eventually, after much disturbance of mind (hinted at in the Swain's description of him), reconciles himself to his probable fate by reflecting that none of the rewards of successful ambition can "sooth the dull cold ear of Death," which comes as inevitably to the great as to the obscure; that a life passed "far from the madding crowd's ignoble strife," though circumscribing the exercise of virtue and talent, may yet be a means of preserving innocence; and that he can at any rate look forward to— what all men desire as a minimum—living on in the memory of at least one friend, while his merits and frailties alike repose "in trembling hope" on the bosom of his Father and his God.[236] Something like this, I think (pedantic as any brief statement of it must sound), is the answer our second critic would give; but the point is that in arriving at it he would be using his theory of possible principles of structure in short poems simply to furnish him with the distinctions he needs if he is not to substitute a structure of his own for the structure Gray achieved.

176

The more extensive and discriminating such general knowledge, therefore, the better the critic's hypotheses are likely to be. But it is also the nature of this kind of theoretical knowledge to be always inadequate, though in varying degrees, to the particulars we use it to illuminate. We can never know in advance all the possibilities, and we can never, consequently, form a hypothesis about a work of any artistic complexity or even about many simpler works without making a shorter or longer inductive leap from the words and sentences before us to the peculiar combination of universals which define their poetic form. And that is why, in this mode of criticism, we can make no separation except analytically between theory and application, the latter being possible only if the former already exists at least up to a certain point and the former being constantly refined and enlarged as we proceed with the latter.

Application, however, is our main problem here, and its success depends upon the extent to which the universal terms of our hypotheses and the perceived and felt particulars of the texts for which they are constructed can be made to fit together. The general conditions are two: first, our ability to keep our explanatory formulae fluid and to submit them to constant revisions in principle or in detail before we transform them into conclusions; and, second, our willingness to use systematically what has been called "the method of multiple working hypotheses."[237] We have to remember, that is, that the value of a hypothesis is always relative, not merely to the facts it is intended to explain, but to all the other variant hypotheses which the same facts might suggest if only we gave them a chance; that the best hypothesis is simply the best among several possible hypotheses, relevant to the same work or problem, with which we have actually compared it; and that unless we make such comparisons a regular part of our procedure, we always court the danger of missing either slightly or altogether what our author was really attempting to do.

There are also, in addition to these very general rules, several more particular criteria. Our aim is an explanation and judgment of poetic works in terms of their structural causes; hence, in the first place, the necessity of so framing our hypotheses that they are not descriptive formulae merely but clearly imply practical artistic consequences, in what the writers must or cannot or

177

might well do in the act of writing, for the details of the works they are being used to explain; that is the character, for example, of Aristotle's definition of tragic plot-form in *Poetics* 13, and I have tried to impart a similar character to the statements above about *Macbeth*. The ideal is to have a central principle of explanation that will enable us to see precisely the functional relations between all the particular problems a writer has attempted to solve and the form of his work as a whole, even though we may have to conclude, in some cases, that the relation is a very tenuous one. In the second place, our aim is an explanation and judgment in terms adapted as closely as possible to the peculiar structure and power of the work before us; hence the necessity of trying to go beyond formulae that imply the work as a whole or any of its parts only generically; as when, for instance, we neglect to distinguish between the different material structures possible in lyrics and treat a particular lyric without regard to such distinctions, or as when we discuss a work like Jane Austen's *Emma* merely as a comedy, failing to see how little this can tell us about its distinctive comic construction. In the third place, we aspire to completeness of explanation; and this means that in framing a hypothesis about any work we must consider everything in the text as significant evidence that involves in any way a free choice on the writer's part between possible alternative things to be done with his materials or ways of doing them at any point. The hypothesis must therefore be complex rather than simple; it must recognize that the same parts may have different functions, including that of mere adornment; and, above all, it cannot be arrived at by giving a privileged position, on *a priori* grounds, to a particular variety of signs of artistic intention, in a complex work, to the exclusion of other and often conflicting signs of the same thing. This last is conspicuously the error of those interpreters of *Macbeth* who have inferred the central form of that play chiefly from the thought and imagery that serve to emphasize the "unnatural" character of the hero's crimes and the inevitability of a just retribution, without attempting to correlate with this the many signs, both in the construction of the plot and in its extraordinarily artful representation, of the distinctive moral quality of Macbeth's actions when

178

these are seen from the inside. There will always be incomplete-
ness in any hypothesis, moreover, or in any criticism that follows
its use, that leaves out of account, as one of the crucial facts, the
peculiar sequence of emotions we feel when we read the work
unbiased by critical doctrine; for, as we have seen, the most
important thing about any poetic production is the characteristic
power it has to affect us in this definite way rather than that.[238]
Completeness, however, is impossible without coherence; hence
our hypotheses, in the fourth place, must aim at a maximum of
internal unity, on the assumption that, although many works are
episodic and although many predominantly imitative works, for
example, also have didactic or topical parts, this can best be
seen if we begin by presuming that literary artists usually aim
at creating wholes.

The only proof there can be of a hypothesis about any particular thing lies in its power of completeness and coherence of
explanation within the limits of the data it makes significant—
and this always relatively to the other hypotheses pertinent to
the same data with which it has been compared. We must be
guided, however, in choosing among alternative hypotheses, by
a further criterion—the classic criterion of economy: that that
hypothesis is the best, other things being equal, which requires
the fewest supplementary hypotheses to make it work or which
entails the least amount of explaining away; it is no recommenda-
tion, thus, for Mr. Knights's interpretation of *Macbeth* that he
has to say of the emotion aroused in most readers as well as in
Bradley by Macbeth's soliloquies in Act V, that this is mere
"conventional 'sympathy for the hero,'" which ought not to be
allowed to distort that dialectical system of values in the play
that is for him "the pattern of the whole."[239] And we must be
careful, further, not to construe our "data" in too narrow a sense
and so be satisfied with hypotheses that clearly conflict with facts
external to the works we are considering but relevant nevertheless
to their interpretation; I mean not only such particular evidences
as we can often find of writers' intentions—for example, Coleridge's statements about the kind of poem he designed *The Rime
of the Ancient Mariner* to be—but also such general probabilities
with respect to the works of a given period or genre or with

179

respect to poetic works of any kind or age as are supplied by either our historical knowledge or our common sense. It is not likely, for instance, that a Shakespearean tragedy intended for the popular stage should really have a kind of basic structure which practising playwrights of any time would find it difficult or impossible to make effective for their audiences.[240] Nor is it ever a sensible thing in a critic to cultivate indifference to common opinion about the works he is discussing. The opinion may be wrong or, as often happens, it may need to be corrected and refined; but in such conflicts—at least when they involve the larger aspects and effects of works—the burden of proof is on him. For the secrets of art are not, like the secrets of nature, things lying deeply hid, inaccessible to the perception and understanding of all who have not mastered the special techniques their discovery requires. The critic does, indeed, need special techniques, but for the sake of building upon common sense apprehensions of his objects, not of supplanting these; and few things have done greater harm to the practice and repute of literary criticism in recent times than the assumption that its discoveries, like those of the physical sciences, must gain in importance and plausibility as they become more and more paradoxical in the ancient sense of that word: as if—to adapt a sharp saying of Professor Frank Knight about social studies—now that everybody is agreed that natural phenomena are not like works of art, the business of criticism must be to show that works of art are like natural phenomena.

It remains, finally, to consider the bearing of all this on judgments of poetic value. And the first thing to observe is that, if our hypothesis concerning the shaping principle of any work is adequate, it will give us a basis for saying with some precision (as my example of Act V of *Macbeth* will perhaps suggest) what are the necessities which such a form imposes on any artist whose aim is its successful realization in his materials. Some of them will be necessities common to all self-contained poetic works of no matter what kind, such as the necessity, if the parts are to cohere, of devices for effecting continuity from beginning through middle to end; others will be more and more specific necessities determined by the nature of the form we assume to have been intended, such as the necessity, if a comic effect like that of *Tom Jones* is to be obtained, of keeping the ridiculous mistakes of the hero from obscuring the sympathetic traits that make us wish him ultimate good fortune. These will all be consequences inferable from our basic definition of the form, and our primary task will be to trace them, in detail, throughout the particulars of the work at all its levels from plot or lyric situation down to the imagery and words. A kind of judgment of value will thus emerge in the very process of our analysis: if the writer has indeed done, somehow, all the essential things he would need to do on the assumption that he is actually writing the kind of work we have defined, then to that extent the work is good, or at least not artistically bad; and we should have to use very little rhetoric in addition to make this clear. But this is only half of the problem, for it is true of most mediocre writers that they usually do, in some fashion, a great part or all of the things their particular forms require, but do little more besides. The crucial question, therefore, concerns not so much the necessities of the assumed form as its possibilities. What is it that the writer might have done, over and above the minimum requirements of his task, which he has not done, or what is it that we have not expected him to do which he has yet triumphantly accomplished? These are the things our analyses ought peculiarly to attend to if they are to be adequate to their objects.

The possible in this sense, as distinguished from the necessary, is that which tends to perfect—to warrant praise of a positive rather than a merely negative kind. We can know it in two ways: by having our minds stored with memories of what both the most and the least perfect of artists have done when confronted with similar problems of invention, representation, and writing; and by considering theoretically the conditions under which any particular effect aimed at in a given work might be better or worse achieved—by asking, for instance, what would in general make a predicament like that of Tom Jones on the discovery of his first affair with Molly seem most completely comic, and then discussing the episode, as it is actually developed by Fielding, in these terms.[241] Both methods are comparative, but the comparisons, if they are not to result in unfair impositions on the writer whose work we are considering, must take account of the fact that the desirable or admirable in literature is never something absolute but is always relative, in any given part of a work, to the requirements of the over-all form and to the function of the part as only one part along with many others: forgetting this, we should make the mistake of Mr. Joyce Cary's critic and demand neatness where clumsiness is what "belongs," vividness and particularity where faintness and generality are needed, doing more than is done when this would be doing too much.

The judgments of value we should thus be trying to make would for this reason always be judgments in kind, grounded on a prior definition of the writer's problems as problems peculiar, at least in their concrete determination, to the formal nature of the work he is writing. They would also be judgments in terms of intentions—what is it that the writer aimed to do here and how well has he succeeded in doing it?—but the intentions we should take as principles would not be those, except accidentally, which the writer had stated explicitly before or after writing or those which can be defined for the writer by saying that he must have intended to write this work because this is what he has written. The common objections to criticism based on "intention" in either of these senses are unanswerable. They do not hold, however, when we identify intention with the hypothesized form of a poetic work and then consider how fully what we know of the necessities and possibilities of this form are achieved in the work, on the assumption that, if the work shows any serious concern with art at all, the writer must have wished or been willing to be judged in this way. There is nothing unfair to the writer in such an approach, inasmuch as we are not engaged in a judicial process of bringing his work under a previously formulated general theory of literary value but in a free inquiry whose aim is simply the discovery of those values in his work—among them, we always hope, unprecedented values—which he has been able to put there. They will always be values incident to the relation between the form of the work and its matter at all of its structural levels; and it will be appropriate to interpret what we find in terms of a distinction between three classes of works considered from this point of view: works that are well conceived as wholes

182

but contain few parts the formal excellence of which remains in our memory or invites us to another reading; works that are rich in local virtues but have only a loose or tenuous over-all form; and works that satisfy Coleridge's criterion for a poem, that it aims at "the production of as much immediate pleasure in parts, as is compatible with the largest sum of pleasure in the whole."[242] These last are the few relatively perfect productions in the various literary kinds, and as between the other two we shall naturally prefer the second to the first.

V

All methods, in any field of study, have their characteristic corruptions when they fall into the hands of incompetent practitioners. The corruption of the historical critic is thus typically some kind of antiquarian irrelevance, as when texts are annotated more learnedly than they need to be or with only a loose pertinence to the problems and difficulties they present. The corruption of the literary critic in the modes of criticism we are chiefly familiar with at the present time is most commonly perhaps a cult of the paradoxical, along with which go, often enough, an addiction to irresponsible analogizing, a preference for metaphorical over literal statement, and a tendency to substitute rhetoric for inquiry as a guiding aim. The critic whose portrait I am drawing in this lecture is less likely, I think, to give way to any of these perversions than to certain others which, though different in kind, are no less to be deplored. In his concern with form, he can all too easily become merely formalistic, attending less to what gives life to poems than to the mechanism of their structural parts; in his concern with poetic wholes, he can be tempted to forget that the wholes have no existence apart from the words through which they are made actual; in his concern with development of theory, he can readily persuade himself that the enunciation of theory, however well established, is more important than the solution of the concrete problems to which it is relevant and so fall into a methodological pedantry as bad as the factual pedantry of the antiquarians.

I do not think, however, that these are inevitable faults, given a certain flexibility of mind, a sensitivity to literary particulars, an ability to resist the spirit of routine and self-satisfaction, and an understanding of the right relation between methods and problems. And when they are not allowed to distort the results, I should contend that the approach I have been describing is capable of giving us more nearly adequate insights into the structural principles and characteristics of poetic works than any of the other modes of critical language with which we have compared it. We may say of these other methods, in terms borrowed from our own, that what they have chiefly concentrated on, in their analyses of structure, has been the matter of poetic works and its generic figurations and techniques rather than their forms. These are essential aspects of the problem, but they are aspects with which we too can deal. We can consider how any element in a poem "works with the other elements to create the effect intended by the poet"; we can discuss the "meaning" of poems in the sense of the thought that is presupposed by or expressed through any of their characteristic devices of statement and representation; we can treat of images and patterns of images and of the subtleties of poetic diction and rhythm; we can find a place for what is sound in the distinction between "structure" and "texture"; and we can make use of all that the "archetypal" critics can tell us about the cultural and psychological universals which poems imply. We can do all these things; but we can also do more, and as a consequence be able to do these things with greater precision and intelligibility.

For we possess what these other methods have conspicuously lacked: a means of isolating and defining those principles of structure in individual poems which distinguish them from other poems or kinds of poems and determine thus in highly specific ways what their distinctive elements are and the artistic reasons that justify the particular configurations we observe them to have. In contrast with our constructive and differentiating procedure, the procedures of these other critical schools have been, in varying degrees, generalizing and reductive. There is reduction, and hence a loss of causal particularity, whenever the only terms critics use in talking about literary structures are terms applicable primarily to the writer as distinct in some way from his product (as in F. R. Leavis' discussions of novels as direct reflections of the "complexity" of the novelists' "interests") or whenever the only source of terms is the psychology of readers (as in Miss Bodkin's definition of the "archetypal pattern" of rebirth evoked for her by *The Ancient Mariner*): what can be discovered in such cases is merely a kind of structure that many poems can have, or even other species of writing. There is reduction similarly in any method that draws its only structural formulae from such things as the common figures of poetical or rhetorical language (as in Cleanth Brooks and the Shakespearean critics who speak of plays as "metaphors"), or the non-poetic forms of myth and ritual, or the supposed patterns of psychic activity. And there is still reduction, though of a less extreme variety, in the critics who equate poetic structure, in all except the most general sense of "aesthetic pattern," exclusively with the conventions of verbal form or thematic arrangement which poets derive from earlier poetic tradition; in the critics, again, who look for fixed and unitary definitions of the poetic genres and discuss individual tragedies, comedies, epics, novels, and lyrics as more or less typical or perfect examples of these various quasi-Platonic forms; in the critics who identify the principles of structure in poems with the "themes" which are either their germinal ideas or moral bases or their underlying schemes of probability; and in the many critics, lastly, who fix their attention on some part of the total structure—on one phase of the action or on the framework of its representation, on a principal character, a "key" passage of thought, a conspicuous train of imagery—and proceed to derive from this their formula for the whole.

What these critics all leave out is thus the very principle we have taken as our starting-point: the shaping principle of form and emotional "power" without which no poem could come into existence as a beautiful and effective whole of a determinate kind. We can therefore talk with a fullness and precision of distinction impossible to them about the particular and widely variant relations which exist in different poems between their formal and their material natures. We are not limited to any one conception of poetic unity or to any one set of concepts for defining structure. We are not forced to speak of the working

185

together of the parts of a poem merely in terms of simple con-
trarieties of theme or tone or in a vocabulary of which the most
exact words are expressions like "goes with," is "associated with,"
or is "related to" or "carries out," "reflects," "repeats," "qualifies,"
"balances," "contrasts with," "contradicts," and so on. We are not
compelled, in order to show our recognition that the best poetry
is not indifferent to thought or "meaning," to interpret all poetic
masterpieces in which ideas are contained or evoked as if they
were compositions of the same order as *The Divine Comedy*, or,
at any rate, in some sense or in some degree, metaphorical or
symbolic expressions, or, at the very least, "studies" of something
or other. We shall be aware that there are indeed many poetic
works to which such descriptions can be applied, but we shall go
on the assumption—which all experience and literary history
surely warrants—that ideas can function in poems in radically
different ways: sometimes as sources of inspiration, sometimes
as formal and shaping ends, sometimes as means for constituting
the characters, purposes, or states of mind of the *dramatis personae*, sometimes as choric devices for enhancing or universalizing
the actions; and the distinctions of our theoretic analysis, and
notably our distinction between imitative and non-imitative
forms, will enable us to discriminate these various uses when we
come upon them and to judge of the significance of the thought
in any poem or passage according as one or another of them is
its primary cause. And finally, in dealing with the problems of
imagery that have been so prominent during the past generation,
especially in the criticism of Shakespeare, we are not restricted to
either a merely material classification and psychological interpretation of images (as in Miss Spurgeon and her followers) or to a
merely generalized and indefinite discussion of their functions in
drama (as in some of the more recent Shakespeareans[243]): with
our basic distinction of object, manner, and means and our more
specific devices for relating the parts of individual works to their
controlling forms, we should be able, at the very least, to introduce greater particularity and artistic intelligibility into the
subject than are apparent in most of the current discussions.

I look upon this approach, therefore, as one likely to repay a
more concentrated effort of research and application than it has

received in modern times. It is not a method that lends itself too easily, perhaps, to the immediate purposes of reviewers and professional critics of current productions, but it is not without its utility even here: there must be many readers of such criticism who would be grateful for more precise indications than they usually get of what are the formal as well as the material and technical novelties to be found in the latest serious novels, plays, and volumes of verse, and above all of the kinds of "peculiar pleasures" they are fitted to give us and why. The method is undoubtedly better suited, however, to the more ample and considered criticism of the literature of the past or of contemporary literature when this is made an object of elaborated study; and there is excellent reason to think that the writing of literary history in particular might be radically transformed, and to great advantage, through the inclusion of what I have called the immediate artistic causes of literary productions along with the relatively more external and remote causes to which historians of literature have mainly confined themselves.

And there is another realm in which these principles might be expected to yield peculiar benefits—that of literary education. They can give us, for one thing, the basis of a teachable discipline of reading and appreciation which would be exempt, on the one hand, from mere impressionism and the evocation of irresponsible opinion and, on the other hand, from the imposition on students of ready-made literary doctrines or canons of taste. Its essence would be simply the communication to students of a comprehensive scheme of questions to be asked about all the different kinds of literary works they might be studying and of criteria for discussing the appropriateness and adequacy of the answers in the light of the particulars of texts and of the students' responses as human beings to what is going on in them. The development of such a discipline, centred, as it would be, in the statement and free comparison of hypotheses, would help to bring into literary studies something they have commonly lacked —a subject-matter, namely, in the sense not merely of facts but of compendent general concepts for their interpretation; concepts, moreover, that can be translated into habits of observation and reflection such as will tend to make the student independent of

187

his teacher: a potential scholar in criticism rather than a disciple or member of a school, and a scholar who would do credit to his training precisely in proportion as he was able to correct and develop further the things he had been taught. I think that this could be done by a kind of practical and inductive teaching which would keep the student's mind centred on the concrete aspects of works and his feelings about them rather than on theoretical matters as such and which would, at the same time, build up in him an increasingly clear understanding of what it means to give a reasoned and warranted answer to a critical question and also, to an extent greater than has been common in the teaching of criticism, of how essential it is, if the answer is to be valid, that it accord with whatever truths the student has learned in the linguistic and historical parts of his education. For it is hard to see how the training I am suggesting could be carried on successfully without bringing criticism and these other disciplines into closer mutual relations than have existed between them for a long time.

We might expect, moreover, that such training would encourage a kind of appreciation of literary masterpieces that has been largely neglected in the critical tradition upon which our teaching has hitherto, in the main, been founded. The strength of that tradition has been its sensitiveness to the qualities and values which literary works share with one another or with other modes of expression—to these rather than to the differentiated characteristics of works which are what they are by virtue primarily of their writers' individual acts of poetic making. And it is not at all to minimize the importance of analogies and common principles in criticism to suggest that any literary culture is incomplete that does not lead also to a discriminating understanding, such as the training I propose is suited to give, of the peculiar principles of construction that contribute to make poetry the complex and richly diversified experience we all feel it to be. We may say indeed that what chiefly distinguishes the genius of literary study, as of the humanities in general, from the genius of science is that it naturally aspires to this kind of completion, not being permanently satisfied with reductions of the individual and the specific to the common, and perpetually feeling the need for distinctions and methods that will help us to do justice to the inventiveness of man and the uniqueness of his works.

And along with this would go a third benefit, in the capacity of our principles to maintain the integrity of literary appreciation without cutting it off formalistically from the life which literary works represent or attempt to guide. It is difficult to keep this balance in any of the critical languages in which the basic distinction for the analysis and judgment of works is some variant of the ancient dichotomy of *verba* and *res*; for if we distinguish thus between art and what art expresses, between poetic language and poetic thought, structure and idea, technique and meaning, symbol and concept, "presentment" and the moral "interests" of writers, we inevitably tend to regard one or the other of these two aspects as primary in importance. Our teaching of literature, consequently, in so far as it is "literary," appears far removed from common experience and human emotion, and in so far as it throws the emphasis on content, on questions of knowledge and behaviour, runs the risk of becoming merely an amateur branch of ethics, psychology, sociology, anthropology, or the history of ideas.

These disadvantages very largely disappear, I think, when we bring to the discussion of poetic works our radically different distinction of matter and form. For form as we conceive it is simply that which gives definite shape, emotional power, and beauty to the materials of man's experience out of which the writer has composed his work. Hence it cannot be separated as mere "form" from the matter in which it exists, nor can we talk about it adequately (as I have tried to illustrate in my discussions of *Macbeth* and of Gray's *Elegy*) without talking at the same time about the human qualities of the actions, persons, feelings, and thoughts the work brings before us and the very human, but no less poetic, responses these evoke in our minds. There can thus be no good "literary" criticism, in this language, that does not presuppose a constant making of moral and psychological discriminations and a constant concern with nuances of thought, as well as with subtleties of language and technique; what keeps it "literary" or "poetic" and prevents it from degenerating into either "studies in character" or excursions into philosophy and social history is the direction imposed on all our questions about the "content" of works by our hypotheses concerning their shaping principles of form. We can agree, therefore, with the critics who hold that we ought to deal with poetry as poetry and not another thing, and we can agree no less with those who insist that one of the main tasks of criticism is to show the "relevance" of poems to "life"; only these, for us, are not two tasks but one. And I would state a further point in the same connection, the bearing of which will be easily evident to those who have grown impatient with the current tendency to reduce all questions of morals and politics to questions of ideologies and beliefs. The counterpart of this "rationalism" in literary studies is the assumption that "relevance to life" in poetry is a matter primarily of "themes" and "imaginative visions," so that no imaginative work can be taken seriously from which we cannot extract a "total meaning" over and above the human particulars it exhibits, which we then set forth as what the work is intending to say. From this narrowing of the scope of literary values to such values as only earnest modern intellectuals can think of greater importance than the spectacle of individual men doing and suffering, we have, fortunately, an effective way of escape in our distinction between imitative and didactic forms. We can accord a proper appreciation, in their own terms, to works of which the formal principles are clearly ideas. But we are free to discuss the others, including notably the tragedies of Shakespeare, in a way that fully respects their seriousness, and the implication of universals in the working out of their plots, without being committed to the dehumanizing supposition that the moral habits and dispositions of individual persons and the qualities and circumstances of their actions are things less valuable for us, as men and citizens, to contemplate in literature than the pale abstractions by which they have been overlaid in the prevailing modes of interpretation. And so we might contribute not only to a more discriminating understanding of what literature as literature can do but to a kind of training in concrete moral and social perception, unbiased by doctrine, such as all who live in a free society would be the better for having.

190

VI

When all this is said, however, it is still true that what I have been talking about in this lecture is only one out of many possible legitimate approaches to the question of poetic structure, not to speak of the innumerable other questions with which critics can profitably concern themselves. I should not want to leave the impression, therefore, that I think it the only mode of criticism seriously worth cultivation at the present time by either teachers of literature or critics, but simply that its development, along with the others, might have many fruitful consequences for our teaching and criticism generally. What distinguishes it from the other modes is its preoccupation with the immediate constructive problems of writers in the making of individual works and with the artistic reasoning necessarily involved in their successful solution; and its great claim to consideration is that it can deal with these matters more precisely and adequately, and with a more complete reliance on the canons of inductive inquiry, unhampered by doctrinal preconceptions, than any of the other existing critical languages. It can give us, consequently, a body of primary literary facts about literary works, in their aspect as concrete wholes, in the light of which we can judge the relevance and validity—or see the precise bearing—of such observations and statements of value as result from the application to the same works of other critical principles and procedures: if the structural principles of *Macbeth* or of Gray's *Elegy* are actually what we have taken them to be, then whatever else may be truly said about these same works, in answer to other questions or in the context of other ways of reasoning about them, must obviously be capable of being brought into harmony with this prior factual knowledge of the distinctive how and why of their construction. Here is something, therefore, which critics who prefer a more generalizing or a more speculative approach to literary works can hardly neglect if they wish to be responsible students of literature rather than merely rhetoricians bent on exploiting favourite theses at any cost. For though it is true enough, for example, that what writers do is conditioned by their personal lives and complexes, their social circumstances, and their literary

191

traditions, there is always a risk that exclusive explanations of literary peculiarities in terms of such remoter causes will collapse and seem absurd as soon as we consider, for any work to which they have been applied, what are the immediate artistic exigencies which its writer faced because of his choice of form or manner in this particular work.[244] These exigencies can never be safely disregarded so long as the genetic relation between art and its sources and materials in life remains the very indirect relation we know it is; and it is perhaps not the least of the utilities to be found in the criticism of forms that its cultivation, in a context of the many other kinds of critical inquiry, would help to keep critics of all schools constantly reminded of their existence and importance.

But the other kinds ought to be there. Of the truth about literature, no critical language can ever have a monopoly or even a distant approach to one; and there are obviously many things which the language I have been speaking of cannot do. It is a method not at all suited, as is criticism in the grand line of Longinus, Coleridge, and Matthew Arnold, to the definition and appreciation of those general qualities of writing—mirroring the souls of writers—for the sake of which most of us read or at any rate return to what we have read. It is a method that necessarily abstracts from history and hence requires to be supplemented by other very different procedures if we are to replace the works we study in the circumstances and temper of their times and see them as expressions and forces as well as objects of art. It is a method, above all, that completely fails, because of its essentially differentiating character, to give us insights into the larger moral and political values of literature or into any of the other organic relations with human nature and human experience in which literature is involved. And yet who will say that these are not as compelling considerations for criticism as anything comprised in the problem of poetic structure as we have been discussing it in these lectures? The moral is surely that we ought to have at our command, collectively at least, as many different critical methods as there are distinguishable major aspects in the construction, appreciation, and use of literary works. The multiplicity of critical languages is therefore something not to be deplored

192

but rather rejoiced in, as making possible a fuller exploration of our subject in its total extent than we could otherwise attain; and for my part I have as fond a regard for Longinus and for the masters of historical criticism as I have for Aristotle, and as strong a conviction of their continuing utility. Nor will there ever cease to be employment for criticism of the less rigorous or more imaginative types—in directing attention to aspects of poems which only a new model or analogy can bring into view, in formulating and promoting new ideals of poetic excellence or new poetic styles, in suggesting to poets unrealized possibilities in subject-matter and language, in relating poetry, for readers, to large non-poetic human contexts of emotion and meaning, in keeping the life of poetry and of taste from declining into orthodoxy and routine.

The best hope for criticism in the future, indeed, lies in the perpetuation of this multiplicity; nothing could be more damaging than the practical success of any effort to define authoritatively the frontiers and problems of our subject or to assign to each of its variant languages a determinate place in a single hierarchy of critical modes. Better far than that the chaos of schools and splinter parties we have with us now! But there need be no such choice; for the great obstacle to advance in criticism is not the existence of independent groups of critics each pursuing separate interests, but the spirit of exclusive dogmatism which keeps them from learning what they might from one another; and for that the only effective remedy, I think, is to take to heart the two lessons which the persistence throughout history of many distinct critical languages ought to teach us. The first is the lesson of self-knowledge: we can attempt to become more clearly aware than we have usually been of just what it is that we ourselves are doing—and why—when we make critical statements of any kind, and at the same time try to extend that clarity, in as intellectually sympathetic a way as possible, to the statements of other critics, and especially to those that appear to be most inconsistent with our own. And it will be all the easier to attain this self-understanding, with its natural discouragements to doctrinal prejudice, if we also learn the second lesson, and come habitually to think of the various critical languages of the past and present, including our own, no longer as rival attempts to foreclose the "real" or "only profitable" truth about poetry, so that we have to choose among them as we choose among religious dogmas or political causes, but simply as tools of our trade—as so many distinct conceptual and logical means, each with its peculiar capacities and limitations, for solving truly the many distinct kinds of problems which poetry, in its magnificent variety of aspects, presents to our view.[245]

NOTES

1. Cleanth Brooks and Robert Penn Warren, *Understanding Poetry* (rev. ed., New York, 1950), pp. xlix–l; Cleanth Brooks, *The Well Wrought Urn: Studies in the Structure of Poetry* (New York, 1947), p. 178.
2. Cleanth Brooks, *The Well Wrought Urn*, pp. 179, 191.
3. For example, John Dover Wilson, in his edition of *Macbeth* (Cambridge, 1947), pp. lii–lxviii.
4. For example, Kenneth Muir, in his edition of *Macbeth* (London, 1951), pp. l–liv.
5. Roy Walker, *The Time is Free: A Study of "Macbeth"* (London, 1949); see especially pp. xiv–xv, 64 ff.
6. Harold Goddard, *The Meaning of Shakespeare* (Chicago, 1951), p. 520.
7. L. C. Knights, "How Many Children Had Lady Macbeth?" in *Explorations* (London, 1946), pp. 16–36.
8. G. Wilson Knight, *The Imperial Theme* (London, 1939), p. 153.
9. I. A. Richards, *Principles of Literary Criticism* (London, 1925), p. 6.
10. For two recent suggestions of this kind see Murray Krieger, "Creative Criticism: A Broader View of Symbolism," *Sewanee Review*, LVIII (1950), 36–51, and R. P. Blackmur, "The Lion and the Honeycomb," *Hudson Review*, III (1951), 494–507.
11. See his article on "Language" in the *Encyclopaedia of the Social Sciences*, IX (1933), 155–68.
12. I borrow these illustrations from Warner A. Wick, "The 'Political' Philosophy of Logical Empiricism," *Philosophical Studies*, II (1951), 51–52.
13. For other statements, in somewhat different terms, of this view, see *Critics and Criticism: Ancient and Modern*, ed. R. S. Crane (Chicago, 1952), pp. 5–12, 148–49, 174–75, 463–545, 546–52. See also Richard McKeon, "Philosophy and Method," *Journal of Philosophy*, XLVIII (1951), 653–82; "Semantics, Science, and Poetry," *Modern Philology*, XLIX (1952), 145–59; and *Freedom and History* (New York, 1952).
14. See *Explorations*, pp. 1–18, and especially pp. 1, 4, 10.
15. A. C. Bradley, *Shakespearean Tragedy* (2nd ed., London, 1929), p. 1.

16. Quoted by Knights, *Explorations*, p. 4.

17. *Biographia literaria*, ed. J. Shawcross (Oxford, 1907), II, 12.

18. See McKeon, in *Critics and Criticism*, pp. 149–68.

19. See his "Poetry: A Note in Ontology," in *The World's Body* (New York, 1938), pp. 111–42.

20. See Elder Olson, in *Critics and Criticism*, pp. 235–59.

21. John Crowe Ransom, *The New Criticism* (Norfolk, Conn., 1941), pp. 270–71.

22. See especially pp. 36–38, 41–46, 111–42, 181–83, 195–211, 278–95.

23. *An Enquiry Concerning the Principles of Morals*, Section I.

24. For examples of this latter mode of definition, see Bradley, *Shakespearean Tragedy*, Lecture I; Maud Bodkin, *Archetypal Patterns in Poetry: Psychological Studies of Imagination* (London, 1934), chapter 1; E. M. W. Tillyard, *Shakespeare's Last Plays* (London, 1938), pp. 16–20; Northrop Frye, *Kenyon Review*, XIII (1951), 103–10, 543–62; Maynard Mack, *Yale Review*, XLI (1951), 84–85.

25. Warner A. Wick, *Philosophical Studies*, II, 53. For a view analogous in part to this see R. G. Collingwood, *An Autobiography* (Oxford, 1939), especially pp. 29–43, 57–76.

26. Rudolf Carnap, "Empiricism, Semantics, and Ontology," *Revue internationale de philosophie*, IV (1950), 20–40.

27. For one recent version of this position see Frederick A. Pottle, *The Idiom of Poetry* (Ithaca, N.Y., 1941; rev. ed., 1946), especially Lecture II, "The Doctrine of Critical Relativism."

28. *The Armed Vision: A Study in the Methods of Modern Literary Criticism* (New York, 1948), pp. ix, 395–407.

29. *Hudson Review*, III, 495–98. Cf. also John Crowe Ransom, *Kenyon Review*, XIV (1952), 656–59.

30. Cf. *Critics and Criticism*, pp. 100–5.

31. Cf. G. Edison, "Plato and Freud," *University of Toronto Quarterly*, XVI (1946), especially pp. 12–15.

32. *The Wheel of Fire* (London, 1949), pp. 32–38. A similar, though less drastic, technique of "explaining away" in the interest of an "abstract" hypothesis can be seen in L. C. Knights's remarks on Bradley's view of the emotional effects of *Macbeth*; see *Explorations*, p. 36.

33. See *Critics and Criticism*, pp. 56–63, 84–107.

34. Cf. Hoyt Trowbridge, *Comparative Literature*, III (1951), 360–61.

35. *Contributions to Analytical Psychology*, trans. by H. G. and Cary F. Baynes (London, 1945), pp. 229–34, 360–61.

36. *An Enquiry Concerning the Principles of Morals*, Section I.

37. J. I. M. Stewart, *Shakespeare Survey*, V (1952), 130, apropos of Clifford Leech, *Shakespeare's Tragedies and Other Studies in Seventeenth-Century Drama* (London, 1950).

38. *The World's Body*, pp. 297–98.

39. F. R. Leavis, *Revaluation* (New York, 1947), pp. 204–7.

40. Cf. especially *Posterior Analytics* i. 7, 9, 32; also *De Anima* i. 1.

41. *Poetics* 6. 1450b5–7; 19. 1456a35.

42. The following account is greatly indebted to the various discussions of the *Poetics* collected in *Critics and Criticism*; see especially pp. 160–68, 176 ff., 463 ff., 552–66. My analysis would have gained in several important

respects had I been able, before completing the revision of these lectures, to read Elder Olson's paper on "The Poetic Method of Aristotle: Its Powers and Limitations," *English Institute Essays, 1951* (New York, 1952), pp. 70–94.

43. Cf. *Poetics* 5. 1449ᵇ18.

44. *Nicomachean Ethics* ii. 2. 1103ᵇ27–28.

45. *Ibid.* i. 1. 1094ᵃ5; ii. 4. 1105ᵃ27 ff.

46. On this division of the sciences see especially *Metaphysics* vi. 1.

47. On the notion of "concrete wholes" and the kind of definitions appropriate to the investigation of them, see *Physics* ii. 2; *De Anima* i. 1. 403ᵃ25–ᵇ8; *On the Parts of Animals* i. 1. 640ᵇ18–29; *Metaphysics* vi. 1. 1025ᵇ30–32; vii. 3. 1029ᵃ3–5, 10–11; viii. 2.

48. Cf. *De Anima* ii. 1. 412ᵇ10–413ᵃ4; *On the Parts of Animals* i. 1. 642ᵃ10 ff.

49. *Metaphysics* vii. 7.

50. Cf. *Posterior Analytics* i. 4–6 *passim.*

51. *On the Parts of Animals* i. 1. 639ᵇ24–640ᵃ37.

52. *Ibid.* 642ᵃ10 ff.

53. *Ibid.* 640ᵇ5 ff.; cf. *Physics* i. 4–5.

54. *Metaphysics* vii. 7.

55. See McKeon, in *Critics and Criticism*, pp. 149–59.

56. *Physics* ii. 8. 199ᵃ15–17; cf. *Meteorology* iv. 3. 381ᵇ6. On the whole question see McKeon, in *Critics and Criticism*, pp. 160–68, and Olson, *ibid.*, pp. 553–54.

57. It should be observed that for Aristotle rhetoric is not, like poetry, an art of making determinate kinds of objects but a faculty (*dynamis*): it is the faculty or power of discovering and using with respect to any subject the available means of persuasion. The discussion begins, therefore, not with certain actualized forms, of which it seeks the necessary internal conditions, but with a consideration of the range of subjects about which we may seek to persuade, the general means of persuasion, and the kinds of audiences and ends that determine the major types of persuasion (deliberative, forensic, and epideictic). It then proceeds, in Book i, to set forth the kinds of premises the speaker ought to seek for each of these three types; in Book ii, to explain how the emotions of audiences may be aroused or directed and how arguments may be constructed; and in Book iii, to deal with questions of style and organization, which is the closest approach possible, in rhetoric, to the forms with which poetics begins. The constitutive parts of any rhetorical composition are consequently three: thought (*dianoia*), including all the devices of argument; style (*lexis*); and arrangement (*taxis*); the principle of construction, in any speech, being the particular thesis, whether deliberative, forensic, or epideictic, concerning which it seeks to persuade its special audience. I should conjecture that had Aristotle dealt anywhere with didactic poems it would have been in terms of some such analytic as this, with the major distinctions those of argumentative means rather than of formal ends.

58. Cf. *On the Parts of Animals* i. 1. 641ᵃ18–33. See *Politics* i. 2. 1253ᵃ24: all things are defined by their working (*ergon*) and power (*dynamis*).

59. *Poetics* 5. 1449ᵃ35.

197

60. *Nicomachean Ethics* vi. 4.

61. Cf. Northrop Frye, *University of Toronto Quarterly*, XIX (1949), 14.

62. The distinction has been blurred through the modern extension of the term "convention" to include anything that imposes restrictions or necessities on an artist once he has accepted it as a kind of thing to be done; thus the choice of verse rather than prose or of a dramatic rather than a narrative manner is often spoken of as a choice between different "conventions"; and poetry or art itself is said to be a "convention" on the ground that it necessarily involves distortions of life. In a stricter meaning of the term, "convention" denotes any characteristic of the matter or technique of a poem the reason for the presence of which in the poem cannot be inferred from the necessities of the form envisaged but must be sought in the historical circumstances of its composition—that is to say, in the habitual practice of other writers or in a prevailing opinion as to what ought to be done. The chorus in Greek tragedy is a convention in this sense, since, although the chorus serves an artistic function or functions in the tragedies which employ it, that function could be—and was in later times, as by Shakespeare —realized in quite different material ways. In relation to the nature and inherent necessities of any kind of poetry a convention is thus an accidental attribute, however long-lived or influential it may be.

63. *Nicomachean Ethics* i. 1. 1094ª1–2.

64. See also *Poetics* 26 *ad fin.*

65. For both of these views see W. Hamilton Fyfe's Introduction to the Loeb Classical Library edition of the *Poetics* (London and New York, 1932), pp. x–xiv, xix.

66. *Nicomachean Ethics* x. 4 *passim*; cf. *ibid.* i. 6.

67. *Poetics* 13. 1453ª35–36; 14. 1453ᵇ10.

68. *Nicomachean Ethics* ii. 6.

69. *Ibid.* ii. 9 *ad fin.*

70. *Poetics* 8; 23. 1459ª30 ff.; 24. 1460ª5 ff., 20 ff.

71. *Ibid.* 4. 1449ª15.

72. *Ibid.* 13. 1453ª25 ff.

73. E.g., 6. 1450ª25, 1450ᵇ7; 18. 1456ª20.

74. Cf. *Rhetoric* ii. 12–17; iii. 7, 16.

75. Especially *Poetics* 6, 7, 9.

76. See above, pp. 14–15.

77. *Poetics* 6. 1450ᵇ18–20; 14. 1453ᵇ1 ff.

78. *Ibid.* 16. 1454ᵇ35.

79. Cf. *Rhetoric* ii. 5, 8.

80. The ethical basis of the plot-form here argued as best is clarified by the discussion, in *Nicomachean Ethics* v. 8, of the various causes of unjust acts.

81. I owe the hint for this interpretation, as well as much else in these lectures, to my friend and colleague, Professor Elder Olson. The distinction is well illustrated in some of Jane Austen's revisions. See Mary Lascelles, *Jane Austen and Her Art* (Oxford, 1939), pp. 99–100.

82. Reuben A. Brower, "The Heresy of Plot," in *English Institute Essays, 1951*, p. 69.

83. *Poetics* 20. 1457ª27–30; cf. *Posterior Analytics* ii. 10. 33ᵇ35; *Metaphysics* viii. 6. 1045ª12.

84. J. W. H. Atkins, *Literary Criticism in Antiquity* (Cambridge, 1934), I, 117.
85. *Ibid.*
86. W. Hamilton Fyfe, ed., *Poetics*, p. xiv.
87. See *The World's Body*, pp. 173–211; *Kenyon Review*, XIV (1952), 651–56.
88. Francis Fergusson, *The Idea of a Theatre* (Princeton, 1949).
89. See above, pp. 28–29.
90. Cf. Crane, in *Critics and Criticism*, pp. 617–20, especially note 7.
91. See the essays by Bernard Weinberg on Robortello and Castelvetro in *Critics and Criticism*, pp. 319–71, and his "Scaliger versus Aristotle on Poetics," *Modern Philology*, XXXIX (1942), 337–60, and "The Poetic Theories of Minturno," *Studies in Honor of Frederick W. Shipley* (St. Louis, 1942), pp. 101–29.
92. Yvor Winters, *The Anatomy of Nonsense* (Norfolk, Conn., 1943), pp. 11–12.
93. *Understanding Poetry*, pp. 1–6; rev. ed., pp. xxxiii–xxxviii.
94. Frederick A. Pottle, *The Idiom of Poetry*, pp. 70, 80; rev. ed., pp. 71–72, 89.
95. Ransom, *The New Criticism*, pp. 279–81; also *A College Primer of Writing* (New York, 1943), pp. 83–86.
96. René Wellek and Austin Warren, *Theory of Literature* (New York, 1949), pp. 141, 152.
97. *Institutio oratoria* III. iii. 1–2. Cf. McKeon, in *Critics and Criticism*, pp. 171–72.
98. See above, note 57.
99. See above, pp. 20–22.
100. *Biographia literaria*, ed. Shawcross, II, 8–10.
101. Philip Blair Rice, *Kenyon Review*, VII (1945), 374.
102. Murray Krieger, *Sewanee Review*, LVIII (1950), 44: "The principal differentiating feature of art (and here as elsewhere I am indebted to the terminology of Eliseo Vivas) is that it deals solely and continually with the primary level of experience. This is to say that the artist cannot allow himself any abstraction or generalization of experience (the rightful function of the philosopher or scientist), but rather must concern himself with his organization of experience in all its complexity, an organization which must lose none of the ambiguities and paradoxes inherent in man's condition. If this integrity of experience is the point which sets imaginative literature off from other forms of discourse, may it not be said that the peculiar function of literature is located in the intuitive grasp of the particulars of existence; that its peculiar value is found in the meaningful organization of the relationships with which it deals? It would seem that Melville's artistic intention in *Moby Dick* lies in this realm. It may be true that he wants to stir us in a given manner by a certain arrangement of incident, character, and diction; but above this is a desire to expose certain problems which he can see not in abstract terms but only in the individuality of that very arrangement." I quote this passage at length because it seems to me to illustrate with admirable clarity the kind of dialectical necessity by which the critics I am discussing in this lecture derive their principles: given the initial division of experience and the allocation of one half of the division to the

philosopher or scientist, how inevitable everything else, including the psychoanalysis of Melville, at once becomes!

103. Rice, *Kenyon Review*, VII, 374.

104. See note 95, above.

105. W. K. Wimsatt, Jr., "Verbal Style: Logical and Counterlogical," *PMLA*, LXV (1950), 5–20.

106. Cf. Olson, in *Critics and Criticism*, pp. 62–63, where the point I have been developing in this section is briefly stated.

107. For a brief general account of Hellenistic poetics see Atkins, *Literary Criticism in Antiquity*, I, 164–94.

108. See McKeon, in *Critics and Criticism*, pp. 260–96 *passim*.

109. Thomas Clark Pollock, *The Nature of Literature* (Princeton, 1942).

110. Cf., e.g., Northrop Frye, *Kenyon Review*, XII (1950), 251 ff.; XIII (1951), 95 ff.; and R. P. Blackmur, *Hudson Review*, III (1951), 487–507 *passim*.

111. Cf. *Critics and Criticism*, pp. 14, 459–60.

112. Cleanth Brooks, in *Critiques and Essays in Criticism, 1920–1948*, ed. Robert Wooster Stallman (New York, 1949), p. xix.

113. Cleanth Brooks, *Kenyon Review*, XIII (1951), 72 (for the first two statements).

114. Wellek and Warren, *Theory of Literature*, p. 141.

115. I. A. Richards, *Coleridge on Imagination* (New York, 1935), p. 220.

116. W. K. Wimsatt, Jr., *PMLA*, LXV, 20.

117. Richards, *Coleridge on Imagination*, p. 202.

118. Richards, *Principles of Literary Criticism*, pp. 261–71.

119. William Empson, *Seven Types of Ambiguity* (2nd ed., London, 1947), p. 1.

120. Philip Wheelwright, *Kenyon Review*, II (1940), 279.

121. F. W. Bateson, *English Poetry: A Critical Introduction* (London, 1950), pp. 48–62.

122. Cleanth Brooks, *The Well Wrought Urn*, especially pp. 8–9, 192.

123. W. K. Wimsatt, Jr., *PMLA*, LXV, 8.

124. Cf., e.g., Cleanth Brooks, "Irony as a Principle of Structure," in *Literary Opinion in America*, ed. Morton Dauwen Zabel (rev. ed., New York, 1951), p. 729.

125. E.g., Cleanth Brooks; see above, note 93.

126. E.g., Northrop Frye, *University of Toronto Quarterly*, XIX (1949), 12–16; *Kenyon Review*, XII (1950), 249 ff.

127. E.g., John Crowe Ransom; see above, note 95.

128. Cf. Brooks, *The Well Wrought Urn*, p. 189.

129. Brooks, "Irony as a Principle of Structure," in Zabel, ed., *Literary Opinion in America*, pp. 740–41.

130. Brooks, *The Well Wrought Urn*, p. 199.

131. The view is implicit in nearly all the critical writing of this school; I take the phrase from Marvin Mudrick, *Jane Austen: Irony as Defense and Discovery* (Princeton, 1952), p. 202, note 8.

132. Cf. Crane, in *Critics and Criticism*, pp. 95–100.

133. Brooks, *The Well Wrought Urn*, pp. 177–96, 199.

134. *On the Parts of Animals* i. 1. 641ª15–17. Cf. above, pp. 45–46.

135. *Ibid.* 640ᵇ5–10.

136. *The Well Wrought Urn*, p. 10. With this may be contrasted the argument, *ibid.*, p. 16, in which Donne's use of "paradox" in "The Canonization" is treated as a necessary means to the expressive end of that poem.

137. *Principles of Literary Criticism*, pp. 249–50.

138. *Biographia literaria*, II, 12. Cf. *Critics and Criticism*, pp. 85–93.

139. *The Well Wrought Urn*, pp. 186–87.

140. Robert Penn Warren, "Pure and Impure Poetry," in *Critiques and Essays in Criticism*, ed. Stallman, pp. 101–2.

141. Cf. Crane, in *Critics and Criticism*, pp. 100–7; Hoyt Trowbridge, *Comparative Literature*, III (1951), 361–62; Charles V. Hartung, *University of Kansas City Review*, Spring, 1952, pp. 181–89.

142. In *Critiques and Essays in Criticism*, ed. Stallman, p. xix.

143. For the antecedents in Romantic criticism of some of the "new" conceptions disseminated by these writers, see M. H. Abrams, *The Mirror and the Lamp: Romantic Theory and the Critical Tradition* (New York, 1953), especially chapter 9.

144. I borrow the phrase from Erich Fromm, *The Forgotten Language: An Introduction to an Understanding of Dreams, Fairy Tales and Myths* (New York, 1951), p. 7.

145. *Contributions to Analytical Psychology*, p. 248.

146. "Symbolism," in the *Dictionary of World Literature*, ed. Joseph T. Shipley (New York, 1942), pp. 565–66.

147. Cf., e.g., Clyde Kluckhohn, "Myths and Rituals: A General Theory," *Harvard Theological Review*, XXXV (1942), 45–79; Stanley Edgar Hyman, "Myth, Ritual, and Nonsense," *Kenyon Review*, XI (1949), 455–75. The following are some of the more general discussions which have had an impact on recent criticism: Sir James Frazer, *The Golden Bough* (1890; 2nd ed. in 3 vols., 1900; 3rd ed. in 12 vols., 1907–15); C. G. Jung, *The Psychology of the Unconscious* (New York, 1916), especially Part II; C. G. Jung and C. Kerényi, *Introduction to a Science of Mythology*, trans. R. F. C. Hull (London, 1951); Ernst Cassirer, *Sprache und Mythos* (Leipzig and Berlin, 1925), translated as *Language and Myth* by Susanne K. Langer (New York, 1946); Lord Raglan, *Jocasta's Crime: An Anthropological Study* (London, 1933) and *The Hero: A Study in Tradition, Myth, and Drama* (London, 1936; New York, 1937); Susanne K. Langer, *Philosophy in a New Key* (New York, 1948); Richard Chase, *Quest for Myth* (Baton Rouge, 1949). For other references see the useful articles of Haskell M. Block, "Cultural Anthropology and Contemporary Literary Criticism," *Journal of Aesthetics and Art Criticism*, XI (1952), 46–54, and of Wallace W. Douglas, "The Meanings of 'Myth' in Modern Criticism," *Modern Philology*, L (1953), 232–42.

148. Cf., e.g., William Troy, "Postlude: Myth, Method, and the Future," *Chimera*, IV (1946), 82–83.

149. Cf. C. G. Jung, *Contributions to Analytical Psychology*, pp. 156–63, 245–49, 261–68.

150. See *Speculum*, XIX (1944), 123–25.

151. E.g., Fromm, *The Forgotten Language*, pp. 18 ff.

152. This appears to be the supposition underlying the discussions of Greek tragedy and comedy in Gilbert Murray's very influential "excursus on the ritual forms preserved in Greek tragedy" contributed to Jane

Harrison's *Themis: A Study of the Social Origins of Greek Religion* (Cambridge, 1912), pp. 341–63; in George Thomson's *Aeschylus and Athens: A Study in the Social Origins of Drama* (London, 1941); in F. M. Cornford's *The Origin of Attic Comedy* (London, 1914); and in Francis Fergusson's *The Idea of a Theatre* (Princeton, 1949).

153. Cf. Northrop Frye, *Kenyon Review*, XIII (1951), 98–110. See also his "A Conspectus of Dramatic Genres," *Kenyon Review*, XIII (1951), 543–62.

154. As in Murray's "excursus" and in Francis Fergusson's discussion of *Oedipus Rex*.

155. For a brief historical sketch of the "Cambridge school," see Stanley Edgar Hyman, *Kenyon Review*, XI (1949), 463–69, and the references in note 152, above. Of the vast literature of "archetypal" interpretations of medieval and modern works, I need mention here only the two which have probably had the widest influence: Jessie L. Weston's *From Ritual to Romance* (Cambridge, 1920) and Maud Bodkin's *Archetypal Patterns in Poetry: Psychological Studies of Imagination* (London, 1934).

156. William Troy, *Chimera*, IV, 83. Cf., among others, John F. Danby, *Shakespeare's Doctrine of Nature: A Study of "King Lear"* (London, 1949), pp. 122–25, and Northrop Frye, "Levels of Meaning in Literature," *Kenyon Review*, XII (1950), 246–62.

157. *The New Criticism*, p. x. See also Ransom, *The World's Body*, p. 173; *The Kenyon Critics* (Cleveland and New York, 1951), pp. vii–viii.

158. L. C. Knights, *Explorations*, p. 6.

159. R. W. Stallman, *Critiques and Essays in Criticism*, p. 506.

160. Robert Penn Warren, "A Poem of Pure Imagination: An Experiment in Reading," in *The Rime of the Ancient Mariner* (New York, 1946), pp. 63–64.

161. Brooks and Warren, *Understanding Poetry*, pp. 118–21; rev. ed., pp. 41–48.

162. Brooks, *The Well Wrought Urn*, p. 122.

163. R. W. Stallman, "The Structure and Symbolism of Conrad's *Victory*," *Western Review*, Spring, 1949, p. 149.

164. See Wimsatt's article cited above, note 105, and the other papers by the same writer mentioned therein. Cf. also Maynard Mack, " 'Wit and Poetry and Pope': Some Observations on His Imagery," in *Pope and His Contemporaries: Essays Presented to George Sherburn* (Oxford, 1949), pp. 20–40.

165. Robert Penn Warren, *The Ancient Mariner*, pp. 87–93. Cf. E. E. Stoll, *PMLA*, LXIII (1948), 216–19, and Olson, in *Critics and Criticism*, pp. 138–44.

166. Brooks, *The Well Wrought Urn*, pp. 27–46.

167. Robert B. Heilman, *This Great Stage: Image and Structure in "King Lear"* (Baton Rouge, 1948). Cf. W. R. Keast, in *Critics and Criticism*, pp. 108–37.

168. Cf. John Crowe Ransom, "The Understanding of Fiction," *Kenyon Review*, XII (1950), 189–218.

169. Roy Walker, *The Time is Free*, esp. pp. xiv–xv, 64 ff.

170. Knights, *Explorations*, p. 23.

171. John F. Danby, *Shakespeare's Doctrine of Nature*, pp. 59, 174.
172. G. Wilson Knight, *The Wheel of Fire* (London, 1949), pp. 3, 10, 119, 139. Cf. Tillyard, *Shakespeare's Last Plays*, pp. 27–40, 44–46, and Danby, *Shakespeare's Doctrine of Nature*, pp. 18–19.
173. Heilman, *This Great Stage*, p. 35.
174. An excellent recent example is Ernest Sirluck's "The *Faerie Queene*, Book II, and the *Nicomachean Ethics*," *Modern Philology*, XLIX (1951), 73–100.
175. See Lawrence Edward Bowling, "The Thematic Framework of *Romeo and Juliet*," *PMLA*, LXIV (1949), 208.
176. *The Time is Free*, pp. ix, 106–7.
177. J. I. M. Stewart, *Character and Motive in Shakespeare* (London, 1949), p. 144. Cf. Hyman, *The Armed Vision*, pp. 405–7, and especially the following (p. 406): "Thus we could take, say, Eliot's symbol of the Waste Land in the poem of that name, a symbol of great depth and complexity, and read it at any level we cared to insert a vocabulary: at the most intimate level, to the Freudian, it would be castration and impotence; at a more conscious level, to a post-Freudian psychology, perhaps the fear of artistic sterility; on the daily-life level, in the biographical terms of Van Wyck Brooks, the symbol of Eliot's pre-conversion state; on a more social level, to a critic like Parrington, the empty life of the artist or the frustration of the upper class; to Eliot himself, the irreligion of the times; in broadly historical terms, to the Marxist, the decay of capitalism; in Jungian terms, the archetypal ritual of rebirth."
178. George Ian Duthie, *Shakespeare* (London, 1951), especially pp. 39–56; see also his remarks in *Review of English Studies*, N.S., II (1951), 79–80.
179. *Shakespeare's Doctrine of Nature*, pp. 121–23.
180. Knight, *The Wheel of Fire*, pp. 2–9; Goddard, *The Meaning of Shakespeare*, pp. 8–13. Cf. also Walker, *The Time is Free*, pp. ix, 106–7.
181. Knight, *The Wheel of Fire*, p. 7. See above, p. 34.
182. *The Meaning of Shakespeare*, p. 642.
183. Northrop Frye, *Kenyon Review*, XII (1950), 257.
184. Maud Bodkin, *Archetypal Patterns in Poetry*, p. 4. For representative statements by Jung, see *Contributions to Analytical Psychology*, especially pp. 111–40, 157–63, 245–48, 278–81, 396, and *Introduction to a Science of Mythology*, especially pp. 99–106, 218–19.
185. *Shakespeare Survey*, IV (1951), 30–31.
186. *The Crown of Life* (London, 1948), pp. 30–31.
187. *Poems, 1938–1945* (New York, 1946), p. 41.
188. Colin Still, *Shakespeare's Mystery Play: A Study of "The Tempest"* (London, 1921).
189. *The Idea of a Theatre*, pp. 13–41.
190. *Character and Motive in Shakespeare*, pp. 135, 138–39. Cf. also *ibid.*, pp. 21–22, on the blinding of Gloucester in *King Lear*: "There is something unmistakably atavic about the play. Like Keats's *Hyperion* it treats of the procession of the generations and the struggle this involves: 'The younger rises, when the old doth fall.' But whereas Keats would use his myth to interpret philosophical and personal problems which are

essentially modern, Shakespeare drives to his story's immemorial core in drama and projects the struggle in that extreme form in which, phylogenetically, it still exists in the recesses of every human mind. The first anthropologist to approach *King Lear*—curiously enough, he seems not yet to have arrived—when he observes how one paternal figure is deprived of his possessions and wits and another of his eyes, will certainly aver that these incidents are symbolical as such things in dreams are symbolical: they veil an unconscious fantasy of the kind classically expressed in the myth of Uranus and Cronus. So at this level again—the deeper level at which tragic drama tends to rehearse archetypal imaginative themes—Gloster's [*sic*] maiming is implicated with the play, cohering with its primitive character as a whole and having a distinguishable relationship to yet more savage deprivations in analogous parent-and-child stories." Cf. E. E. Stoll, *Modern Philology*, XLVIII (1950), 122–32.

191. R. W. Stallman, *Western Review*, Spring, 1949, p. 149.

192. Northrop Frye, *Kenyon Review*, XII (1950), 258. See also Richard P. Adams, "The Archetypal Pattern of Death and Rebirth in Milton's *Lycidas*," *PMLA*, LXIV (1949), 183–88, and Caroline W. Mayerson, "The Orpheus Image in *Lycidas*," *ibid.*, pp. 189–207.

193. Edith Sitwell, *A Notebook on William Shakespeare* (London, 1948), pp. 84, 90–91.

194. *Character and Motive in Shakespeare*, pp. 33–37.

195. *Contributions to Analytical Psychology*, p. 40.

196. Cf. Bodkin, pp. 48–54, and Jung, *Contributions to Analytical Psychology*, pp. 34–44.

197. See especially pp. 16–26.

198. On this see A. W. Pickard-Cambridge, *Dithyramb, Tragedy and Comedy* (Oxford, 1927), especially pp. 185–208, 329–49. The rejoinder of Lord Raglan to such criticism of Murray's theory as that of Pickard-Cambridge is to the effect that the theory must be accepted because we can't prove that it is false. See *The Hero* (New York, 1937), p. 283: "The well-considered attempts of Professors Gilbert Murray and F. M. Cornford to reconstruct from the dramas the ritual upon which they were based have been met by the criticism that their theories are valueless, since no such rituals are known to have been performed. This criticism sounds plausible enough, but when analysed it is found to be based on the belief that we are in possession of full knowledge both of early Greek ritual and of the development of the Attic drama. Such evidence as we have, however, is traditional, and therefore has no historical value." We can continue, therefore, to believe what we wish to believe.

199. Erich Fromm, *The Forgotten Language*, pp. 221–28.

200. Richard Chase, *Herman Melville: A Critical Study* (New York, 1949), p. 43.

201. The interpretation is Dr. Franz Alexander's in an essay which I have been unable to see; I borrow the statement from Lionel Trilling, *The Liberal Imagination: Essays on Literature and Society* (New York, 1950), p. 51. "An analysis of this sort," Trilling comments (pp. 51–52) "is not momentous and not exclusive of other meanings; perhaps it does no more than point up and formulate what we all have already seen. It has the

tact to *accept* the play and does not, like Dr. Jones's study of *Hamlet*, search for a 'hidden motive' and a 'deeper working,' which implies that there is a reality to which the play stands in the relation that a dream stands to the wish that generates it and from which it is separable; it is this reality, this 'deeper working,' which, according to Dr. Jones, produced the play."

202. Bodkin, *Archetypal Patterns in Poetry*, chapter 2, "A Study of 'The Ancient Mariner' and of the Rebirth Archetype." The quotation is from p. 54.

203. *Kenyon Review*, XIII (1951), 544.

204. See above, p. 33.

205. *Selected Essays, 1917–1932* (New York, 1932), p. 96.

206. *New York Times Book Review*, April 30, 1950, p. 1. There is of course much to a similar effect in the notebooks and prefaces of Henry James; cf., for example, the Preface to *The Awkward Age* (London, 1922), especially pp. vi, xvii, xix, xxv.

207. See above, pp. 104–6.

208. These types are discussed, with references, in Ransom, *The New Criticism*, pp. 235–54.

209. For example, that of Kenneth Burke in his "Lexicon Rhetoricae"; see Stallman, *Critiques and Essays in Criticism*, pp. 234–38.

210. Robert B. Heilman, "More Fair than Black: Light and Dark in *Othello*," *Essays in Criticism*, I (1951), 315–35.

211. *Hudson Review*, III (1951), 497.

212. See above, pp. 44–45, and note 47.

213. *On the Parts of Animals* i. 1. 640^{b}25–29; *Metaphysics* vii. 17. 1041^{b}5–8.

214. Jane Austen, *Emma*, chapter 12.

215. See above, pp. 91–92.

216. See above, pp. 45–46.

217. See above, pp. 57–63.

218. *An Autobiography*, p. 2.

219. On the kind of criticism which refuses to grant to an artist the "subject" he has chosen, see the remarks of Henry James in his preface to *The Portrait of a Lady*.

220. See above, pp. 47–49, and Olson, in *Critics and Criticism*, pp. 65–68, 69–70, 588–92.

221. See above, pp. 50–57.

222. Cf. Crane, in *Critics and Criticism*, pp. 621–22, 632–45; Olson, *ibid.*, 563–66.

223. Cf. Olson, *ibid.*, pp. 71 ff., 562–63. With the remarkable development, in modern literature, of elaborate representational means for making effective relatively simple or universalized plots, the problem of distinguishing the two is sometimes a delicate one; there has been a good deal of confusion, consequently, in some of the discussions of works like *Ulysses*, *A Passage to India*, and Hemingway's "The Killers."

224. See above, pp. 67–68, 70–73.

225. Cf. Olson, in *Critics and Criticism*, p. 592, for brief definitions of the principal types.

226. Cf. Norman Maclean, *ibid.*, pp. 408 ff.
227. Cf. Olson, *ibid.*, p. 560, and his forthcoming book on the shorter poetic forms.
228. Cf. Olson, *ibid.*, pp. 555–56; Crane, *ibid.*, pp. 636–38. But these are merely hints.
229. One of my former students, Mr. Richard Levin, is completing a study of the plot-forms of these and other similar works in Renaissance English drama.
230. See above, pp. 76–77.
231. Cf. Crane, in *Critics and Criticism*, pp. 641–45.
232. Cf. Olson, *ibid.*, pp. 68 ff., 567 ff.
233. Cf. above, pp. 7–8.
234. See, in addition to what follows, Wayne C. Booth, *Journal of General Education*, VI (1951), 21–25. For a somewhat similar discussion of an episode in *King Lear*, cf. Maclean, in *Critics and Criticism*, pp. 595–615.
235. Cleanth Brooks, *The Well Wrought Urn*, pp. 96–113.
236. I borrow here the substance and many of the words of a note of mine in *Critics and Criticism*, p. 99.
237. By T. C. Chamberlin, in a paper with this title, first published in *Science*, Old Series, XV (1890), 92–96; reprinted in the *Journal of Geology*, XXXIX (1931), 155–65. The "method of multiple working hypotheses" is contrasted with "the method of the ruling theory" and "the method of the working hypothesis."
238. Cf. Keast, in *Critics and Criticism*, pp. 131–36.
239. *Explorations*, p. 36. Cf. above, pp. 33–34.
240. Cf. Keast, in *Critics and Criticism*, pp. 135–37.
241. Cf. Crane, *ibid.*, pp. 639–40.
242. *Coleridge's Shakespearean Criticism*, ed. T. M. Raysor (London, 1930), II, 66–67; cf. *Biographia literaria*, II, 9–10.
243. E.g., U. M. Ellis-Fermor, *The Frontiers of Drama* (London, 1945), pp. 77–95; M. M. Morozov, "The Individualization of Shakespeare's Characters through Imagery," *Shakespeare Survey*, II (1949), 83–106; R. A. Foakes, "Suggestions for a New Approach to Shakespeare's Imagery," *ibid.*, V (1952), 81–92.
244. An instance in point, verging on caricature of the fault I speak of in the text, is a recent discussion of the character of Jane Austen's Darcy. Why, the critic asks, "is he, among the major figures in *Pride and Prejudice*, the only one disturbingly derived and wooden?" And the answer, in terms of his psychoanalytical thesis, is given at once, without any consideration of the great difficulties that must have arisen, for the novelist, from the role which Darcy had to play in the first part of the plot and from the fact that the choice of point of view prevented even later any direct or sustained disclosure of his unspoken thought: "The reason seems to be the same as that which *compelled* Jane Austen to falsify her tone and commentary concerning Wickham's seductions and to supply Elinor and Marianne Dashwood with such nonentities for husbands. The socially unmanageable, the personally involving aspects of sex, Jane Austen *can* no longer treat with irony, nor *can* she as yet treat them straightforwardly. Darcy is the hero, he is the potential lover of a complex young woman much like the author

206

herself; and as such Jane Austen *cannot* animate him with emotion, or with her characteristic informing irony. She borrows him from a book; and, though she alters and illuminates everything else, she *can* do nothing more with him than fit him functionally into the plot." Marvin Mudrick, *Jane Austen: Irony as Defense and Discovery*, p. 117; italics mine.

245. I have discussed some of the practical consequences of this view in an essay, to be published soon, entitled "Questions and Answers in the Teaching of Literature." The "soon" of the preceding sentence has at this reprinting (June, 1967) become fourteen years; but any reader who may still wish to see the promised essay will find it, slightly revised, in *The Idea of the Humanities and Other Essays, Critical and Historical* (Chicago, 1967), II, 176–93.

INDEX

Abrams, M. H., 201
Absalom and Achitophel, 157
"Abstract" methods in criticism, xvi, 23–25, 37–38, 47, 113, 139, 147, 149, 154, 156, 167–68
Adams, Richard P., 204
Alchemist, The, 159
Alexander, Franz, 136
Alexander, W. J., 3
Allegory, interpretation of, 122–23
Ambiguity, 33, 99
Analogy, uses of, in criticism, 5–6, 92–94, 100–1, 109, 138–39
Anthropology, influence of, on contemporary criticism, 8, 110–14, 129–39, 201–2
Antigone, 136
Aquinas, St. Thomas, 114
Archer, William, 7
"Archetypal" criticism, 24, 32, 109–14, 128–39
"Archetypal patterns," 116, 128–39 *passim*
"Aristotelian" criticism in the Renaissance and after, 80–83, 94–95
Aristotle, xvi, 3, 4, 5, 6, 7, 18–19, 23, 28–29, 38, 39–79, 80–83, 85–89, 93–94, 98, 104–6, 116, 118, 149–64, 170–71, 178, 193
Arnold, Matthew, x, xi, 96, 98, 192
Ars poetica, 29, 82
Atkins, J. W. H., 77, 200
Augustine, St., 29, 94
Austen, Jane, 151, 162, 178, 206

Bateson, F. W., 92, 101
Beauty, conception of, in Aristotle, 58–63
Blackmur, R. P., 28–29, 78, 100, 115, 119, 149
Blake, William, 137
Block, Haskell M., 201
Bloomfield, Leonard, 9
Bodkin, Maud, 32, 109, 129, 134–35, 136, 185, 196, 202
Boileau, 143
Booth, Wayne C., 206
Bowling, Lawrence Edward, 124
Bradley, A. C., 5, 7, 14–17, 196
Brooks, Cleanth, 4, 5, 84, 92, 96, 98, 99, 100, 101, 102, 103, 104, 105, 107, 109, 118, 119, 120, 175–76, 185
Brothers Karamazov, The, 65, 117, 162
Brower, Reuben A., 74
Browne, Sir Thomas, 109
Burke, Kenneth, 5, 78, 109, 205
Butcher, S. H., 78

Cambridge school of classical anthropologists, 78, 113
Carnap, Rudolf, 26, 30
Cary, Joyce, 142–43, 182
Cassirer, Ernst, 110, 201
Castelvetro, 95
Catharsis in tragedy, 41, 54, 56–57, 63, 71–72, 82, 171–73
Cazamian, Louis, 91

209

211

24, 38, 78, 85, 88, 92–93, 100, 102, 115, 196, 202, 205
Reduction terms in contemporary "thematic" criticism, 123–26, 148
Reductive methods in criticism, 24, 33, 36–37, 89, 110, 112, 184–85. *See* Constructive methods in criticism
Relativism, historical and sociological, 27–28
Relativity of critical statements to questions and "frameworks," 26–27
Representation, manner of, 23, 76–77, 144, 159, 163–64, 173
Rhetoric, 43, 49, 74, 89, 95, 118–19, 125–28, 197
Rice, Philip Blair, 91
Richard II, 135
Richard III, 7, 160, 162, 170
Richards, I. A., 9, 96, 98, 99, 100, 101, 106, 107, 149
Rickword, C. H., 14, 16
Rime of the Ancient Mariner, The, 120, 125, 136
Ritual, patterns of, in poetry, 6, 32, 111–14, 128–39 *passim*
Robortello, 94
Romantic criticism, 97–98, 201
Romeo and Juliet, 124
Roper, Gordon, xvii
Russell, Bertrand, 8
Rymer, Thomas, xii

Sainte-Beuve, Auguste, x
Sapir, Edward, 11
Scaliger, 95
Scepticism, 8, 27–28
"Semantic" criticism, 98–100; two principal schools of, 100–14, 116
Shakespeare, William, 4, 6–8, 9–10, 12, 14–18, 30, 32, 34–35, 38, 65, 66, 67, 73, 75, 116, 117, 119, 120, 121, 122, 124, 125, 126–28, 130–33, 134–35, 136, 138, 146–48, 160, 162, 164, 166, 169–73, 178–80, 189, 190, 191
Shelley, Percy Bysshe, 38
Sidney, Sir Philip, 81
Sirluck, Ernest, 203
Sitwell, Edith, 133

Sophocles, 63, 132, 136, 138
Species of poetry as a concept in criticism, 5, 46–47, 49–54, 57, 61, 86, 95, 103–5, 117, 158–62, 170, 182. *See* Comedy; Lyric poetry; Tragedy
Spenser, Edmund, 54, 123, 165
Spurgeon, Caroline, 186
Stallman, Robert Wooster, 115–16, 118, 133, 138
Stevenson, Robert Louis, 53
Stewart, J. I. M., 126, 132, 133, 196, 203–4
Still, Colin, 132
Structure in poetry, how defined in contemporary "semantic" criticism, 102–9; variant conceptions of, 4–8. *See* Form; Symbolic structure; Tension
Subject-matter, how constituted in criticism, 17–19; how related to method, 19–20, 25
"Symbolic structure," 116–28 *passim,* 165
Symbols, modern interest in, 11, 96, 98–100

Tartuffe, 53
Tate, Allen, 100
Tempest, The, 132, 135
"Tension," 99, 106–8, 124–25
Theme as an analytical concept in criticism, 99, 102–3, 115, 117–18, 119, 120–39 *passim,* 165, 190. *See* Meaning; Total meaning
Theory, indispensability of, in criticism, xi–xiv, 146
Thomson, George, 202
Thought in poetry, 42–43, 67, 69, 73–74, 154, 186
"Three Ravens, The," 118
Tillyard, E. M. W., 134–35, 196
"To His Coy Mistress," 21, 176
Tom Jones, 53, 159, 181
"Total meaning," 99, 103, 117, 123, 190
Tragedy, 6–7, 15–16, 25, 53–54, 65–77, 133–34, 136, 159–60, 162, 170–71. *See* Catharsis
Trilling, Lionel, 109, 204–5

213